AFRICAN MEDIA AND DEMOCRATIZATION

PETER LANG
New York • Washington, D.C./Baltimore • Bern
Frankfurt • Berlin • Brussels • Vienna • Oxford

Yusuf Kalyango, Jr.

AFRICAN MEDIA AND DEMOCRATIZATION

Public Opinion, Ownership AND Rule of Law

PETER LANG
New York • Washington, D.C./Baltimore • Bern
Frankfurt • Berlin • Brussels • Vienna • Oxford

Library of Congress Cataloging-in-Publication Data
Kalyango, Yusuf.
African media and democratization: public opinion, ownership & rule of law /
Yusuf Kalyango, Jr.
p. cm.
Includes bibliographical references and index.
1. Mass media—Africa. 2. Mass media and public opinion—Africa. 3. Mass
media—Political aspects—Africa. 4. Democratization—Africa. I. Title.
P92.A4K35 2011   302.23096—dc22   2010050483
ISBN 978-1-4331-1207-2

Bibliographic information published by **Die Deutsche Nationalbibliothek.**
Die Deutsche Nationalbibliothek lists this publication in the "Deutsche
Nationalbibliografie"; detailed bibliographic data is available
on the Internet at http://dnb.d-nb.de/.

The paper in this book meets the guidelines for permanence and durability
of the Committee on Production Guidelines for Book Longevity
of the Council of Library Resources.

Table of Contents

List of Figures

List of Tables

Preface

This book is suited for both academic and nonacademic readers, particularly students, educators, internationalists, and envoys to Africa, who are interested in an informed and empirical analysis of media performance and ownership, democratization, rule of law, and political control in Eastern and Southern Africa (ESA). It features extensive research including public opinion data from 3,339 citizens, discussions from 24 focus groups, and content analyses of media coverage. It offers a hard-hitting assessment of the region's media performance and effects in an era when many African regimes are transitioning from authoritarian and militarized states to democratization. It encompasses Burundi, Ethiopia, Kenya, Rwanda, South Africa, Tanzania, Uganda, and Zambia. The role of media in democratization has been understudied in these countries, except South Africa. A comparative nested case study of Nigeria and Uganda as well as an analysis of the link between African media and the political economy of development in 30 countries are also included.

The book reveals public attitudes on highly controversial political and societal issues that are considered deadly taboo topics in Africa by the state actors. They include press freedom, state authoritarianism, presidential supremacy, dictatorship, political expression, social and economic injustice, and political patronage, as well as state control, extrajudicial killings, and ethno-political sectarianism. This work is the first of its kind to explore these issues through a triangulation of research methodologies[1]—public opinion surveys, focus groups, interviews, and media content analyses—which provides readers with a comprehensive understanding of African political discourse, media effects, state control, and governance. This work comes at a critical time when most Sub-Saharan African nations seek international and regional state legitimacy. The analysis is explorative, empirical, and also critical to a great extent.

The public opinion data were collected from July to August 2007 and December 2008 to January 2009 in all eight countries.[2] The statistical analyses in several chapters extrapolate media effects and public attitudes, as well as examine how archaic policies and laws, self-censorship, and patronage impact the media. The scholarly information is presented in a straightforward manner that is accessible to both academics and nonacademics. Whenever it is appropriate, the author provides a few personal anecdotes that serve as a point of context or introspection. The theoretical underpinnings and empirical analyses are contextualized not only from the author's firsthand knowledge as a former international journalist, war correspondent, and influential television political talk-show host in East Africa, but also through a host of real-world in-depth interviews.

The case studies and critical analyses seek to shape the debate by challenging ESA governments to protect free speech, political expression, and unfettered media discourse. The author clearly is not an apologist for any of the countries and governments examined here, and the issues are discussed in a fair and reasoned manner. The purpose of this research is to empower Africans, who are too often inadequately informed, to critically evaluate how they are governed, the legitimacy of the regimes, and how their basic human rights are upheld.

Abstract of the Contents

The book's early chapters unravel the different layers of governance and regimes, the current struggles with democratization, and the perception of democracy in each ESA country. Ethnic favoritism and cleavages, as well as sectarian politicking at the national and regional levels, are also explored. The early chapters offer new insights into largely unexplored areas of political conflicts, political and judicial volatility, and specific un-adjudicated cases of prominent African journalists who are languishing in prisons.

The remainder of the book makes a persuasive case for the utility of an unfettered and autonomous media. It also links the central role of media to inform and educate citizens to democratic rule and articulates how the rule of law, ethno-politics, regime legitimacy, economic liberalization, and other factors are key elements to achieving substantive democratic governance. It discusses how governments and state actors use the media to deflect the political ambitions of opponents. It details the state of the media in ESA and posits the necessary alternative actions that regimes should establish to ensure a free, robust, and independent media environment. State-owned, community, and privately owned media are examined.

The influential African scholarly works of Berger, Bratton, Eribo, Gyimah-Boadi, Hyden, Kaiser, Ocitti, Okumu, Lindberg, Mamdani, Rubongoya, Young, and others have been acknowledged in the wide-ranging reflections on previous research on African politics, governance, and the media. Their work is primarily grounded in political science, sociology, anthropology, history, and media studies. The author advances their theories with a central argument that ESA countries can achieve democratic consolidation only if the regimes and governments enforce the principles of equality in political competition, free speech, free markets, and the separation of state powers from other autonomous institutions, press freedom, and due process under the rule of law.

Mass communication literature and political theories from Western scholars such as Diamond, Dahl, Huntington, Iyengar, Lippman, McCombs, Norris, O'Donnell, Scheufele, Shaw, Schiller, Wanta, and others are also referenced and comparatively tested. Theories include agenda setting, agenda building, liberal and substantive democracy, and state militarization. As modernization theorists have consistently concluded, democracies are more likely to emerge in developed nations with well-informed citizenry than in underdeveloped dictatorial regimes. Dictatorship survives when citizens are poor, uneducated, and largely depend on state patronage for their survival. Considering the vital role of the media, sensitization of citizens about the continent's economic potential can contribute to sustainable development, and may lead to the creation of a middle class that is necessary for democratic consolidation.

Some of the principal questions addressed in the chapters are: In what ways do citizens in Eastern and Southern Africa (considering their region, level of education, socioeconomic status, and other individual characteristics) evaluate the media, the regimes, and their governments? Do citizens understand their basic rights? Do politicians use the media to influence favorable attitudes, or do they control the media and use them to reinforce ethno-political isolationism, sectarianism, and other political hyperbole? What attitudes do citizens hold towards the president or the government regarding governance, the regime, or political power?

The conclusion to the first nine chapters (see table of contents) provides an integrative assessment of the media's survival and how the regimes can consolidate democratic rule by safeguarding the rule of law, building a strong civil society, and providing an enabling environment for a free and robust media. The last chapter discusses prospects for the future role that the news media in the eight countries, and in Africa at large, should play in shaping public opinion to identify, advocate, and agree on state legitimacy and democratic governance. The author firmly argues that such an outcome would benefit both the African media and the regimes because a laissez-faire societal structure and decentralized or autonomous institutions would relieve some of the domestic political pressures and international condemnations that the governments endure.

The book also identifies the free independent media, rule of law, political expression and participation, modernization, and free markets as necessary components at the heart of good governance and state accountability. It is a highly recommended resource for anyone interested in the cutting-edge debates surrounding the challenges facing contemporary media, third world politics, and democratization. It offers readers much-needed knowledge about how the media should mobilize the public to make informed political choices that strengthen and foster good governance and the rule of law in Africa's transition to democratic rule.

Notes

[1] See a section devoted to the challenges of conducting research and collecting data in Africa in the Appendix at the end of the book. Also visit the author's website at www.kalyango.com to learn more about the methodologies used and to access some of the datasets.

[2] More information about the research design is detailed in the Appendix at the end of the book and on the author's website, www.kalyango.com.

Acknowledgments

The data gathered for this book, often collected under harsh field circumstances in eight African countries, would not have been possible without the financial support of Sue H. and Charlie Ragan of Ely, Minnesota; the John D. Bies International Travel Fund at the University of Missouri (MU); the research incentive funds provided by the Scripps College of Communication at Ohio University (OU); and the Honors Tutorial College (HTC) at OU. I am forever grateful for the generosity of the 3,339 citizens of Eastern and Southern Africa (ESA) who were surveyed, as well as those who participated in focus groups and in-depth interviews. Besides dozens of field survey coordinators and research assistants whom I name on my website, www.kalyango.com, and other scholars whose work I cite, I would like to personally thank several colleagues and friends who have contributed to this project.

I would like to believe that my scholarly contributions are, to a great extent, a consequence of my interactions with colleagues like Petya Eckler, Wayne Wanta, Cary Frith, Fred Vultee, Steve Howard, Uche Onyebadi, Joseph Kizito, and a few others. As I write these acknowledgments, I have come to appreciate that scholarship is never accomplished in isolation or without the relentless support, criticism, and solidarity of academic friendships like the ones I have made over the years. This book is as much a product of the scholarly community, whose members have reviewed and critiqued my contributions to journals and book chapters over the years, as it is my individual effort.

Among those who provided invaluable feedback on the research that evolved over several years into this book are members of my doctoral dissertation committee: Wayne Wanta at University of Florida (international media), Stephanie Craft at MU (qualitative research), Minion K. C. Morrison at Mississippi State University (African politics and democratization), Peggy E. McGuinness at St. Johns University (international and comparative law), and Paul Bolls at MU (quantitative research).

I wish to extend my appreciation to Cary Roberts Frith (E. W. Scripps School of Journalism at OU); who copyedited and commented on the manuscript. The conceptual and analytical narratives were clearly improved as a result of her detailed edits. Her professional work as a magazine journalist and two years as a Park Fellow at the University of North Carolina at Chapel Hill studying political communication and quantitative methods have paid dividends in this project. It has been a real pleasure working with Cary, who shares my passion for political communication research.

Also, I am grateful for the wealth of suggestions provided by the external reviewers who read the manuscript for Peter Lang Publishing, especially Osabuohien Amienyi, dean of the College of Communications at Arkansas State University. I also appreciate Musa Wakhungu Olaka (Holocaust and Genocide Studies Center, University of South Florida) for his incisive thoughts on appropriate literature that I reviewed and many suggestions on the first four chapters of my book. I also extend my deepest thanks to one of my research assistants at OU, Darcy Higgins (political science), who spent endless hours in the library searching for literature, summarizing some readings, and formatting all chapters. She worked with me as a research apprentice, sponsored by the HTC at OU. She even continued to work on this project after the HTC funds dried out. I hope that the experience Darcy gained from this project was beneficial to her studies as she explored social justice and other problems of transitioning countries using democratic theory. Darcy's work ethic and charisma will make her an invaluable global citizen. Aisha Mohammed at the E. W. Scripps School of Journalism also dependably delivered on several assignments pertaining to Chapter Three and Four. Robert Stewart and Eric Rothenbuhler at OU also remarkably supported this endeavor. I commend Gregory Shepherd's leadership as dean of the Scripps College of Communication and thank him most profoundly for creating an enabling environment for me to finance and complete this book.

The acknowledgments cannot be complete without crediting my fiercest critic and ardent research supporter, Petya Eckler (University of Iowa), who played the very active roles of reviewer and judicious critic on this book for several years. I am forever thankful for the time she expended on countless phone calls and e-mails when she served as a sounding board for many of the propositions and research ideas in this book. Petya and I also collaborated on a number of other research endeavors, which were related to some of the question stems and variables used here. My work as an international comparative scholar would not be exciting without her aptitude.

I also would like to thank Steve Howard, head of the Center for African Studies at OU. Steve helped clear ambiguities in the early stages of conceptualizing the main ideas for this book. He kindly shared his work and was a helpful resource as I prepared the final manuscript. There is no doubt that Africa is still daunted by many socioeconomic and political challenges and has a long way to go towards achieving democratic consolidation. Steve's decades of indirect support and dedication to spread knowledge through training Africa's future leaders at OU should not go unnoticed.

Special thanks to John Sentongo (Makerere University), Musa Olaka (University of South Florida), Henry Ngilazi (Zambia), Samuel Gummah (Uganda), Joshua Wamwara (Kenya), Rosemary Faraja (Tanzania), Gerald Mputwe (South Africa), Jean Pierre Kabanda (Rwanda and Burundi), and Tesfaye Berhane (Ethiopia) for their lead in managing and coordinating dozens of field survey assistants. I am proud to be able to call all these internationalists my colleagues and friends.

My greatest and immeasurable debt is owed to my family—Jenny and our sons, Ragan and Isaac—who have had to endure long periods of my absence at the lunch table and whenever I traveled to Africa to collect data. A special thanks to my dear wife, Jenny, to whom I am indebted not only because of the extra responsibilities she took on while I sat at the dining table past midnight for endless days, but also because she provided the indispensable moral support I needed to finish this project. I am also grateful to my sister, Fatuma (Fat), whose help and encouragement enabled me to stay focused and complete this project on time. I would not have been able to marshal the tenacity required to contribute my share of social justice and knowledge for the betterment of Africa without my family's profound love, resilience, and affection.

I thank the almighty God for the extraordinary fortune of reaching this milestone.

Abbreviations

ADI	Africa Development Indicators
AFRICOM	Africa Command
AMREF	African Medical and Research Foundation
ANC	African National Congress (South Africa and Tanzania)
ANOVA	Analysis of Variance
ANP	Afrikaner National Party
APHRC	African Population and Health Research Center
CBR	Centre for Basic Research
CBS	Central Broadcasting Services
CCK	Communications Commission of Kenya
CCM	Chama Cha Mapinduzi (Tanzania)
CNC	National Communication Council (Burundi)
CNDD-FDD	National Council for the Defense of Democracy–Forces for the Defense of Democracy (Burundi)
COMESA	Common Markets for Eastern and Southern Africa
COPE	Congress of the People
COSATU	Congress of South African Trade Unions
CPJ	Committee to Protect Journalists
CUF	Civic United Front (Tanzania)
DP	Democratic Party (Uganda)
DRC	Democratic Republic of Congo
EAC	East African Community
EACU	East Africa Customs Union
EPRDF	Ethiopian People's Revolutionary Democratic Front
ESA	Eastern and Southern Africa
FDD	Forces for Democratic Defense (Burundi)
FOIA	Freedom of Information Act (United States)
FRODEBU	Burundian Democratic Front

FXI	Freedom of Expression Institute (South Africa)
GDP	Gross Domestic Product
GGR	GDP growth rate
GLM	general linear models
HLM	hierarchical linear modeling
HTC	Honors Tutorial College at Ohio University
ICASA	Independent Communications Authority of South Africa
ICC	intraclass correlation
IDP	internally displaced person
IMF	International Monetary Fund
IR	inflation rate
IREX	International Research and Exchanges Board
IRI	International Republican Institute
IV	independent variable
KANU	Kenya African Union
KIMC	Kenya Institute of Mass Communication
KNCST	Kenya National Council for Science and Technology
KTN	Kenya Television Network
KUJ	Kenya Union of Journalists
KY	Kabaka Yekka (Uganda)
MDDA	Media Development and Diversity Agency
MISA	Media Institute of Southern Africa Zambia
MMD	Movement for Multi-Party Democracy (Zambia)
MP	Member of Parliament
MWASA	Media Workers Association of South Africa
NCC	National Council of Communication (Burundi)
NEB	National Electoral Board (Ethiopia)
NEPAD	New Partnership for Africa's Development
NGO	Non-governmental Organization
NIJU	National Institute of Journalists of Uganda
NPN	National Party of Nigeria
NRA	National Resistance Army (Uganda)
NRM	National Resistance Movement (Uganda)
ODM	Orange Democratic Movement (Kenya)
OLS	ordinary least squares
ORINFOR	National Information Office of Rwanda

PAC	Pan Africanist Congress
PARMEHUTU	Party of the Hutu Emancipation Movement
PCG	per capita GDP
PNU	Party of National Unity (Kenya)
RPA	Radio Publique Africaine
RPF	Rwandan Patriotic Front
RTLM	Radio-Télévision Libre des Milles Collines
RTNB	Radio-Télévision Nationale du Burundi
SABC	South African Broadcasting Corporation
SADC	Southern African Development Community
SPSS	Statistical Package for the Social Sciences
SUNY	State University of New York
TANU	Tanganyika African National Union
TBC	Tanzania Broadcasting Corporation
TBN	Trinity Broadcasting Network
TVT	Televisheniya Taifa
UBC	Uganda Broadcasting Corporation
UCLA	University of California in Los Angeles
UDJP	Unity for Democracy and Justice Party
UJSC	Uganda Journalists Safety Committee
UJU	Uganda Journalists Union
UNDP	United Nations Development Program
UNESCO	United Nations Educational, Scientific and Cultural Organization
UNIP	United National Independence Party (Zambia)
UPC	Uganda People's Congress
UPDF	Uganda People's Defence Forces
UPRONA	Union for National Progress
USC	University of Southern California
USD	United States Dollars — $
USIU	United States International University
VOA	Voice of America
WBS	Wavah Broadcasting Services
WDI	World Development Indicator
ZARD	Zambia Association for Research and Development
ZNBC	Zambia National Broadcasting Corporation

Chapter One

Evolution of the News Media in Eastern and Southern Africa

Understanding the impact of mass media on public opinion and the democratization process is vital to the fortitude of African democracy and its people. This book examines three media-related phenomena that highlight the central dilemmas in the consolidation of democracy in Eastern and Southern Africa (ESA). First, many ordinary citizens in different parts of Africa have expressed their discontent about media performance, particularly the content delivered by various news outlets. Second, the wrath of state retaliation often falls upon ordinary citizens who are politically engaged in media discourse and are motivated to obtain knowledge about democratic rule and governance. Third, journalists have had to endure strict, archaic media policies and harsh conditions in different authoritarian and democratizing regimes. As an Africanist and former journalist, my scholarly interest in the link between media and democratization comes from experiencing these three phenomena firsthand.

On several occasions in 1999 and 2000, my father, or *mzee* as I call him, pressed me to change my career from journalism to a more "rewarding" profession. His argument was that although I had worked in national and international media for more than a decade, he did not trust the news organizations for which I worked. Nor did he trust the other competing media in East Africa because they did not provide him with the information he needed to carry out his social, fiscal, and democratic obligations. My father knew well my great passion for journalism, but he made it absolutely clear that he disparaged the news media. He scorned news coverage about current affairs with comments such as, "The news on radio and television is inept." "We all notice that the news coverage of politics in newspapers creates antagonistic partisanship."

My father's colleagues also found fault with the news, remarking that it is tainted by state propaganda and that some journalists contribute to enduring ethnic and regional insurrections. Ordinary citizens also weighed in. When I was the head of news and current affairs at Wavah Broadcasting Services (WBS) television in the mid-1990s, my colleagues and I received about ten letters and several e-mails and faxes every week from viewers who consistently expressed similar sentiments. These comments, from my immediate family members and our viewers, made me wonder whether such attitudes resonated with other citizens.

At the start of the invasion of Zaire (now the Democratic Republic of Congo or DRC) in November 1996, I attended a regional media conference in Nairobi, Kenya, which addressed media coverage of the refugee crisis in Eastern Zaire. That meeting turned out to be a rebuke of the state-owned media of Burundi, Rwanda, Tanzania, Uganda, and Zaire. Participants condemned the national media for their active support of their governments' involvement in regional and transitional insurrections. At that time, most African governments had overwhelming control of the media through ownership, media policies, and outright disregard of press freedoms and the rule of law. When Rwanda and Uganda led a coalition of ESA nations[1] that overthrew President Mobutu Sese-Seko of Zaire for unclear reasons, neither of their national media questioned or extensively covered the mass killings and wanton destruction of property and resources in Eastern Zaire. Hundreds of thousands of civilians have been killed in internal conflicts and civil wars in Burundi, Ethiopia, Rwanda, South Africa, Uganda, and recently in Kenya. It should be noted, however, that because of the violence, the media in these countries have also been the victims of dictatorships that have curtailed their ability to expose evils and to enlighten uninformed ESA citizens.

Such condemnation of media performance and strong public attitudes toward the influence of government on political expression and media discourse have persisted for more than three decades, even as some communities and ethnicities suffer at the hands of their elected governments.[2] In 2001, for example, during a visit to Addis Ababa, Ethiopia, my good friend Desta Getachew told me that authorities had imprisoned his brother, Dahnay, a journalist, on charges of participating in unauthorized meetings and for spying on the government. Desta later learned that the unauthorized gathering was actually a meeting of student organizations who were opposed to government policies on the education system. He assured me that his brother would be safe and that the government would not come after him. He believed in Ethiopia's system of governance and hoped for better days ahead. Desta may have said that in order to mitigate my concerns for the safety of his brother. In April 2002, security operatives roughed up Desta and Dahnay at their home in Arat Kilo, a suburb of Addis Ababa. In May 2002, I received an e-mail from another Ethiopian journalist, whom I will identify only as Tesfaye, informing me that Desta and his family had all disappeared without a trace.

Burundi and Rwanda are among the countries that I covered extensively as an international journalist. Because of Burundi's record of human rights violations, it was always a challenge for my cameraman, Ibrahim Mugwanya, and me to work in Bujumbura. Incidents of intimidation against Burundian journalists were whispered about around hotel lobbies and bars, although the local media never reported any cases of journalists who were charged by the government for exposing the regime's human rights abuses. During our coverage of the Burundi and Rwandan conflicts between 1995 and 2002, we talked to dozens of politicians, members of civic organizations, and human rights defenders about the safety of journalists and the independence of the media. Some activists and international observers intimated that journalists were arbitrarily arrested and charged with treason if they mentioned government activities that were not sanctioned by the Ministry of Information and Broadcasting. For example, Jean-Claude Kavumbagu, editor of *Net Press*, was arrested in September 2008 and charged with defamation for reporting about graft in state institutions and criticizing a presidential trip to the Beijing Olympics.

Another case in point is an acquaintance, Ismail Mbonigaba, whom I met in Rwanda in February 2001. Mbonigaba said that he had faced harassment and overnight detention in private security cells on six different occasions. In 2003, he was arrested and imprisoned for more than fifty days on charges of inciting division and discrimination. Civilians in both countries told me about the decline in the quality of political discourse and about partisan political reporting that hyped the state agenda on national issues. However, some citizens would go to great lengths to disagree with me about the value and impact of the news on all broadcast stations in Rwanda and Burundi. Gerard Ndiyuhira, a promi-

nent trader in Kigali, Rwanda, told me during an interview[3] that Rwanda's radio
and television media were interested only in unimportant issues such as "where
President Paul Kagame has visited and who he has met. This is a lead story—
day after day, and night after night." His argument was that following the
whereabouts of the president and cabinet was not newsworthy and that deliver-
ing television and radio news was a waste of time and resources. He was interested in political satire and business news.

While my examples are somewhat dated, journalists continue to share anecdotes of fear and intimidation at social gatherings and bars across communities
and cities in Kenya, South Africa, Tanzania, and Zambia. Local law enforcement agencies continue to close or ban media organizations, intimidate media
personnel, and arrest journalists.

Scope and Context

This book aims to provide empirical evidence in support of conjectures
about media performance and how media are governed. It examines eight countries in ESA, focusing on media coverage of nationally important issues. It also
assesses how citizens evaluate the different national media, their regimes, and
their elected government officials during the democratization era in Africa. It
encompasses Burundi, Ethiopia, Kenya, Rwanda, South Africa, Tanzania,
Uganda, and Zambia. These countries—except South Africa—remain largely
understudied in the important area of mass communication. They are all part of
either the East African Community (EAC) or the Southern African Development Community (SADC) region.

The rationale for focusing on the two ESA regions is multifold:

- Seven countries are the most understudied in mass communication research.
- The two eastern and southern regions, EAC and SADC, have set up regional economic and political communities.
- The EAC and SADC are engaged in advancing transnational peace and
mitigating interstate conflicts in the two regions.
- Through mass media and civic education, the potential exists for multilateralism in the area to empower and liberate citizens from ignorance and
backwardness.

The EAC and SADC also formed the Common Markets for Eastern and Southern Africa (COMESA). COMESA's purpose is to create a wider free market among member states that is dedicated to consolidating commercial services and industrial ventures. This multilateralism would include promoting socioeconomic development, sharing physical infrastructure, and protecting the environment. Multilateralism, however, comes at a greater cost for EAC and SADC member states as they try to calibrate their governments to foster political stability, security, human rights, and democratic governance.

One of the central claims of democratization theory is that individuals can work collectively to promote personal growth and alleviate poverty. However, some African leaders use state-sponsored terror to reassert their political authority and to frustrate progressives and assertive citizens.[4] In every election cycle, citizens face the wrath of authoritarian regimes when the state feels threatened or its institutions and political ideologies are challenged through media discourse. During the wave of democratization in the 1980s and 1990s, authoritarian regimes in ESA clamped down on the vibrant media and working-class individuals who posed a threat to the status quo.

My father is one of thousands of Africans who bear the scars of extrajudicial persecution, handed out by their governments for being commercially vigilant and politically attentive citizens. Three successive regimes have charged my father with political rebellion and thrown him into prison even though he has never run for elected office, has never actively engaged in political activism, and has never made threatening public comments through the media.

Security personnel of former Ugandan president Idi Amin Dada's State Research Bureau threw my father in prison for three months in 1977 on fabricated charges that he was supplying farm produce to enemy Jews and other "European imperialists." In 1983, the military special force of former president Dr. Apollo Milton Obote imprisoned him after he turned down an offer to operate a food export business with Colonel Murshidi Orala, an army officer. My father languished in prison for six months. Then in 2000, under Ugandan president Yoweri Museveni, my father and dozens of other civilians and businesspersons endured another detention without trial in military barracks and unregistered places of remand, which the media ironically dubbed "safe houses." Despite the brutality and harsh conditions that my father endured, he still pledges his unwavering support for the Ugandan regime and professes his love of President Museveni. He does not hold any grudges against Museveni or the Ugandan government, whose security men threw him in a military prison without charges or trial. Such tolerant love of an undemocratic system defies logic and common sense.

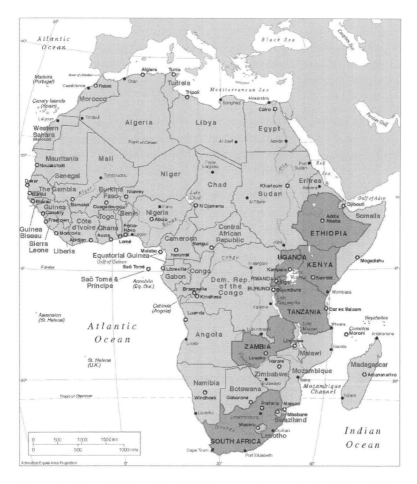

Figure 1.1. Map of Africa—All eight ESA countries are shaded. Map of Africa showing the eight countries—highlighted in dark color. Source: Designed and produced by maps.com exclusively for this author. Copyright: Yusuf Kalyango 2010.

Throughout ESA, there are many more untold stories even worse than my father's. According to the last twenty years of Human Rights Watch reports, civilian men and women from all eight countries have languished in jail and been constantly tortured, and some have died in detention without ever standing trial. Regardless of this abrogation of human rights and civil liberties, a majority of citizens continue to support their government, and even vote the incumbent president and government back into power. These government supporters include citizens whose families have been kidnapped, inhumanely tortured, and even killed by state authorities and law enforcement agents. In this era of democratization, why do an overwhelming number of Africans continue to support autocratic leaders and tyrannical regimes?

Since the role of the press is to educate citizens and to shape political awareness, why is it that citizens in these countries do not positively react to messages that enlighten them about their fundamental human rights, their civil liberties, the rule of law, and the benefits of a truly democratic state? How does the news media in these African nations shape the political and socioeconomic agenda on issues of democratization? What impact does the news media have on public attitudes towards citizens' respective governments, neighboring countries, and the heads of state? To what extent do the media shape the public agenda and attitudes towards regime legitimacy, the rule of law, and government accountability? Does the public perceive their government as the builder of national policy agendas? In answering these questions, I proceed under the assumption that the media in these countries do not perform their duties with a clearly defined agenda regarding the broader issue of democracy and good governance. I also assume that media products are not equally accessible to everyone across all regions in the EAC and SADC.

It is imperative to note from the outset that there is not enough space in this book to make all arguments and counterarguments at the depth necessary to fully explicate what is happening in the region. Therefore, this book focuses on eight countries in these two regions and narrows its conceptualization of democratic governance and media performance to address the most critical variables. To go beyond this constraint, and broaden the scope and content of the volume, would fatally distract from those central theories and issues. Therefore, this volume will deal only with how the media perform in these eight countries during the current wave of democratization.

Post-colonial Evolution of the News Media

Throughout the 1970s, the early years of the post-independence era, the national state-owned media in ESA continued with their journalistic tradition of protest for social justice, emancipation from state oppression, and support for equality.[5] This type of journalism, primarily in the print media, was rooted in the expression of dissent, which started during the anti-colonial struggle from the 1950s through the mid-1960s.[6] In the early 1980s through the 1990s, some ESA countries, particularly Kenya, South Africa, and Zambia, enjoyed rapid growth of the print media, particularly newspapers and magazines. Yet most of the print media were primarily elitist, only catering to upscale urban audiences who were literate in French—in the case of Rwanda and Burundi—and in English for the other six countries.[7] In most of ESA during the late 1980s and early 1990s, radio became a potentially powerful influence in news and political commentary.[8] In this period most countries, except Rwanda and Burundi, allowed private entrepreneurs to launch commercial FM radio channels. Before the liberalization of telecommunication and mass media sectors in all eight countries, most broadcast networks were run by the government. These governments, through their state-appointed directorate (ministry) of information, on average required broadcast corporations to devote 95 percent of their content to the arts and social development.

Following is a synopsis of the broadcast and print media in each of the eight ESA countries, with particular attention to the plight and resilience of the media as they transitioned from fully state-controlled to liberalized outlets.

The Media and the Governments in ESA

Burundi

When Burundi gained its independence from Belgium in 1962, the interim government established a constitutional monarchy. Four years later, the government of President Michel Micombero abolished the constitutional monarchy and set up a military state. A series of one-party regimes followed until 1992. Throughout those thirty years under the ruling Union for National Progress party (UPRONA), internal conflicts grew into armed rebellions between the authoritarian Tutsi governments and the militia groups led by the Hutu opposition.[9] Much of the oppression in Burundi occurred at the hands of the Tutsi minority on the Hutu majority; whereas in Rwanda, the Hutu majority suppressed the Tutsi minority until 1994. Both Burundi and Rwanda have a Francophone legacy, while the rest of the six countries adopted English traditions handed down from their British colonial rulers.

In post-colonial Burundi, the new regimes demanded and received favorable coverage from the national media. When Jean-Baptiste Bagaza became president in 1976, his government set up media policies that severely restricted press freedom. For two decades, journalists who were critical of the government were arrested. Some news publications run by civil society, as well as by foreign news organizations, were either suspended or shut down.[10] Attacks included frequent intimidation and imprisonment of journalists and all media professionals. The Committee to Protect Journalists and other various media-monitoring and free-press advocacy groups show that since 1980, more than fifty local and foreign journalists have been killed or disappeared in Burundi. Dozens have been imprisoned for months without trial. Jean-Claude Kavumbagu, Bob Rugurika, Christelle Ruvari, Serge Nibizi, and Domitile Kiramvu are among the top independent journalists who have served time in Burundi's prisons in the last decade.

The country's political and economic conditions have severely hurt the media. Most of the journalists who have disappeared without a trace have worked for privately owned media. One of the missing journalists is a well-known reporter, Corneille Nibaruta, who is believed to have been picked up by security agents in 2006. My cameraman, Ibrahim Mugwanya, and I first met Corneille in 1999 when he was affiliated with *Radio-Télévision Nationale du Burundi* (RTNB). On two occasions, Corneille visited us at Novotel Hotel in Bujumbura to talk about human rights, ethnic politics, and prospects for independent media ventures. His disappearance occurred just three months after his return from forced exile. I lost contact with Corneille in 2003 when I went to graduate school in Columbia, Missouri. The National Council of Communication (NCC), which oversaw press freedom and respect for the law, closed two newspapers and suspended the license of a private FM radio station in 2007 in order to control messages considered extreme and dangerous to national security.[11]

The current Burundian government headed by Pierre Nkurunziza still controls the nation's only radio and TV station. The main media outlets are RTNB, *Le Renouveau* newspaper, and an official weekly, *Ubumwe*. In 1994, there were twenty-two newspapers, but by 1999 the number had been reduced to four, and another thirteen appeared irregularly.[12] The only privately owned and partially independent newspaper is *Ndongozi*, which is owned by the Catholic Church and enjoys some international financial backing.

Like Rwanda, Tanzania, Uganda, and Zambia, radio has been the most important source of information for ordinary Burundians. Private radio stations have played an essential role in promoting pluralism.[13] Unlike in Rwanda, where radio became the medium of state propaganda, newspapers in Burundi were the "weapons of war" during political campaigns and were responsible for reinforcing ethnic stereotypes.[14] Since joining the EAC in 2007, the Burundian government has vowed to establish a working environment conducive to a free and independent press. President Nkurunziza said in a 2008 national address that promotion of political expression and press freedom will be realized through policy reforms that ensure all state institutions adhere to the rule of law and protection of human rights. That rhetoric is yet to be followed by appropriate action.

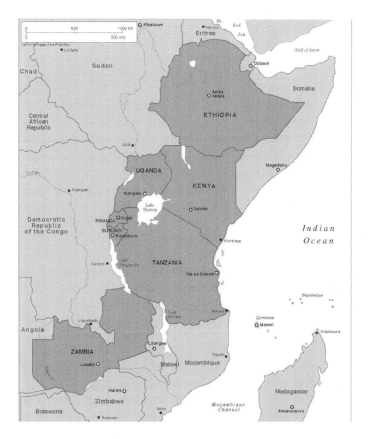

Figure 1.2. Eastern Africa—Geographic location of Eastern Africa. Map showing the Eastern African countries: Burundi, Ethiopia, Kenya, Rwanda, Tanzania, and Uganda. The capital cities are spotted with white-in-black star. Source: Designed and produced by maps.com exclusively for this author. Copyright: Yusuf Kalyango 2010.

Ethiopia

In 1974, Ethiopian army major Mengistu Haile Mariam overthrew the government in a military coup that collectively killed sixty aristocrats and officials of the imperial regime.[15] Mengistu dismantled a centuries-old imperial monarchy and set up a Marxist government. He led Ethiopia into a totalitarian communist regime, supported by the Soviet Union and assisted by Cuba. President Mengistu had established a military state by 1975 and nationalized private farmlands and religious properties, as well as abrogated its bilateral relations with the United States.[16] He consolidated his power through dictatorship by ordering the assassination of his opponents and members of the Derg Political Council. He also drafted a new constitution.

The first crackdown on the press occurred even before Mengistu took power, when Ethiopia annexed Eritrea in 1962 under Emperor Haile Selassie.[17] From 1962 until the early 1990s, Ethiopia banned Eritrean political parties, closed some of the vocal gutter press, and arrested journalists who raised concerns about Ethiopia's hegemony.[18] The gutter presses are defined here as newsletters that are poorly researched and terribly written in local vernacular and in English. Some are written in Swahili and offer propaganda about politicians involved in promiscuity, corruption, and other scandals. Throughout the period under President Mengistu (1974 to 1991), a protracted civil conflict cost an estimated 100,000 lives, and more than 50 journalists were imprisoned or disappeared inside the country.[19] In 1991, the Ethiopian People's Revolutionary Democratic Front (EPRDF) overthrew Mengistu, which escalated the conflict with Eritrean separatists and weakened the military's supremacy.[20] Eritrea ultimately gained its independence in 1993, but discord between the neighbors has continued since then.

A few independent and institutional religious media outlets never survived the autocratic regimes. A case in point is the Lutheran broadcasting station in Addis Ababa, which owned and operated a radio outlet and current affairs periodical in the 1970s. Both were seized by the Mengistu government for what the regime classified as distorted content and "journalistic disobedience." Even the foreign press was considerably censored in the 1970s and 1980s because the government required all foreign journalists to file their foreign bureau reports through the Ethiopian News Agency.[21] Those who disobeyed this policy were fined and even expelled. In the past three decades, Ethiopian governments—particularly under the current head of state, Prime Minister Meles Zenawi—have strategically appointed politicians to work as editors of the Ethiopian News Agency. Their main duties, however, were to censor content or build the government's agenda in newspapers and broadcast outlets. In addition, the governments also banned books and periodicals that were deemed adversarial to the spirit of Ethiopian nationalism and revolution.

In 2005 there were about forty-six newspapers and magazines in Ethiopia, but the private press has been struggling under restrictive press laws. Since then, sixteen newspapers were banned and fourteen others were shut down by their proprietors in a government crackdown on the critical press. In some instances, state-owned printing presses refused to print the privately owned papers. As of December 2008, Ethiopia had one privately owned daily newspaper, six main radio news stations (two privately owned), and one national television station. Just like Rwanda and Burundi, Ethiopia launched its first truly privately owned commercial radio stations in early 2007. Two stations, *Sheger Radio* and ZAMI FM, went on the air in mid-2007. The government imposed stringent restrictions, especially for ZAMI FM, which was licensed to provide news and talk shows. The government required the new ZAMI FM and other privately owned media to hire news managers from the state-owned national broadcasts.[22]

Radio programming in Ethiopia is a key source of news and current affairs, but it is often weak because personnel are underpaid and poorly trained.[23] Draconian media laws have been used to close news outlets and to arrest editors and journalists.[24] Journalists covering state affairs have suffered punitive sentences for exposing corrupt public officials, indiscriminate killings of civilians, and human rights violations.[25] For example, journalists Eskinder Nega and his pregnant fiancée Serkalam Fassil languished in jail for over six months before any charges were brought against them. In the past two decades more than 100 journalists, including prominent journalists Andualem Ayle, Nardos Meaza, and Amare Aregawi, spent thirty days on average in Ethiopian prisons for failing to pay either police bond or court bail or because they lacked the funds to hire lawyers to represent them. Dozens of independent journalists went into hiding or fled the country in the past decade. Privately owned media continue to operate under restrictions and have no access to most official records, while state-owned media were given privileged treatment and even allowed to sell information to the privately owned media.[26]

Kenya

In post-colonial Kenya, Jomo Kenyatta, the first president of the republic, ruled with an autocratic style and increased restrictions on freedom of speech and expression.[27] At that time, the media in Kenya were divided and targeted a particular audience. The top press served the white settlers who claimed Kenyan citizenship; the secondary press served the Indian community; and the gutter press served the Africans. Ironically, Kenyatta was a prominent gutter-press journalist and editor before he became Kenya's president.[28] Since the early 1960s, Kenya's print media were the only privately owned media in East Africa, and the commercially successful presses were foreign owned. But after the death of President Kenyatta in 1978, the domination of the print media by the private sector changed. Daniel Toroitich arap Moi took over the presidency that year in a peaceful succession, and later, in 1983, his party, the Kenya African Union (KANU), bought Hillary Ng'weno's *Nairobi Times* and named it *The Kenya Times*.[29] Moi maintained Kenyatta's autocratic leadership.[30] His regime exercised immense intolerance to political dissent from opposition politicians, academics, and other elite members of civil society.

Opposition politicians and the civil society in Kenya used the gutter press to express dissent against the government. The gutter press in Kenya's major cities of Nairobi and Mombasa has been vibrant for three decades, but these publications last for only a short time. They are mostly sold on newsstands and often on the street corners of Nairobi, the capital city, for half the price of a newspaper. Security personnel have previously harassed news editors, and some of their writers have either spent several months in prison or disappeared. For example, John Wandetto of the *People* spent eighteen months in prison, Victor Nzuma of the *Nation* was beaten and shots were fired over his head during three different incidents in one year, and Andrew Mwangura was imprisoned four times between 2005 and 2008. The journalists mentioned here all lost their professional equipment—video, still cameras, and tape recorders. Dozens of journalists have suffered the same fate in every decade of the democratization era.

Throughout the 1980s and early 1990s, President Moi's regime continued to promote its own party's political agenda and kept state control by dividing the opposition and instigating ethnic and regional cleavages through the national broadcast media.[31] Nevertheless, the Kenyan government also subscribes to the development-communication paradigm that seeks to promote the interests of the nation by engaging in only positive and constructive criticism. In the 1990s, Moi's government banned any publication for disloyalty to the office of the president and to nationalism in general.[32] The regime restricted political expression through the press and criminalized some critical journalists and their media outlets through sedition trials. For instance, in 1989 alone, four independent presses were banned, including the *Financial Review*, *Beyond* magazine, *Development Agenda*, and *Nairobi Law Monthly*. Between 1987 and 1992, at least thirty news outlets were banned in Kenya and some of the editors were arrested.[33] From 1995 to 2005, more than thirty news outlets were temporarily shut down or paid heavy fines for exposing corrupt government practices, using draconian laws such as the Press Council of Kenya Bill (1995) and others.

Rwanda

The Republic of Rwanda is a prominent case study of the detrimental societal effects of the media's failure to inform citizens about state affairs. The events of the 1994 genocide in Rwanda have been well documented in several books and documentaries. I witnessed part of that conflict as I covered the post-genocide angst in Rwanda for Sanyu Television from late 1994 through 1997 and followed the reconstruction and reconciliation process. I also reported on the concentration camps in the Eastern Democratic Republic of Congo, which were constructed for genocidal Hutu militias.

Initially, throughout the 1980s, the Rwandan government led by President Juvénale Habyarimana used national radio and television to promote public health, public safety, and modern farming. Throughout the post-colonial period, France even provided financial aid to the Rwandan government so that it could purchase thousands of cheap radios and batteries in order to disseminate civic education and promote modern farming techniques.[34] In the late 1980s and early 1990s, Rwanda also built stronger radio transmitters and repeater transmission towers to cover the entire country.[35]

From the early 1990s, the Rwanda government owned the only television station and local radio stations in the country, under the umbrella of the National Information Office of Rwanda (ORINFOR). The only non-state broadcast media in Rwanda at that time were international outlets like *Radio France Internationale* and *Radio Deutsch Welle International*.[36] In their early efforts to fuel hatred between ethnic groups, most of the state agencies, including the Rwandan national army, used their authority and control over the state-owned media to unite the majority Hutu ethnic group against the minority Tutsi.[37] When the Rwandan Patriotic Front (RPF) invaded Rwanda in early 1990, *Radio Rwanda* began to promote the killing of Tutsis in regions surrounding Kigali, the capital city.[38] This media incitement, using ethnic propaganda fronted by the regime, led to political violence. Instead of reporting on state accountability for this atrocious propaganda and the collapse of the state, *Radio Rwanda* spread fear, rumors, and terror by engaging in kill-or-be-killed rhetoric.[39] The media set off the killing of more than one-half million Tutsi people and gave instructions to the Hutu majority about how to do it.[40] *Radio-Télévision Libre des Milles*

Collines (TRTLM) and ORINFOR predominantly instigated ethnic cleansing. The two news organizations were owned and controlled by associates of late Hutu president Juvénale Habyarimana and the Rwandan government, respectively.

Fifty-two Rwandan journalists who were identified as Tutsi or moderate Hutu were killed during the genocide.[41] Yet the media failed to provide non-biased coverage of the conflict.[42] Consequently, the government of the new Rwandan Patriotic Front, which overthrew the late Habyarimana's government and ended the genocide, faced an enormous challenge in its attempt to rehabilitate the national media. Major General Paul Kagame, who has presided over the Government of Rwanda since the 1994 genocide, has gradually transformed and reformed the media both as a public and a private press.[43]

Shortly after the genocide, I spent much of late 1994 and 1995 investigating the causes of such hatred and its impact on Rwandan society. During the interviews with survivors of the genocide, I noticed a great deal of mistrust, frustration, disgust, indignation, and continued hatred of the political elites and the media. I still have memories of angry survivors, who pointed fingers and made fists at me simply because I was a broadcaster interviewing them. They berated me with comments such as, "You [the media] are responsible for the death of my relatives. Your colleagues on TV and radio in Kigali are responsible for these atrocities. They asked our elders, our men, our local councilors, our soldiers, and even children to pick up machetes to kill our people." When I first interviewed then vice president General Paul Kagame in late 1996, he vowed never to allow a free and independent radio in Rwanda.

After the genocide, the Rwandan government under President Kagame passed a media law in July 2002, which established a new body called the High Press Council, whose ostensible purpose is to guarantee freedom of the press. Yet this body regulates electronic broadcasting and imposes censorship on the press with the legal guideline of preventing a repeat of the 1994 hate speech.[44] As a result, the regime has been very forceful and proactive in stopping any inflammatory content and critical statements against any individuals in government. The regime is also keen to protect state and commercial institutions from "damaging reports" in the media. Just like the Burundi government's strategy against the independent press, attacks on Rwandan journalists include frequent intimidation, interrogation, and imprisonment of outspoken journalists and news editors. For example, the editors of the *Umuseso* newspaper, Emmanuel Niyonteze and Gérard M. Manzi, have been in Rwandan prisons a combined eleven times. Agnès Nkusi-Uwimana spent a year in jail on frivolous charges of sectarianism and libel. The editor of the *Umuvigizi* newspaper, Jean Bosco Gasasira, was brutally beaten with iron bars by unknown assailants for being critical of the ruling party, the RPF. It has been confirmed by various media advocacy groups that in the post-genocide era more than thirty Rwandan journalists, including prominent journalists Emanuael Munyemanzi in 1998 and Esther Mukamusoni in 2001, have been killed in the line of duty or disappeared without a trace.

In the last ten years under Kagame's leadership, seventeen well-known journalists are known to have been incarcerated without trial on charges of treason, inciting genocide, and hate speech. Rwanda does not even have a daily independent newspaper. The government forbids coverage of some topics and institutions, such as the Rwandan military, the Justice Department, and the State House. Exposing any tyrannical acts committed by the RPF is also taboo. The first privately owned independent radio station was established in 2004, but all private broadcast and print media face government restrictions, and generally exercise self-censorship.[45] Some proprietors of the so-called privately owned press are members of Rwanda's governing council, with close ties and patronage to the presidential State House.

South Africa

In South Africa, the anti-apartheid newspapers such as *South* and the *Weekly Mail* were well known for their adversarial approach, and were primarily established to promote political expression and the struggle for black independence.[46] Presses run by black South African activists took on a new role of countering the state agenda of the apartheid regime, led by the National Party.[47] Apartheid was mainly propagated through state-owned news corporations such as the South African Broadcasting Corporation (SABC). However, during the second term of President Marais Viljoen, the South African government banned newspapers and radio from politicizing segregation issues through commentary and opinion.[48] That happened at the height of the anti-apartheid struggle in the early 1980s when the government took stringent measures to crack down on political activists from the African National Congress (ANC).

Viljoen's government enforced media regulations that restricted press freedoms in South Africa. The Publications and Entertainments Act of 1963 and the Internal Security Act of 1982 were used to suppress newspaper reporting of any demonstrations against the National Party's apartheid regime.[49] These regulations also censored the media's exposure of human rights abuses within the prison system.[50] In March 1982, during the apartheid era, the Executive Prime Minister of South Africa, Pieter W. Botha, declared that any national newspaper or any entity of the state-owned broadcast corporation who reported on the conditions of ANC prisoners or inside the prisons would face closure, and their journalists would be incarcerated.[51]

In the post-apartheid era, since the historic democratic elections of 1994 that ushered in Nelson Mandela as the first black president of South Africa, the national media were expected by the new "government of national unity" to be a part of the nationalism transformation. The South African government, just like the other countries examined here, expected the news media to be supportive of the new government by exclusively focusing on nation building. Both the independent and state-owned national media ignored the call for developmental journalism, which literally meant promoting social development without monitoring and holding the government accountable.[52] The South African media, particularly the private press owned by white South Africans, became even more watchful and aggressive in exposing state incompetence and political scandals.[53] The growing independent and libertarian press has intensified its adversarial and watchdog role of the South African government in this millennium, following the civil outcry that corruption in state institutions was thriving unhindered.[54]

Tanzania

In the United Republic of Tanzania, press coverage of political affairs was exclusively controlled by the ruling Chama Cha Mapinduzi party (CCM) from 1965 until the mid-1990s. In essence, the government and its CCM would simply command the full services of the national media in mobilizing citizens to build the regime's agenda. For more than three decades, both the media and the Tanzanian government have shared an informal belief that news that is detrimental to national pride and patriotism must be withheld for the public good.[55] In the 1970s through the 1990s, that indulgence between the government and the state-owned media led to the alienation of the regime from ordinary citizens.[56] Even worse, it created an ill-informed public vis-à-vis good governance and public accountability, and reinforced the negative attitude that state-run media cannot be trusted.

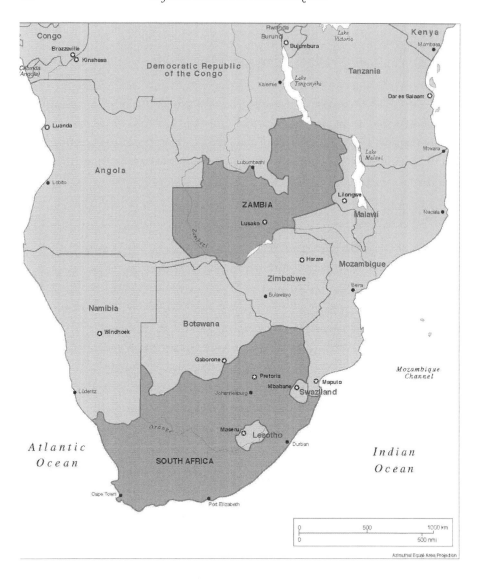

Figure 1.3. Southern Africa—Geographic location of South Africa and Zambia. Map showing Zambia and South Africa in the southern region of Africa. The capital cities are spotted with white-in-black star. Source: Designed and produced by maps.com exclusively for this author. Copyright :Yusuf Kalyango 2010.

After the liberalization of the press in 1995, the media in Tanzania, just like the other countries examined in this volume, increasingly exposed political corruption and the misappropriation of public and donor funds by the state.

Nevertheless, during the era of former president Hassan Mwinyi from 1985 until 1995, vigilant press investigations of corruption and state incompetence were regularly suppressed (and coerced into retractions) by law enforcement agents under the directive of the Ministry of Information. In the late 1980s to mid-1990s some journalists, especially editors such as Praxeda Mtani of *Televisheniya Taifa* (TVT), Hamis Hamad, a photographer with the daily *Uhuru* newspaper, and Emmanuel Muga of the *Express* magazine, were under intense pressure to stop the publishing of critical reports about the government. In fact, these three journalists, and dozens of others, were jailed, physically tortured, and fined for publishing stories related to land-grabbing, expropriations, and corruption by CCM party leaders and other government officials.[57] They were obliged to mobilize citizens for a collective promotion of the *Ujamaa* principles, which is similar to "development journalism." *Ujamaa* is a Tanzania axiom that refers to the family-based concept of socialism, introduced by former president Julius Nyerere in 1964, as a distributive policy associated with socialist communal livelihood.[58]

A 2004 study on the state of the press in Tanzania indicated that press freedom was taking root, but free access to information was still held by public officials such as the police and city or district councilors.[59] The news media in the semi-autonomous archipelago of Zanzibar is still not free. Since independence, politicians in Zanzibar continued to crack down on newspaper and radio journalists who expose their activities.[60] In a country that had more than 100 newspapers registered in 2005, including 11 daily newspapers and 59 weeklies, and more than 30 radio stations, authorities there continued to muzzle the media. In 2003 and 2004, for example, Tanzania's former cabinet Minister of Information Mohammed Seif Khatib implored Parliament to repeal the media law, even though it prohibited the electronic media from covering more than a quarter of the country. Despite the existence of 20 commercial TV stations, the electronic media still do not cover even half of the country, and journalists are still subjected to constant harassment.[61] The government and the CCM still own and control a national radio station, *Radio Tanzania, Dar es Salaam*; a national television station, *Televisheniya Taifa*; and two national newspapers, the English-language *Daily News* and the Swahili-language *Uhuru*.[62] The local authorities continue to make life difficult for the few independent news media based in the archipelago.

Uganda

Uganda became East Africa's inspirational story with a flourishing economy and an educated African middle class. Unlike Tanzania and Kenya, British colonial rulers granted Uganda independence in 1962, without a struggle. However, all of the political opportunities and accolades were reversed during the post-colonial era. During successive regimes from the late 1960s until the mid-1980s, Uganda turned into a political theater of military coups and mass killings, based on ethnic cleavages and political dissent. The military rule of President Idi Amin in the 1970s and Milton Obote in the 1980s marked the brutal pinnacle of unrelenting political instability, suppression of liberties, and massive civilian deaths. The Amin and Obote regimes pursued militarization and despotic politics, which led to legitimacy deficits and socioeconomic and political demise. In Uganda, values such as trust, patriotism, and self-determination were obliterated by state-inspired and institutionalized political conflicts, as well as by ethnic cleavages.[63] That explains the numerous successful coups and violent overthrows of regimes between 1966 and 1986. Uganda was the only African country in the last century to stage a successful internal guerrilla war, which lasted a record five years.[64]

In 1986, Yoweri Museveni overthrew the government of General Tito Lutwa and set up institutions such as the Inspector General of Government, and anti-corruption laws, such as the Public Finance and Accountability Act of 2003 and the Leadership Code Act of 2002 through which his regime and government could be held accountable. Starting in 1995, President Museveni entrenched hegemonic presidentialism, diminished political contestation, and promoted mass mobilization.[65] From 1995 until late 2009, Museveni co-opted independent institutions in order to entrench his grip on presidential power. For example, the inspector general of government is now a presidential appointee. The judiciary, which had been upright, has been weakened, and a previously vibrant human rights commission is relatively powerless.[66] Apparently, several sections of civil society include elites who are prone to state patronage,[67] and a previously independent media have become a muzzled press.[68] Moreover, throughout the 1990s, countless quack journalists were appointed by the state, and their mission was to destabilize newspapers and TV stations for the benefit of the regime.[69]

In the mid- to late 1990s, independent journalists in Uganda were ferried in and out of police detention on weekends so regularly that their wives knew where they had been upon returning home with a peculiar jail scent. For exam-

ple, top Ugandan journalists Andrew Mwenda, John Njoroge, and Joseph Kig-
gundu were blindfolded and arrested by security agents for investigating and
exposing government torture at alleged secret detention centers. In the past
decade alone, as a result of his investigative journalism, Mwenda has been ar-
raigned or prosecuted more than 20 times on sedition and defamation charges.
Other top political journalists such as Charles Onyango Obbo have been harassed and prosecuted more than 100 times under Museveni's regime.

The Ugandan government still owns and controls the *New Vision* newspaper, *Radio Uganda*, and the *UBC* television station. In Uganda, journalists working at state-owned media are government employees. They are the main source
of presidential and ministerial statements, and the lowest paid journalists in the
industry.[70] Media reports claim that Museveni rewards state-owned media practitioners with exclusive interviews and presidential statements. Some FM stations run by the president's friends and by military personnel operate illegally
without a broadcast license. This practice allows the president's friends to evade
broadcast licensing fees and avoid being scrutinized by the broadcasting council
that regulates electronic media.

During the 2006 general elections, popular FM radio talk shows, which had
broadcast open forums through live interactive call-ins and allowed people to
express themselves on a wide range of subjects, were shut down indefinitely.
The ban affected many radio stations, including the four most popular FM stations: *Central Broadcasting Service, Radio One, K-fm,* and *Radio Simba.* The National
Institute of Journalists of Uganda (NIJU) reported that radio stations critical of
the president and his lieutenants would not be allowed to operate. Before the
2006 elections, there were more than 100 FM radio stations registered, and
most of them did not respect the government's election coverage guidelines.
Journalists protested and petitioned government officials a month before Election Day, with more than 6,000 signed petitions opposing the ban. The ban was
lifted after the elections were over.

Zambia

The Republic of Zambia has experienced similar political upheavals since it
attained independence from British rule in 1964. Kenneth B. Kaunda and his
United National Independence Party (UNIP) became Zambia's first head of
state. Kaunda's regime relied heavily on colonial practices and bylaws because
many politicians lacked legislative and governance expertise. In 1972, Kaunda
outlawed all other political parties.[71] Zambia continued to hold regular elections

but only UNIP members could run for office, which created a one-party government.[72]

As Zambia marked the anniversary of its forty-fifth independence, touting its libertarian democratic governance, it is imperative to note that none of the existing media genres—print, radio, and television—are free of state interference. State-owned radio and television have dominated the country's airwaves for over three decades, while privately owned broadcast stations offer little investigative coverage to hold the regime, and all state institutions, accountable. Zambia is no different from the other countries examined in this book in the way its leaders force their agenda on media performance. While the other seven Sub-Saharan African countries expected the news media to be supportive of the governments by focusing on nation building, the Zambian government under the reign of Kaunda established the philosophy of humanism.[73] Humanism is the government expectation that the press will promote and advance the ideas of traditional African communal values in the larger context of nation building.[74]

Radio has made the greatest strides in promoting independent views and political discourse, in spite of the Zambian government's legal authority and control over the licensing of radio stations.[75] The state-owned Zambia National Broadcasting Corporation (ZNBC) is the only national broadcaster, while the privately owned *Radio Phoenix* broadcasts in only four provinces. When the government liberalized the media sector under the Zambian National Broadcasting Act, the number of radio stations increased to thirty-four in 2008.[76] In the last decade, Zambia's Roman Catholic Church has emerged as a dominant radio proprietor with fourteen stations. Many other investment moguls and politicians who own community radio stations and privately owned commercial radio stations have followed the Church's lead. The state-owned ZNBC continues to propagate the government's agenda and elite political perspective, while the new privately owned radio stations provide more diverse programming.[77]

Zambian journalists and the media in general have also been prone to harassment, threats, and physical harm. In 1996, for example, three top independent journalists and editors, Fred M'membe, Bright Mwape, and Lucy Sichone, were sentenced to indefinite imprisonment by the parliament and the president's office for probing into the businesses operating out of the vice president's office. A week after their incarceration, the High Court of Zambia released the three journalists on a ruling that the detention was illegal. Parliament fought back with an appeal, and the vice president's office swung into action and re-arrested them on a different charge.[78] From 2003 to 2008, the Media Institute of Southern Africa Zambia (MISA) documented ninety-nine incidents of physical attacks on journalists, including beatings with batons and verbal hostility from police and other security agents. Tensions between the independent press and government worsened shortly after the untimely death of President Levy Patrick Mwanawasa. In 2009 alone, sixteen journalists were beaten on the streets of Lusaka, the capital city, in broad daylight. Rupiah Bwezani Banda, the current president, resorted to outdated laws and threatened to use his presidential authority to ban independent media for undermining national interests. President Banda has applied more punitive measures than his late predecessor, including relentless threats from the Movement for Multi-Party Democracy (MMD) to suspend broadcast licenses and close down printing presses.

Chapter Summary

This chapter has mapped out the evolution of the media and their performance in ESA within the context of each country's political and historical background. It has described the plight and resilience of the media as the eight nations transitioned from fully state-controlled to more liberalized, market-driven economies. It has also foreshadowed the content of subsequent chapters. Although radio, television, and newspapers have evolved as they have moved from a closed economic system regulated and run by the government to a relatively liberalized open market system during the democratization phase, they have nonetheless continued to struggle. These struggles are primarily due to intervening factors stemming from media policies, the rule of law, state corruption, and presidential hegemony. This chapter has briefly discussed the political cultures and struggles of that period in each of the eight ESA nations, and has illuminated how conflicts and presidential supremacy engendered civil strife, political expression, and press freedoms in each country.

It is important to recognize that many past leaders of these eight countries have engaged in geopolitical construction of regional identity to sustain their grip on political power. Identity politics and sectarian politicking shaped ethnic cleavages at the national and regional levels in ESA. The next chapter briefly reviews some important cases of geopolitical sectarianism in each country. It explicates how regimes, politicians, and governments used tactics of ethno-political isolationism since they gained independence.

Ethnicity and Mass Communication

Anderson famously suggested that nations and ethnic groups are imagined communities, and they are *imagined* because "the members of even the smallest nation will never know most of their fellow members, meet them, or even hear of them, yet in the minds of each lives the image of their communion."[79] Through media or mass communication and shared art, a belief in community and commonality emerges among strangers. This is evidently a departure from the original community, in which members physically knew and interacted with each other. Although such communities are imagined, that does not mean that they are imaginary.

Many international news stories on ethnic conflicts reflect a more primordial explanation of ethnicity than Anderson's. Primordial approaches to ethnicity, such as those of Connor and Geertz,[80] see ethnic groups as natural, organic communities that have strong resonance with members because of deep-seated kinship and shared history. An argument can be made for a more political explanation. In Zambia, for example, Chewa and Tumbukas are allies, but in neighboring Malawi these same ethnic groups are pitted against each other. Perhaps, as Posner argued, this is because Chewa and Tumbukas are too small as groups to be a useful political support in Zambia, while in Malawi, they each make up large enough segments of the population to be useful coalition bases.[81] Clearly, these identities are not primordial or inherent, but dependent on the political environment and how they communicate and interact within the public sphere.

It is better to understand ethnicity as socially constructed and often changing. In this era of communication technology such as radio, television, and especially televised theatrical drama, elites use various media genres to construct identity and sociopolitical parochialism. Ethnicity is also responsive to situations that make it a useful identity. Ethnic identities that depict themselves in primordialist language are based on rational responses to their situations. Ethnicity can be a resource for pursuing or defending one's interests in alliance with others. The more critical are in-group interests, and the greater the threat to the internal security of actors and their circle of relatives, the stronger is the identification with their ethnic in-group.[82] Political elites manipulate ethnic identities and encourage factionalism for their own power and benefit. Political elites use this strategy during times of change in economic and political power, against domestic challengers.[83] One of the modern means through which the elite and national actors propagate ethnic sectarianism is through both entertainment media and current affairs media. But that is not the only means through which ethnic manipulation takes place.

While the sensation of common culture can be manipulated and constantly redefined, it is not entirely manufactured from elites or elders. Similarly, African youths from notable and often monarchic ethnic groups, such as Ashanti (Ghana), Baganda (Uganda), Bakongo (Democratic Republic of Congo), Batutsi (Burundi and Rwanda), or Yoruba (Nigeria), were found to have more ethnocentric attitudes than the youths from other ethnic groups.[84] While state actors and politicians have successfully manipulated ethnicity, and in many situations enflamed regional conflicts, it seems inconceivable that voters find their sectarian political arguments laudable or persuasive enough to elect them. The next chapter briefly reviews some important cases of geopolitical sectarianism in each country. It explicates how regimes, politicians, and governments have used tactics of ethno-political isolationism since they gained independence.

Chapter Two

Sectarianism and Ethnicity in Politics

It is important to examine the role of sectarianism and ethnicity in politics because Africa is overloaded with a myriad of ethnic societies. It is also somewhat politically burdened by grievances of ethnic victimization and fragmentation. Many families, including my close and distant relatives, have been victims of these fragmentations and of ethno-political disenfranchisement. In some post-colonial African states, politicians who seek national power use all means to attain it, including ethno-regional appeals.[1] Ethnicity is one of the main critera by which sociopolitical groups are characterized and defined in ethnic-diverse nations. Some scholars have argued that political elites politicize ethnicity and sectarianism in order to influence the state and secure a share of national resources for their regions.[2]

When ethnicity is labeled by the state or a legal mandate, it competes and overlaps with several characteristics of identity such as language, culture, or shared history. These labeled attributes, based on physical and geographic identification, do not necessarily describe a person's true ethnicity because they are not subject to alteration or conversion.[3] Politically, ethnic characterization must be based on objectivity because subjectivity is detrimental to the principles of governance.[4] It is important to emphasize that ethnic structures do not necessarily determine or indicate behavior. Behavior may be symptomatic of fragmentation due to polarization from either internal or external forces.[5] In most cases, ethnic polarization emerges when political actors employ divisive tactics or are responsible for inequality along fault lines of geography, caste, gender, kinship, and religion.[6] This is one of the major problems with African politics, especially in Eastern and Southern Africa (ESA), and this chapter highlights some of these problems.

Many African leaders in previous regimes engaged in politics of injustice based on regional economic imbalance and misallocation of resources, which gave rise to geopolitics and regional identity.[7] In every one of the twenty-three African countries I have visited so far in my lifetime, I saw how neglected citizens yearn to remove such regimes. In ESA, the politics of injustice were sustained because the opposition advanced the argument of ethno-regional imbalance and declared that they were themselves victims of such oppressive structures.

Figure 2.1. Prehistoric world of Africa's traditions and daily life. A symbolic impression of the stone-age era in Eastern Africa before European explorers and missionaries settled in the region, and ultimately colonized the region. Photo taken in Arusha, Tanzania, by Yusuf Kalyango, January 2009.

Historians contend that using ethnic grouping as a political tool in Africa is quintessentially a colonial legacy, which was used to divide and rule, control, and diffuse the administratively cohesive kingdoms and empires and their resources.[8] Western European colonizers readjusted the cohesive African kingdoms into distinctive clusters by introducing administrative units that were subsequently identified in ethnic, religious, or tribal terms. The exposure to colonial order and incorporation into ethnic cleavages by Europeans set the stage for political opportunism, punctuated by ethno-regional inequalities and discord.[9] The next section explores the meaning of ethnicity.

Understanding Ethnicity and Its Cleavages

One of the first definitions of ethnicity came from Weber, who called ethnic groups, "those human groups that entertain a subjective belief in their common descent because of similarities of physical type or customs or both, or because of memories of colonization and migration."[10] Whether any provable genetic connection exists is beside the point; often it does not. What matters is what people perceive to be their social identity. There are many symbolic and cultural elements that ethnic groups may make central to their identity, such as religion, family traditions, geographic regions, language, and physical appearance. Yet many groups may be defined by one of those elements without being an ethnic group, and a recognized ethnic group may identify with many or none of these elements. Consequently, these elements are not very useful in defining ethnicity. The symbolic elements associated with a given ethnic group are also constantly changing depending on time, place, situation, and politics, and cannot be considered definitive, definable traits. In many respects, belief in a shared descent or history has been a consistent and more reliable defining characteristic of ethnicity.[11]

Ethnic communities in Africa see themselves as distinct; yet outsiders also assign them a distinct identity. A group of people often does not identify itself as an ethnic group until it is situated in contrast to another. Ethnicity cannot exist in isolation because it would be meaningless as a source of identity if no alternative identities existed. So, the mutual recognition of an ethnic group's existence by insiders and outsiders means that ethnicity operates as a social fact. As Brown put it:

> When the state organizes parliamentary representatives, regional structures, interest associations, or identity documents specifically on a racial, ethnic or nationality basis,

such institutionalisations come to define the ideological parameters for those who function within them.[12]

The perception of ethnic identities creates filters for reality. However, that does not mean that ethnicity is not socially constructed. In ESA political actors, via mass media, use tactics such as ethno-political isolationism and political hyperbole to get people to judge them favorably, while judging others harshly.

Ethno-politics in Burundi

Politics in Burundi were dominated by ethnic divisions between the Tutsi (Batutsi) and Hutu (Bahutu) ethnic groups. The Batutsi make up about 14 percent of the population in Burundi, and the Bahutu about 85 percent. The remaining 1 percent of the population comes from an aboriginal ethnic group called the Batwa. All three ethnic groups share the same culture and speak the same language, Kirundi. The differences among them are mainly based in their historical experiences. Traditionally, the Batutsis were cattle-herders and the Bahutus were farmers. Before the arrival of the Europeans, Burundi was generally ruled by a Mututsi (Batutsi) king and a system of princes and chiefs. The king and his chiefs allocated land, thereby concentrating most of the land in the hands of fellow Batutsis.[13] A patronage system with Batutsis as patrons and Bahutus as clients prevailed. The army was also composed almost entirely of Batutsi, and this Batutsi monopoly of force through the military continued until quite recently. While there are ethnic histories attached to the words *Tutsi* and *Hutu*, these words really signified socioeconomic divisions akin to castes or classes before the Belgians colonized the country.[14] Both ethnic groups tend to choose an interpretation of pre-colonial history that speaks in their favor and interests.

As movements for independence swept across the continent, the Union for National Progress (UPRONA) party was jointly formed by Batutsis and Bahutus as Burundi's nationalist party. In the 1961 elections that determined the ruling party of an independent Burundi, UPRONA won 58 of 64 seats in parliament. Nevertheless the Tutsi king, King Mwambutsa IV, remained in control of the country with the power to appoint the prime minister. The UPRONA party fell into internal division and conflict when its leader was assassinated by the opposition.[15] Meanwhile, ethnic violence in Rwanda caused an influx of Batutsi refugees into Burundi in 1959. The overthrow of the Batutsi by Bahutu in Rwanda was felt deeply by Burundians of both ethnic groups. When ethnic

Bahutu politicians won a majority of seats in parliament in 1965, King Mwambutsa rejected the outcome of the parliamentary elections and appointed a Mututsi prime minister. A small group of the Bahutu reacted with a coup attempt. A large number of Bahutu politicians and army officers were executed by Batutsi ministers in response to the failed coup.

In 1966, Michel Micombero overthrew the monarchy in a coup, starting a successive line of three Batutsi presidents, all from the same Bahima clan and the same village in Bururi. Micombero (1966–1976), Jean-Baptiste Bagaza (1976–1987), and Pierre Buyoya (1987–1993; 1996–2003) all served as Batutsi presidents of Burundi. Under Micombero, UPRONA became the only authorized party of the Batutsi-Bahima elite. Parliament was abolished, and government positions were restricted to Batutsis. The ruling elite reflected an even narrower segment of the Batutsi than the rest of the population, and fear of a Bahutu revolution was central to their ability to maintain power.[16] In 1972, Micombero used several murders of Batutsi in the south as a pretext to purge all Bahutu left in the army and civil service, and then killed many educated Bahutu in the country. Some capable Bahutu were forced into exile, and somewhere between 100,000 and 300,000 Bahutus were killed.[17] By 1972, the army was entirely a Tutsi institution. The violence crystallized the country's ethnic identities and created a climate of mutual fear.

From 1988 to 1992, there were several Bahutu outbreaks of violence. Bahutus attacked and killed thousands of Batutsi ordinary citizens, army officers, and politicians. The Burundian army, which was dominated by the Batutsis, retaliated by killing vastly more Bahutus.[18] Refugees from both ethnic groups fled into surrounding countries. During the period from 1988 to 1992, President Buyoya made political overtures under international pressure to open the government to democratization and liberalize the media and state enterprises. Buyoya formed a "government of national unity," composed of twelve Bahutu and twelve Batutsi government ministers, but kept control of the military and judiciary. He left critical decisions entirely in the hands of Batutsi.[19] A "Charter of National Unity" was issued to enforce Burundian unity across ethnic groups and was often used to silence any reference to the 1972 massacres.[20]

The Burundian Democratic Front (FRODEBU), which was a largely Bahutu party, emerged as the primary opposition to the Batutsi-dominated UPRONA. In June 1993, the first presidential elections in Burundi were held, and a Muhutu candidate with FRODEBU, Melchior Ndadaye, won with 65 percent of the vote. Less than four months after his democratically elected government assumed office, President Ndadaye was assassinated.

Unrest erupted across the country following Ndadaye's assassination. The Bahutus in the north and south in particular killed thousands of Batutsis, and the army responded by killing thousands of Bahutus. The tension was exacerbated by the 1994 genocide of the Batutsis in Rwanda. Rumors spread that the Rwandese president of Hutu origin, Juvénal Habyarimana, and President Ndadaye had been plotting genocide of the Batutsis in Burundi and Rwanda.[21] A series of negotiations over power, the presidency, and ministerial positions ensued between 1994 and 1996 in Burundi. A president was appointed in January 1994 only to die that April in the plane crash that also killed President Habyarimana of Rwanda. Former military leader Major Buyoya returned to power in another *coup d'état*.

From 1993 to 1995, ethnic civil war continued in Burundi at varying degrees of intensity. More than 300,000 people died in the war.[22] Hundreds of thousands of Burundians became refugees in Rwanda, Tanzania, and Zaire, and many were internally displaced.[23] In 2001, former South African president Nelson Mandela negotiated power-sharing between the warring parties in Burundi. These negotiations provided for a transitional government that rotated the presidency and vice presidency every eighteen months between the Bahutus and the Batutsis. Only the minority Batutsi groups signed the agreement. The Bahutu rebel groups rejected it because they have the majority population. A Muhutu politician, Domitien Ndayizeye, took office in 2003. He signed a cease-fire with the main Bahutu rebels of the Forces for Democratic Defense (FDD) in the same year. The Bahutu rebel forces were integrated into the national army, ending Batutsi control of the military. In 2005, the former FDD rebel leader Pierre Nkurunziza won the presidential elections. According to the 2005 Africa Research Bulletin, the democratic ascension of a Muhutu president to office was widely regarded as a marker of the end of the war, although violence and conflict are still a problem.

Ethno-politics in Ethiopia

The current constitution of Ethiopia has divided the nation into ethnically based regions united in a federalist system. Ethiopia has extensive ethnic diversity with somewhere between sixty-seven and eighty-four ethnic groups. Two ethnic groups, the Oromo and the Amhara, make up over 62 pecent of the population.[24] The third-largest ethnic group, at just 6 percent of the population, is the Tigray. The Tigrays have been the dominant ruling group since 1991. Two different interpretations of the history of Ethiopia as a nation exist. In one interpretation, Ethiopia has existed as a nation for thousands of years, with the Amhara and Tigray core cultures assimilating and uniting diverse ethnic groups. However, Oromo nationalists see Ethiopia as a colonial empire that is controlled by the Abyssinia region. Ethiopia historically evolved and expanded as a non-colonial empire-state through the incorporation of various kingdoms.

From 1974 to 1991, Ethiopia was ruled by General Mengistu Haile Mariam and a totalitarian communist regime known as the Derg. A pan-nationalist Ethiopian agenda assimilated and forced the Amharic language and culture, and the Abyssinian Orthodox Church, on all citizens. This provoked subordinated groups to organize ethnic movements in various regions of Ethiopia. While some gestures towards regional culture were made between 1974 and 1983, the totalitarian authority of the central state was absolute and severe. Opposition groups that waged war against the Derg were based on ethnic movements. Pluralistic ethnic nationalism was one of the major consequences of, and threats to, the military rule of General Mengistu. The Derg caused great suffering by misusing food aid for political purposes during the 1984–1985 famine. This drove many groups that had previously accepted the Derg's rule to support the rebel fighters.[25] While many other groups were fighting for representation and overthrow of the government, the Eritrean People's Liberation Front was fighting for complete independence. The Eritrean region had only been part of Ethiopia since 1962, and Eritreans saw themselves as part of a separate political history.

In 1995, the Ethiopian People's Revolutionary Democratic Front (EPRDF) took control of the government and Meles Zenawi became prime minister. Creating pluralistic ethnic federalism was the major project of the new government and the new constitution. The EPRDF government designed the ethnic federalist state with the goal of maintaining a united Ethiopian state and avoiding secession, which had been the goal of many of the groups that had fought with them against previous military juntas.[26] Many Oromo groups, in particular, still feel that they have been mistreated historically and remain committed to secession. Seats in the legislature are distributed ethnically, one for each of the sixty-seven recognized ethnic groups, plus one more seat for each additional one million members of the ethnic group. Local ethnic parties manage state government and administration, leaving little but foreign affairs and defense to the central government. Local governments are also in charge of running the polls during elections, contributing to election irregularities.[27]

Ethnic identities have changed and are often overlapped and mixed. Some groups that were previously classified as clans of one ethnic group have now been declared separate ethnic groups.[28] It has become quite difficult for the ethnic federalist system to determine which ethnic groups are classified as independent. The Amhara ethnic group, for example, is arguably better defined as simply a group of people who all speak Amharic. Many speakers of Amharic, who are legally considered Amhara, also identify themselves with other ethnic groups. Ethnic violence among many groups has continued since the 1990s, including violence over election rights, violence between Amhara and Oromo, violence between the Amhara and Tigray, and other attacks against the Tigray. At the same time, strong currents of pan-Ethiopian nationalism still exist. However, pan-Ethiopian identity suffers from being mostly rooted in the Amharic experience.[29]

Although the political system opened up to multiple parties after Mengistu's departure, opposition parties—nearly all of which are based on ethnicity—refused to participate in elections leading up to, and after, the transition. They claimed that the ruling EPRDF was illegitimate, it monopolized power in the hands of the Tigrayan ethnic group, and its commitment to ethnic self-determination was either not genuine enough or too oriented towards deconstructing the state.[30] Although EPRDF is a coalition of several ethnic political parties, the Tigrayan party is undeniably in charge.[31]

In 2007, the UN Committee on the Elimination of Racial Discrimination issued a report criticizing Ethiopia for very serious violations of human rights along ethnic lines. The report accused Ethiopia, and especially the ruling party, of systematically targeting certain ethnic groups, including the Oromo and the Anuak, for arbitrary detention and execution, torture, rape, and destruction of livelihood.[32] The report identified political tensions and competition over basic resources as fuelling the abuses. It identified a lack of faith in political processes and a perception among the Ethiopian people that political opposition equates to armed resistance.[33] Furthermore, many researchers criticized the ethnic federalist system as cementing ethnic identities and encouraging ethnic conflict.[34]

Although the government proclaimed its commitment to lessening ethnic conflict, any reduction of ethnic conflict at the federal level pushed it to the local level—or redefined it as a local problem.[35] At the very least, the ethnic federalist system does not effectively defuse ethnic tensions. The main opposition party in 2005 and its successor, the Unity for Democracy and Justice Party

(UDJP) in 2010, were two of the few parties to organize on issues that mobilized across ethnic groups. This is an ongoing need for the country's democracy.

Ethno-politics in Kenya

At least five large ethnic groups account for 70 percent of the Kenyan population. The Kikuyu ethnic group is the largest, with about 21 percent of the population. The Kalenjin is the second largest, but not significantly bigger than the Kamba, the Luhya, and the Luo. These latter groups have an average population of about 13 percent.[36] Within the major provinces, some of these ethnic groups are structured as the primary form of alliance or coalition for recognition and political competition. For instance, Kenya has had three presidents since independence, two of whom were Kikuyu: Jomo Kenyatta and Mwai Kibaki. The second president, Daniel Toroitich arap Moi, was a Kalenjin, and his grip on power was uninterrupted for twenty-four years because he strategically fanned anti-Kikuyu sentiment.[37] The Kikuyu ethnic group is strategically located in the central provinces and Nairobi province, the central seat of the government.

In the early 1970s, political emissaries of former president Kenyatta and his cabinet members used to insinuate that only Kikuyu women can give birth to Kenyan presidents.[38] This created discord from other regions over the Kikuyu hegemony. After the colonial days, many people continued to believe that social injustices and regional parochialism were responsible for underdevelopment, and the economic woes afflicting them and their societies.[39] For example, contemporary political candidates regard the disproportionate control of the manufacturing industry by the minority Asian community (less than 2 percent of the population) to be deplorable and detrimental for the national economic landscape. While Asians have contributed considerably to the development of the Kenyan economy since independence, the persistent underrepresented participation of indigenous Kenyans in the mainstream entrepreneurial and manufacturing industry is a major source of political rhetoric that is fanning ethno-political conflicts.[40]

The Kikuyu is not only the largest centrally located ethnic group, but it is also the richest. The Kikuyu elite have dominated politics and the trade and manufacturing sectors since Kenya attained its independence in 1963.[41] Politicians and their kinship in Kenya have increasingly become more militant and influential in shaping and imposing their sectarian ethnic agendas.[42] Political and economic favoritism toward the Kikuyu ethnic group has been demonstrated in the appointment of government personnel and the awarding of lucrative government tenders.[43] In order to outbid the large ethnic groups, therefore, political parties further their platform on sectarian ethnic politics by building alliances with the economically deprived.

This political tactic is based on what a minority ethnic group brings into the political coalition in order to increase the potential of winning an election. It does not, however, consider how inclusive or accommodative the candidates are to the diverse ethnic interests of their electorate. Although Kenya is regarded as one of the most developed and stable countries in Eastern Africa, the December 2007 general elections exposed its ethnic stigma and susceptibility. The main opposition leader, Raila Odinga of the Orange Democratic Movement (ODM) party, is a Luo, while the incumbent, President Mwai Kibaki of the Party of National Unity (PNU), is a Kikuyu. Opposition parties, especially the ODM, have accused Kibaki's government of continuing former president Moi's legacy of nepotism.[44] As a result of regional economic imbalances during Moi's blanket use of patronage, ethno-marginalization punctuated by a culture of corruption plunged Kenya into an economic crisis. Politicians resorted to exclusionary ethnic or religious appeals, patronage, and social class in order to compete for the allocation of scarce resources.[45] Simply by taking advantage of frustrations over Kibaki's Kikuyu dominance and politicizing the frustrations of most Kenyans, the ODM party mobilized some of the political elites in marginalized ethnic groups to join the opposition.

During the late 1990s in Burundi, Kenya, Rwanda, and Uganda, heads of state declared that multiparty politics elevates sectarianism based on ethnic or religious identity and that a single-party political system would guarantee nation building and national unity. During the EAC Summit of 2007, heads of state committed to eliminating the use of ethno-political contestation at the constituent level because it undermined regional integration at the expense of underprivileged people. The discord inherent in geopolitical sectarian formations, particularly in Burundi, Kenya, Rwanda, and Uganda, epitomized the vexing questions of power sharing and its related demands for political accommodation and self-determination.[46] Similar measures were undertaken by member-states within SADC. All rival groups, notwithstanding their geopolitical characteristics, measured the legitimacy of these governments by the level of access to state resources.[47]

In the December 2007 elections in Kenya, voting between the ODM and PNU was split along ethnic lines. Periods of election violence and sporadic turbulence erupted during and after the elections, due to suspicions of election rigging. The Kenyan press reported that opposition party supporters vowed to shed blood should Odinga lose the elections.

More ethno-political conflicts erupted in major towns across the country when the incumbent was declared a winner. In the capital city of Nairobi, the media reported that some opposition supporters, mainly non-Kikuyu but identified as ODM Youth Brigade, attacked some slums and residential estates, stoned several Kikuyu residents, and burned down kiosks that they said belonged to Kikuyu retail traders. The Kenyan police shot and killed dozens of protestors. Sympathizers of Kibaki and his PNU party, largely Kikuyu, deployed vigilantes to patrol their neighborhoods in response to the threats from ODM supporters. Rioting spread across the country, particularly in the western town of Kisumu, an opposition stronghold. In Nairobi, the Kenya Television Network (KTN) reported that on December 31, 2007, police patrolled residential neighborhoods while announcing on loudspeakers that they would shoot dead anyone found loitering on the streets. Most independent broadcast media in Kenya were temporarily shut down. Amidst all of the political mayhem, much of the fighting pitched Odinga's Luo group against the Kikuyu group of President Kibaki. Minister of Information John Michuki banned live broadcasts and threatened journalists who criticized the Electoral Commission and blamed the government for the violence.

Ethno-politics in Rwanda

The ethnic history of Rwanda through the colonialist period is very similar to that of Burundi. The population of Rwanda is made up of 84 percent Bahutu, 15 percent Batutsi, and 1 percent Batwa. A Tutsi kingdom also ruled precolonial Rwanda. Unlike Burundi, Rwanda had several Hutu kingdoms in what is now northwestern Rwanda. These Hutu kingdoms fought against aggression from the Tutsi kingdoms after the colonialists arrived. The Belgians gave the Batutsi military aid and incorporated the Hutu kingdoms into a Tutsi-dominated Rwanda. Belgians also divided and ruled Rwanda by putting the Batutsi in power over the Bahutu. They believed in the racial superiority of the Batutsi, believing that they were born leaders, hardworking, and more intelligent than the Bahutus. Belgian colonialists required ethnic identity travel documents and relied on quasi-scientific measurements of skull and nose sizes. The colonial documentation of identity enabled differentiation of the otherwise culturally indistinguishable Bahutus and Batutsis, and fueled prejudice between the two ethnic groups during the struggle for independence.

The Tutsi monarchy was overthrown and Rwanda claimed independence in 1962, as the Belgians supported and fronted the Bahutu revolution because they were fearful of elite, radical, and anti-colonial Batutsis.[48] In the first legislative elections, an anti-Batutsi Hutu liberation party called the Party of the Hutu Emancipation Movement (PARMEHUTU) swept Parliament. Thousands of Batutsis fled the country in 1962. When some Batutsi refugees attempted to return via guerilla attacks through the mid-1960s, the Bahutu-dominated Rwandan government responded with mass killings of innocent Batutsi citizens.

Grégoire Kayibanda was the first president of Rwanda from 1962 to 1973. In 1973, Maj. Gen. Juvénal Habyarimana took power in a *coup d'état* and ruled exclusively until his death in 1994. Habyarimana was periodically "re-elected" in staged elections, where he received 95 percent to 98 percent of the vote. International development agencies portrayed the country as the perfect recipient of aid, with steadily improving statistics on public health and education, although in reality these resources seemed unevenly distributed.[49] The Hutu government maintained the colonial system of requiring ethnic identity papers and instituted quotas limiting the number of Batutsis allowed in educational institutions and state jobs.

Habyarimana's government used two arguments to justify his military rule. First was the ethnic argument: Rwanda was rightfully and originally for the Bahutu, who had been brutally subjugated for centuries by the "evil" Batutsi, and the government was the sole defense against Batutsi attempts to re-enslave the Bahutu. Since the Tutsi government had been feudal and undemocratic, the new government pushed for democratization and economic development. At the beginning of the 1990s, the Rwandan Patriotic Front (RPF), whose soldiers were mostly descendents of the Batutsi refugees from the 1960s, invaded Rwanda from Uganda. At the same time, dissent and challenge were growing in the south. Southerners were displeased with the monopoly of power and investment that Habyarimana had given to the north. Like Buyoya in Burundi, Habyarimana was also facing international pressure to democratize and share power with the RPF and the internal political opposition. Reviving ethnic fears was a way to unite people around the government and to fight the RPF, the opposition, and national elections.

The government of Habyarimana intensified its propaganda and fear mongering. His government also maintained the rhetoric of demonization, stereotyping the Batutsi as hungry to return to power and to subjugate the majority Bahutu. It became easy to whip up fear during these national emergencies, especially during the RPF rebel offensive. Since the Batutsi-dominated RPF was a threat to the Hutu-led government, all Batutsi civilians within Rwanda were implicated as enemies, and any moderate or opposing Muhutu was also declared an enemy of the state. Thus only Bahutu who supported the government, and its agenda of hatred, were not traitors or dangerous. The newspaper *Kangura* and the now infamous *Radio-Télévision Libre des Milles Collines* (RTLM) carried the government's message and advocated violence, giving instructions to the "good Bahutu" to eradicate the enemy. Both the military and some Bahutu journalists circulated lists of names of people to be killed. The massacres of Batutsis occurred from 1990 to 1993 and were directed by local authorities, national politicians, and the police. The RPF continued to fight for military victory as reprisals were carried out on Batutsi civilians within the country. Power-sharing agreements between the RPF and Habyarimana's government were held in Arusha, Tanzania, as fighting continued. The Arusha Accords were signed in 1993 but were not implemented until after the genocide.

When the plane carrying Habyarimana was attacked by a rocket that killed all passengers aboard, the Rwandan government immediately accused the RPF and its rebel leader, Paul Kagame, of carrying out the assassination. Kagame argued that Bahutu extremists shot down the plane to ruin peace negotiations and to create an excuse for the genocide that followed. In 2010, President Kagame's government released a report with testimony from over 600 witnesses to support his claim. The assassination of Habyarimana triggered genocide of Batutsis and sympathetic Bahutus. The Rwandan military and militia groups (especially the group called Interahamwe and its youth wing) prepared extermination plans, made lists of Batutsis across the country, and went into action. The media called upon Bahutu civilians to help them slaughter Batutsis. About 800,000 Batutsis were killed en masse within three months, the majority of them in the first two weeks.[50] Without calling the situation "genocide," intervention was not within the scope of the UN peacekeepers' mandate. The genocide ended when the RPF took the capital of Kigali and overthrew the Hutu government. About 2 million people, mostly Bahutu, fled Rwanda when the RPF captured the seat of government, due to fear of reprisal from the new Tutsi-led military state.[51]

The RPF set up the new government based on the power-sharing structures that had been agreed upon in the Arusha Accords but amended them to ensure RPF dominance in government and the presidency. Meanwhile, international tribunals prosecuted the highest profile perpetrators of the 1994 genocide. But most of the accountability and reconciliation process occurred in Gacaca courts. These local community courts were used as empowering approaches to reconciliation but were also venues for reprisal, acting out local politics, and a tool for government manipulation.[52] Another wave of departures from Rwanda's Bahutu national politicians and the Tutsi-dominated RPF occurred in 2000. The speaker of the house, prime minister, and president, Pasteur Bizimungu, all resigned and sought asylum, except for Bizimungu, who died in prison. Major General Paul Kagame, the military leader of the RPF, assumed the presidency. The first presidential elections in 2003 were heavily controlled by the RPF, and Kagame's presidency was overwhelmingly maintained. Kagame accused the opposition of being ethno-"divisionists," which is a political propaganda tool or myth used to create fear of another genocide in order to silence dissent.[53]

Figure 2.2. A typical image of Africa's traditions and daily life. Phiri Mwesi plays his African xylophone at the Victoria Falls entrance, Mosi-ao-Tunya, in Zambia. Photo taken by Yusuf Kalyango, December 2010.

He again won the presidential elections by over 80 percent of the vote in 2010, while using intimidation and violence. Top opposition candidates were disqualified on charges of engaging in "genocide speech" and ethnic politics.

Ethno-politics in South Africa

Ethnic conflicts and sectarianism in South Africa were primarily grounded in the struggle for natural or economic resources and settlement security between the Afrikaners (white settlers) and the native Bantu (or black) South Africans.[54] Afrikaans, a dialect of Dutch, developed as the main language of the settlers, which was influenced by the Malay, Bantu, and Khoisan languages. Afrikaner landowners, known as Boers, expanded from the coast into the interior and fought with the local Khoikhoi for control of farmland and grazing land.[55] Social roles and class were heavily restricted and directed by race in the interior and the more established Cape Town.

The discovery of mines in the second half of the twentieth century transformed parts of South Africa into an industrial economy. New laws and company policies restricted non-whites from managing or investing in the mining industry—especially disenfranchised black migrant workers—in order to keep profits in the hands of white owners.[56] Afrikaner nationalism was a tool for white workers to guarantee themselves skilled work and better working conditions.[57] Segregation as a policy goal emerged in the 1930s. It was an effective way to unite whites across class lines.

As economic forces increased and blacks flowed into the cities, the Afrikaner National Party (ANP) was elected into power in the 1940s and instituted apartheid in 1948. Although white supremacy was crucial to the economic interests of Boer farmers, actual segregation had not been an issue until the 1920s and 1930s, when cheap African labor began to leave their farms. Policies that segregated native South Africans into artificial "homeland" reserves thus ensured a continued migrant, and therefore cheap, system of labor for white capitalists and landowners.[58]

Segregation was also a response to increased militancy and conflict among workers in the 1920s. The apartheid system was defended for years as a defense against communism. The fear of the "Black Peril" encouraged white supremacist and capitalist leaders to return the black population to communal farmland. At the same time, liberals with non-racial intentions also advocated for black homelands as a way to protect traditional African culture from industrial society.

Ethnic fragmentation and apartheid divided all South Africans by race as white, black (also called "Native," "Bantu," or "African"), or colored (mixed race or Indian). Sexual contact or marriage between whites and non-whites was banned. Residential segregation resulted in the forced removal of many populations, especially in the cities, into separate townships. Public facilities and education were also segregated, and free and compulsory education was only available to whites. The education system available to native South Africans stressed Bantu culture and was designed to prepare them for manual labor. Laws required the natives to carry documents at all times. Starting in 1959, the ten homelands created by government had little resemblance to any historical settlements. These "Bantustans" were nominally independent but under South African control. There was no economic viability. The natives were forcibly relocated to one of the homelands and were only allowed in white South African areas with the status of migrant worker. In this way, white leaders hoped to break apart broad African nationalism using tribal identities.[59]

The African National Congress (ANC) was the main voice of black resistance in South Africa. The ANC was founded in 1912, but black protest intensified in the 1960s and 1970s. The Indian Congress and South African Colored People's Organization, which represented the Indian and colored populations, increasingly allied with the ANC against apartheid, although they often felt restricted by a desire to avoid facing discrimination as great as that faced by blacks. In Sharpeville in 1960 police fired on a group of non-violent protesters; 69 were killed and 180 were wounded. The Sharpeville shootings were a turning point and were followed by increased strikes, resulting in reconsideration of non-violent resistance. The ANC and Pan Africanist Congress (PAC) were banned in 1963. While this impeded structured organization, the philosophical rise of black consciousness filled in some of the gap. In 1976, a government decision to teach the curriculum in black schools in Afrikaans triggered protests among students in Soweto. Police raided and killed protesters as they attacked police and administration buildings, and boycotted national services during several weeks of unrest known as the Soweto Uprisings. The conflict spread to nearby towns and eventually to the Cape. At least 575 people died and 2,389 were wounded.[60]

As protest increased during the 1980s, the state relied on military presence, detentions, and increased repression to maintain control, which only added to the alienation of much of the country.[61] The state encouraged vigilante action against activists, which was then portrayed in the media as black-on-black violence. The Afrikaner base of the National Party was also fracturing, since many English-speaking whites now supported the National Party while Afrikaner workers, farmers, and small-scale traders were marginalized. Attempts were made to restructure apartheid to placate opponents without threatening white hegemony but this only increased resistance from opponents.[62] The international community added pressure to the South African government in 1985 when foreign banks called in all their loans and foreign states imposed economic sanctions. The rand collapsed, and South African business leaders grew angry with the government.

The economic crisis in 1991 was a major reason behind the National Party's reversal when President Fredrik de Klerk announced that the ANC, PAC, and South African Communist Party were free to operate as political organizations. Political prisoners, including Nelson Mandela, were also released. Key pieces of apartheid legislature were repealed, and the government entered negotiations with opposition parties to create a new, universally democratic constitution. Nelson Mandela and de Klerk shared leadership of a transitional government until 1994. In April 1994, the first inclusive elections were held. Mandela became the first native South African president when the ANC won the elections with 62.6 percent of the vote. The National Party held on to 20 percent of the vote. The international community immediately embraced the "New South Africa." The Truth and Reconciliation Commission, led by Archbishop Desmond Tutu, was established to achieve reconciliation between all South Africans and create a society free of racial divisiveness and ethno-politics.

Economic inequalities did not disappear with enfranchisement. An equitable distribution of resources is still a challenge. While non-blacks have become "more reconciled" to blacks since the end of apartheid, support for policies aimed at creating equality has been low.[63] While coloreds and Indians sometimes called themselves "black" as a gesture of solidarity in the decades leading up to apartheid's collapse, this largely stopped in 1994.[64] Actual intergroup relationships remain low, with opportunities for cross-ethnic socialization occurring mostly in wealthy areas and in some higher educational institutions.[65] In the 2008 and 2009 elections, the ANC's share of the vote declined for the first time, due to the emergence of the Congress of the People (COPE), a breakaway party. In 2008, the *Economist* attributed COPE's success to frustration with a lack of economic progress under the ANC.

Ethno-politics in Tanzania

There are more than 120 ethnic groups and languages in Tanzania. Some of the major ethnic groups are the Chagga, Haya, Luo, Makonde, Makua, Masai, Nyamwezi, Sukuma, and the Yaho. The Luo are in western Tanzania and southwestern Kenya. Tanzania also has the largest concentration of citizens of Middle Eastern decent (Arabs) and Shirazi (Persian) in East Africa. Religion plays a big role in Tanzania's politics, especially on the Zanzibar archipelago, which accommodates the biggest concentration of Tanzanian Muslims. The western and northern regions are predominantly Christian whereas the southern regions including Zanzibar and most provinces along the eastern coast are predominantly Muslim.

During the colonial era from the early 1900s until the mid-1950s, policies of divide and rule in Tanganyika and Zanzibar (which together form contemporary Tanzania) created divisions within communities on the basis of racial or ethnic consciousness. The escalation of ethnic identification and the partitioning of land and regions resulted in the establishment of ethnic groupings.[66] Over twenty ethno-political associations were formed in the early twentieth century.[67] Some of the strongest ethno-political groups that were allowed to function by the colonizers during that time included Shirazi, Indian, African, and Arab associations.[68] These ethno-political associations fought for the interests of their kinship but consequently came to form the nationalist political parties that contributed to the demise of colonial hegemony. The Tanganyika African National Union (TANU), founded by late president Julius Nyerere, called for a rejection of ethnic identities and made efforts to unite all ethnic, racial, and religious groups.

Tanzania has been ruled by only one non-ethnic party since the country attained independence in 1961. The first president of Tanzania and "father of the nation," Nyerere introduced multiparty politics in 1992. His Chama Cha Mapinduzi (CCM) party has controlled state power and sustained the regime's grip on power for over thirty years. In the 1980s, Nyerere dismantled regional identities using public policies that supported national unity. When he stepped down as president in 1985 and introduced regular presidential and parliamentary elections, he was regarded as a statesman and nationalist throughout Africa. He fostered a sense of nationalism in Tanzania and encouraged East Africans to give legitimacy only to governments that allowed reconciliation, national representation, and accountability.

When Nyerere allowed multiparty politics in the 1990s, the composition of most political parties at that time was multi-ethnic. Due to that composition, including the ruling CCM party, equal ethnic and regional representation has since characterized the civil service and cabinet of all successive governments. When the regime under the CCM political mantra embarked on nation-building efforts, it also abolished traditional leadership like the feudal lords and fiefdom chiefs.[69] Another important consideration when discussing national unity in Tanzania is the fact that in contrast to other ESA nations, no acute income inequalities exist between individual regions twenty years after independence. Opposition politicians, who were concerned about regional factionalism and inequality, have also resisted the fueling of ethno-regional sentiments by raising the politics of social imbalance.[70] As a result, the CCM has been quite successful at embracing the politics of inclusiveness by giving cabinet portfolios and institutional sector representation to all major ethnic groups.

The CCM in Tanzania encourages all of its members who seek parliamentary seats and who have aspirations of holding national positions within the party to contest elections in constituencies outside of their ethnic strongholds. This arrangement allows the CCM to claim legitimacy as a party that embraces ethnic coalitions, rather than ethnic fragmentation and sectarianism. Political actors are forced to work with politicians and campaign coordinators from other ethnic groups who deemphasize the role of ethnicity in politics. CCM remains a dominant and semi-autocratic political party that shapes regimes and state institutions. However, because of ethnic coalitions, its successive governments promote plurality and sustain the spirit of *Ujamaa*.

Geopolitical sectarianism and state patronage in Tanzania are more likely to be based on regional politicization because none of the 120 ethnic groups is politically or demographically dominant. State actors in Tanzania perpetuated factionalism by shifting patronage groups based on client relationships, which then became increasingly polarized into regional sects.[71] Media reports indicate that one of the major factional groups that has emerged includes the Muslim (religious) block from the eastern coast region. In the western region called the lake zone, factionalism and other divisions emerged between parliamentarians from the southern and northern regions of the province. Although the Tanzanian electorate does not vote along ethnic lines, a third of the opposition parties won most of their seats from the home regions of their leaders.[72]

The multiparty politics of the last two presidential elections were affected by political violence resulting from religious and regional factionalism. In the semi-autonomous island of Zanzibar and Pemba, political volatility and election malpractices have undermined the legitimacy of Tanzania's claim to free and fair elections. In the last three general elections, CCM has been accused of instigating electoral fraud and violence to challenge its main political opponent, the Civic United Front (CUF).[73] In January 2001, Zanzibar and Pemba experienced indiscriminate killings of citizens who were protesting the outcome of the October 2000 elections, in which CCM was declared a winner.[74] Media reports put the death toll at 59, while the government's official report claimed that 23 people were killed in the protests.

Elections have been inherently violent in Tanzania, especially in the semi-autonomous island of Zanzibar because political parties are adversarial and often unhappy with the outcomes.[75] Constant clashes between political parties were reported at campaign venues in the last two national elections, in which hundreds died. In September 2005, the *Guardian* newspaper in Tanzania reported that during one week, more than thirty demonstrators were shot dead at five different campaign rallies. State aggression, including police brutality and intimidation of citizens supporting the opposition, led to sporadic political violence between the opposition's followers and the supporters of CCM.[76] The ruling party controls state resources and uses them to reward those who join the government. All opponents who could potentially create new and lasting coalitions to challenge the ruling CCM party were destroyed politically by friends of the president through media rhetoric.[77] In addition to the semi-autocratic governance by the CCM party, successive alternation of presidential power to three different state leaders and the symbolic distribution of power and representativeness created a false sense of electoral trustworthiness in Tanzania.

Ethno-politics in Uganda

Uganda is a multi-ethnic society with more than forty ethnic groups and dialects. These groups have a multiplicity of internal divisions based on religion, class, gender, and others. The historical background explains the beginnings of sectarianism and the struggle for power and supremacy in Uganda. For one, the numerous religions that were introduced by European explorers led to hostile factionalism in the early twentieth century. The colonizers found some well-established indigenous political structures, including the Kingdoms of Ankole, Buganda, Bunyoro, Busoga, and Toro. When the British set boundaries that later established the Ugandan territory, over time they also empowered the Kingdom of Buganda as the most dominant and strategic region for the central authority and management of the colony.[78] The British colonizers deliberately recruited the people of Buganda Kingdom (Baganda) for the civil service in a political tactic that was labeled "divide and rule."[79] During that time, the northern groups were largely recruited into the army, while the southwesterners and westerners were left to keep livestock and grow crops.[80]

The leaders within the Kingdom of Buganda collaborated with the British in their occupation. As a payback for their loyalty, the British monarchy built up the southern-central region of Buganda as the largest, richest, most coherent, and most assertive political entity in the country.[81] Other regions, such as Lango and Toro, resisted Buganda's total authority and supremacy in the political arena. During the early founding of political organizations in the 1950s, the British allowed native Ugandans to set up political parties, but these organizations were largely linked with religious and ethnic affiliations. Geopolitical sectarianism became a central factor in post-colonial Uganda, and ethnic dissonance increased when the army, dominated by northerners and led by Brigadier General Idi Amin, attacked Buganda Kingdom in 1967 and forced King Edward Mutesa into exile.[82] Even as recently as the early 1980s after the fall of Idi Amin, political parties mobilized the faithful for votes on the basis of ethnicity, religion, and regionalism.

When General Yoweri Museveni fought guerilla warfare and captured power from Major General Tito Okello Lutwa in 1986, one of his National Resistance Movement's (NRM) manifestos was to eliminate ethnic and religious divisions in Uganda. Museveni devoted most of his efforts in the first years of his presidency to developing a sense of national identity around a shared goal of stability and poverty reduction. In the late 1980s, he made a case to citizens, civil society, and international donors that the conduct and actions of multiparty politics worsened conflicts and wasted opportunities to unite and confront socioeconomic underdevelopment.[83] Museveni has persistently stated that the British colonizers were architects of identity formation in Africa and that they fostered ethnic sectarianism and political repression. In 2010, a message on Museveni's presidential (State House) website read as follows:

> Long before colonialism, our communities had evolved a very sophisticated civilization in terms of language, culture and governance. The only great weakness of our traditional rulers was their inability to get together to confront the foreign invaders when they came to this area after 1850 AD. Once the foreigners had taken over this area, they planted a new seed of poison. Both Islam and Christianity were introduced, whose intolerance and narrow-mindedness were in marked contrast with the practices of these areas of ours, whose characteristic was symbiosis. Seeds of sectarianism involving

Catholics, Protestants and Moslems were planted so much that when the political parties started in the 1950s, they automatically took on the character of that sectarianism.
DP [Democratic Party] was for the Catholics, UPC [Uganda People's Congress] for the
Protestants and KY [Kabaka Yekka] for only Baganda. The British, before they left in
1962, organized the first multi-party elections in 1961 and 1962, which were badly organized, and by 1966 the regime had collapsed. This sectarianism was, partly, responsible for the coming into power of [Idi] Amin and for his stay in power for 8 years.[84]

Ethnic sectarianism also manifested as a campaign tool used for political competition and state influence in many East African provinces instead of as a social order that would uplift the citizenry and engage in nation building. In the
1980s, despite the fact that 70 percent of the population was peasant farmers
and unemployed citizens, political parties in Uganda were organized based on
regional and religious interests. In other words, the central characteristic of the
political party orientation and agenda was not based on social class, as one
would expect. Political elites engaged in sectarianism, which gave rise to a system of patronage, perpetuated by the leeching of state resources. Political leaders swindled state resources through revenue barreling, rent seeking, and
corruption, and the plunder was distributed among their regional kinfolk.[85]

In the late 1980s and early 1990s, Museveni and his government imposed
legal restrictions on multiparty activities in order to suppress political dissent. In
the 1990s, he outlawed most activities related to political parties. Electing party
leaders and cadres, operating division offices, and holding rallies and member
conferences were all banned.[86] A new constitution was even promulgated with
restrictions on political parties. Museveni argued that a return to the multiparty
democracy of the late 1960s and early 1980s was bound to be a return to the
ruthless days of ethnic politics, sectarianism, and dictatorship.

Meanwhile, the political culture under a "one-party" NRM regime continued to fuel ethnic and religious sentiments. Politicians seeking public offices in
parliament or district leadership polarized regions for political gain, arguing that
other political contenders would commit religious persecution and marginalize
them.[87] What is also visible in the twenty years of Museveni's rule is the depri-
vation of basic social services in education and health, along with economic
marginalization in the northeastern and northwestern regions. There is also a
perception that the western and southwestern regions, from which President
Museveni hails, have benefited from the NRM regime more than other regions,
in terms of commercial investments, and political and civil appointments.

A major dispute that has tainted the political culture in Uganda is the competition for control of the state between the military, who participate in civilian governance, and the civilian political elite, who oppose the status quo. Museveni is a military general who allows his commanders to serve in his cabinet, parliament, and other state institutions. This causes disconformities in democratic values. Two army generals at the helm of the Uganda Police Force, for example, have militarized the Uganda Police. Between 2005 and 2007, the government conducted illegal suppression of civilian protests by having army officers wear police uniforms, disguising themselves as law enforcement officers.[88] On November 25, 2005, the *Daily Monitor*, a privately owned independent newspaper, published photos of two military Special Forces wearing police uniforms, alongside earlier photos when they were clad in army attire. The army officers had been deployed along with thousands of police and special force military to forcibly quell civilian protests and mass riots, which had spread throughout the capital city after the government had arrested the main opposition politician, Dr. Kizza Besigye.

At the beginning of 2008, four opposition members of parliament expressed discontent over the government's biased job appointment policy. They said that the regime undermines harmony in the country. They demanded that Museveni review the national appointment policy as part of wider efforts to curb sectarianism. They presented evidence that more than 70 percent of top government agencies are headed by people from the president's western region. The members of parliament said that such ethno-political favoritism and nepotism undermined nationalism, worsened regional imbalances, and promoted discontent. Museveni dismissed the evidence as allegations and never agreed to investigate the matter.

Chapter Summary

In light of these ethnic structures and ethno-political fragmentations in ESA, various political and cultural interest groups have tried to mobilize citizens on the continent to forge national unity. Successive leaders in ESA have so far embraced the plurality of the people they govern and have somewhat come to terms with this reality by adopting certain forms of democratization. They engage citizens in the political process of electing and legitimizing their governments. But how does democracy take root and endure with the pervasive ethno-politics?

The following chapter conceptualizes the structures of democratization as they relate to ESA. It is theoretically important to understand what democracy and democratization mean in these eight countries and how different regimes have applied them. The chapter offers both the functional and procedural approaches employed in these countries on the basis of democratic rule.

Chapter Three

Structures of Democratization

Before discussing theories about democracy and the broad idea of democratization and its processes, a personal account of how I became interested in this important topic is necessary. At the start of my journalism career in the then dusty streets of Kampala, Uganda, I believed that voting in elections was the only yardstick for measuring a true democracy. This was especially true, I thought, when people voted for their chosen representative, regardless of fairness and other constraints of the election process. By the end of 1992, which marked the start of my journalism vocation, I had not yet witnessed a single national parliamentary or presidential election. At that time many Ugandans of my generation and those of the older generations understood democracy to rightly mean "government of the people by the people." They did not, however, think of it in terms of its consequential value.

The term *democracy* and its functional nephew *democratization* were alien words to many citizens like my father, a run-of-the-mill trader and agriculturalist. My father used to discuss politics in terms of the amount of sugar and paraffin a particular candidate had promised him and other residents as a reward for casting a vote in a local village council committee or municipal election. According to him and his circle of friends, "Those were good democratic days." Throughout the 1990s, the naïve assumptions of my immediate family and friends instilled in me a sense of astonishment and misgiving about the true nature of democracy and its utility. Such claims primed me to wonder what other ordinary citizens across the region understood democracy to really mean. Did they connect democracy to other important national treasures such as good governance and the rule of law? These are people in rural areas and on farmlands who are poor, predominantly less educated, and only rarely participants in the broad decisions that affect their daily livelihoods.

In 1993 I covered a story about a municipal council by-election in the Kampala suburb of Kasubi, and my sources bluntly said that they were saddened that democracy was fast approaching. When I probed further as to why they were disappointed by the upcoming municipal elections, they responded that they enjoyed the goodies that the candidates delivered in the middle of the night, such as bars of soap and candles, and that such enticements would end on Election Day. I started to wonder and inquire how the media in Uganda, and in Africa as a whole, could handle coverage of an issue as complex as the emergence of democracy in an environment where the audience's notion of democracy was often simplistic and at odds with good governance.

Models of Democracy in ESA

Scholarly interest in democracy and the democratization process in Africa as a whole has grown in recent decades.[1] However, studies have documented considerable variation in the degree of democracy that citizens enjoy across states.[2] This chapter examines that variation across the individual regimes in the eight Eastern and Southern African (ESA) nations using classic models of democracy—liberal and procedural versus substantive. The former represents an ideal and the latter provide criteria for developing democracies. Procedural elements are more basic than substantive ones, and a combination of these elements must be present before substantive liberal democracy can be achieved. The chapter also discusses public opinion toward democracy and democratization based on extensive surveys conducted across the region.

The notion of liberal democracy necessitates that regimes be responsive to democratic values such as freedom of speech, assembly, and religion; the right to private property and privacy; equality before the law; and due process under the rule of law. (Chapter Four examines the rule of law.) These elements are mainly focused on the question of regime legitimacy and leadership qualities. Liberal democracy is the highest level of democratic rule that can be attained by the ESA nations. The electoral elements focus on the regimes' ability to provide basic rights of expression, organization, and assembly out of which politicians seek votes in regular competitive elections to fill administrative and legislative offices. More than half of the countries examined here—particularly Kenya, South Africa, Tanzania, Uganda, and Zambia—have made legitimate efforts to achieve liberal democracy.

My colleague Eckler and I examined several elements of liberal democracy in a study of media performance and democratization in Eastern Africa.[3] We focused on the challenges faced by the East African Community (EAC), which encompasses Burundi, Ethiopia, Kenya, Rwanda, Tanzania, and Uganda. Liberal democracy in the framework of political liberalization begins with the transition stage. In that study, we defined transition as a process of dissolving authoritarian regimes and replacing them with political contestation. This enables citizens and groups to compete for political power and economic resources under some form of an egalitarian system.

Procedural democracy is understood to mean the practices of regimes that shape the design and operation of a political administration, as well as institutions that respect the will of the majority, bestow justice, and discern best practices for the management of state affairs. The state assumes the responsibility of engaging citizens so that governance is shared as a collective, yet sovereign, power. Democratic states and regimes abide by a constitutional arrangement for arriving at political decisions that account for the will of reasonable individuals to control their public affairs in the interest of the common good and the common welfare of a sovereign country. Common good in the African situation may mean economic satisfaction, a "healthy" nation, equal justice for all, universal education, and other social and public services. Such a classical definition of democracy in procedural terms does not address other elements such as representation, participation, or the capitalist approach.

The idea of a procedural model is that as long as elected officials meet formal requirements, their conduct is assumed to be democratic and does not require evaluation based on actual representativeness. This procedural model fits the democratization process for Ethiopia and Rwanda. For instance, the Ethiopian Federal Constitution provides for an independent National Electoral Board (NEB), which manages elections at the federal level and within regional provinces and administrative districts. The procedural provisions in both the Rwandan and Ethiopian constitutions include voter eligibility and rights, qualifications for political contestants, structures of constituencies, supervision of ballots, conduct of actual elections, and dissemination of the results.

Substantive democracy is a process of governance that regulates power in order to maximize equal participation for all citizens.[4] Democratic theorists such as Held argue that the substantive model is primarily about an active civil society, and widespread public participation and self-determination in political life.[5] It emphasizes values that go beyond the formal aspects of a procedural democracy. These values include socioeconomic justice and legitimacy of the political regime, stability of alternation, and sovereignty of the people.[6] In describing the political situation in Uganda, Rubongoya notes that there is no stability of power at the presidential and parliamentary level.

Rubongoya's assessment of the situation in Uganda bears anecdotal resemblance to the reality in Burundi and Rwanda. In Burundi, particularly, the political situation is so marred by volatility—due to the country's history of ethno-sectarianism—that very often, the alternation of power is not primarily determined by the election outcome. The victor cogently "bargains" with the incumbent government before a new regime takes over. The substantive model of democracy dispels the notion of procedural democracy.[7]

Any universal definition that focuses on one element of democracy over another can be faulted for espousing a minimalist view. On the particular issue of the requirements of democratization, procedural, substantive, and liberal conceptions of democracy should not be considered in isolation or one viewed as more important than another in ESA. Consequently, the argument here is that the substantive and liberal models are complementary in dealing with the dynamics of democracy, the rule of law, and regime legitimacy in the ESA.

In Ethiopia during the first phase of modernization from the late 1950s through the late 1960s, the imperial regime of Haile Selassie established a parliament and provided a written constitution. During that heightened period of restructuring the state and its institutions, Emperor Selassie also introduced a national electoral system under universal suffrage. However, all other institutionalized branches of government had no formal power, and the parliament acted as a sounding board for the imperial regime. For instance, between the early 1950s and the mid-1980s, Ethiopia's monarchies and political regimes banned political dissent and the formation of political parties, and used the constitution to affirm the emperor's absolute rule. Even in the first decade of the twentieth century, the multiparty system was undermined by the government's Leninist leanings and excessive constitutional power granted to the executive over the other branches of the federal system.

Ethiopia is not the only country with excessive constitutional power for the executive at the expense of the autonomy and authority of other crucial branches of government and civil society. Just as the power of Ethiopia's prime minister is constitutionally unprecedented over other arms of government, the same is true for Burundi, Kenya, Rwanda, South Africa, Tanzania, Uganda, and Zambia. In fact, throughout ESA, and particularly in Burundi, Ethiopia, Rwanda, and Uganda, presidents have overarching command of the executive branch. The dominant parties in each of the countries are chaired by, and are accountable to, the head of state. In Burundi, President Pierre Nkurunziza, a former rebel fighter, is the leader of the CNDD-FDD party, which also dominates the parliament.

Rwanda's president, Paul Kagame, is a military general who controls the Rwandan Patriotic Front (RPF) party and the Rwanda Patriotic Army. More than 70 percent of the members of parliament belong to the RPF. Uganda's story has a similar political tune. President Yoweri Museveni is a lieutenant general and his ruling Movement government was created twenty-five years ago from former guerrilla forces, which later evolved into the National Resistance Army (NRA), and the movement's political wing called the National Resistance Movement (NRM). In South Africa, the African National Congress (ANC), which ushered in Nobel Laureate Nelson Mandela to the presidency in 1994, now dominates virtually every level of government. Tanzania's ruling party Chama Cha Mapinduzi (CCM) has also sustained its monopolistic influence on governing state institutions, including the executive, the legislative, and even the judicial branches.

Consequently, the political parties mentioned above came to power by means of militaristic revolution inspired by some form of rebellion against societal oppression. These parties control the parliament and determine the legislative agenda. They also have amended or interpreted their constitutions in ways that give the executive branch of government excessive power. Their party apparatuses recommend, and the party leaders (president or prime minister) appoint, the commissioners of most independent state institutions such as the electoral commission. The heads of state appoint Supreme Court justices and the auditors general. Hence, the presidents or heads of state of all eight countries examined here inadvertently usurp significant power by influencing the judiciary and other important institutions that are vital for checks and balances in state systems and the government. The control of all independent state institutions by a single dominant party makes the power of the head of state unaccountable to the legislature, the judiciary, and other civic institutions.

Africans in this study of media and democratization not only displayed low levels of confidence in the voting process, but they also felt that other parts of the political process needed to be strengthened. The majority of Ethiopian and Ugandan respondents, in particular, indicated that intimidation of politicians was a major problem and political actors could not contest freely. Many citizens complain about political suppression during the campaigns. Security agents routinely interrogate political candidates when they try to engage in voter education and registration. Qualitative in-depth interviews with local municipal politicians in the capital cities of Addis Ababa, Ethiopia; Kampala, Uganda; Nairobi, Kenya; and Lusaka, Zambia, revealed a belief that central governments systematically manipulate the electoral process by confusing voters, and hindering political opposition and engagement.

Tables 3.1 and 3.2 illustrate how the procedural model of democratization is overwhelmed by dominant-party systems, which methodically enforce executive power that is concentrated in the heads of state. These types of regimes in ESA have shattered institutional structures that are essential to substantive democratic elements.

Recall that the primary elements of a substantive model should reflect a greater influence of legal and political alternatives in conjunction with accessibility to government, citizens' rights, and political participation that informs democracy. In some countries, like Burundi, Ethiopia, Rwanda, and Tanzania, the legislative branches do function as lawmaking institutions, but their governments and heads of state regularly issue decrees that trump legislative efforts. In certain instances, ruling-party-dominated parliaments pass laws that contravene their constitutions. It is important to note that evaluating these emerging democracies under the rubric of substantive democracy leads to an unfair assessment of their efforts. It is also fair to say that substantive democratic elements are not the only yardstick for measuring democratic values or the only way to achieve democratic consolidation. Yet, despite this caveat, most ESA countries, with the relative exception of South Africa and Tanzania, do not meet the minimum requirement of procedural democratic elements. Critics argue that substantive conceptions of democracy run the risk of being at loggerheads with normative indicators of democracy, such as sociopolitical variables and due process under the rule of law.[8]

Table 3.1. Unicameral parliamentary and legislative political structures

COUNTRY	TYPE	MPs	EXECUTIVE VERSUS LEGISLATURE
Kenya	Unicameral	222	• President appoints 12 members of parliament • Manifest checks and balances for the executive • Attempts in last 10 years to trim executive power • Freedom of consultative public assembly hampered
Tanzania	Unicameral	323	• Zanzibar has a branch of House of Representatives • Weak system of checks and balances; CCM dominant • CCM leverages and dominates legislative proceedings • Opposition is very weak but treated fairly in assembly
Uganda	Unicameral	319	• Women occupy two-thirds; president appoints 10 MPs • Weak system of checks and balances; NRM dominant • No level playing field: presidential supremacy • Freedom of consultative public assembly hampered
Zambia	Unicameral	160	• Women occupy two-thirds; president appoints 10 MPs • Attempts at checks and balances for the executive • Attempts in last 10 years to trim executive power • Opposition is tough but influenced by the executive

Both the procedural and substantive approaches in third world politics fail to recognize the notion that democracy means the governance or rule of people, just as much as it implies that people should benefit by governing themselves.

One other major criticism of procedural and substantive democracies is that they are based on the principle of popular control and equality, but they do not consider other elements such as separation of powers and economic liber-

Table 3.2. Bicameral parliamentary and legislative political structures

COUNTRY	TYPE	MPs	EXECUTIVE VERSUS LEGISLATURE
Burundi	Bicameral	162	• President appoints 12 senators; president dominant • No system of checks and balances • Lawmaking by presidential decree, but not absolute • President can suspend the National Assembly
Ethiopia	Bicameral	546	• Prime Minister can dissolve the parliament • Weak system of checks and balances • No formal lawmaking powers • No level playing field: executive supremacy
Rwanda	Bicameral	104	• World record as the first to have majority of women • No system of checks and balances • Assembly usurps judiciary to empower president • President can suspend assembly on "security grounds"
South Africa	Bicameral	400	• ANC leverages and dominates legislative proceedings • Unequal playing field for women politicians • Checks and balances are minimal in provincial legislatures • Aisle-crossing without compulsory by-elections

alization.[9] It is at least anecdotally evident that even minimal standards of procedural democracy are not met by some African countries.

For example, Rwanda has not fully created an environment that would enable political parties to oppose arbitrary power, and the few existing political organizations are too encumbered to compete freely and fairly in parliamentary and presidential elections. Many international election observers and members of the international community regard the electoral commissions of Uganda and Zambia as susceptible to governmental interference.[10] In Burundi, Ethiopia, and Kenya, the judiciary and the parliament are not fully independent from state manipulation and are not fully empowered to safeguard the constitution, strengthen the rule of law, or protect citizens against human rights abuses.

As far as the procedural elements of democracy are concerned, the only exceptions are Tanzania and South Africa. These two countries have successfully regulated their parliamentary and presidential elections, and have also institutionalized their electoral commissions, which are regarded as autonomous from government interference. The two countries have their own political pitfalls, but research shows that the two states are not only shining African examples of the successful procedural conduct of free and fair elections, but that they are also on the road to substantive democracy.[11] The conceptualization of substantive and procedural democracy captures the processes by which each country has constructed democratic forms of political organization and governance. A combination of these two concepts in the study of the ESA's democratization process opens up the possibility for assessing public opinion on these two important factors.

Measuring the Procedural and Substantive Elements

It is imperative to turn to contemporary accounts, including the opinion of citizens, when accessing Africa's democratization process. No previous studies of ESA have addressed how ordinary citizens observe, orient, and respond to the key principles of procedural and substantive democratic elements in their countries. Field coordinators who were involved with residents of the sample communities conducted face-to-face surveys across the eight countries (see the Appendix for a detailed explanation of the methods employed, including sampling and questionnaire design). Before soliciting citizens' opinions, the field coordinators clearly explained each conceptual question, along with the scale for indicating how strongly respondents felt about a particular issue, ranging from strongly agree to strongly disagree.

Clarifying these universal concepts uniformly to each respondent provided an opportunity to put respondents at ease with the instrument and also helped the field coordinators to avoid imposing their own understanding of democratization on the respondents. (Note: The level of preponderance in the following analysis simply means that the country where the majority of respondents received a higher response value on an issue or outcome variable was listed first.) The social context in which the opinions were formed and expressed was taken into account by some of the supplementary items on the instrument. For example, some respondents who are accustomed to a particular system of authoritarian rule may not have recognized the distinctions between procedural and substantive democracy. In addition, respondents may have assumed that the evaluation of procedural or substantive democracy may not even be a pressing issue of concern to them. Moreover, some respondents may have believed that learning about the elements of democracy may not be of any benefit to them and that their *true* opinions did not really matter.

Africans in all eight ESA countries placed varying importance on the elements of procedural and substantive democracy. The data show that South Africans, Tanzanians, and Zambians (in that order of preponderance) placed regular contested elections at the core of procedural democracy. The same countries also placed multiparty politics at the heart of a legitimate democratic society. In the same vein, Burundians, Ethiopians, and Rwandese did not regard multiparty politics as crucial to attaining substantive democracy, and the majority of citizens in these three countries indicated that they prefer dominant single-party rule in their national assemblies. Public opinion in the eight countries indicates that the majority of citizens strongly agreed that their elected representatives in parliament do not enact laws that limit government (executive) power.

The majority of citizens in Zambia, Ethiopia, Uganda, and South Africa (in that order of preponderance) also supported the idea that politicians need to be changed through the voting process of regular elections based on accountability and the interests of the majority. In Burundi, Ethiopia, and Rwanda, the majority of citizens endorsed a substantive pluralist model, in which autonomous institutions like the judiciary have authority to limit the political actions of the majority, by allowing minorities to rule.

In Burundi, Kenya, Rwanda, and Tanzania, more than half of all individuals preferred a majoritarian model that permits the government to implement cohesive political actions that can limit the voices and priorities of the minority. The origin of these attitudes could be that public expectations are shaped by recollections of previous regimes, which did not promote the benefits of civic engagement in local governance and political representation. A renowned theorist of democracy, Dahl, argued that democratic governance and its consolidation is successful in the United States and a few other Western societies because the citizenry are highly engaged in local governance.[12] This is practically referred to as decentralization, whereby central governments do not conduct all key decisions concerning people's livelihoods. The contention here is that when African governments decentralized political and administrative authorities, they provided local government leaders the opportunity to interact with their constituencies and provided some power to the citizenry in controlling their local political and economic agendas.

In Ethiopia, Kenya, South Africa, Uganda, and Zambia, such actions diminished the power and autocracy of leaders in the central government. Between the early 1960s and the late 1970s, for example, local governments handled the collection of selective local taxes; the administration of primary education, private land, and agricultural cooperatives; and local law enforcement. However, the heads of these African countries retained the control and administration of policing and the local district courts. By the mid-1980s, all the countries tactfully usurped local governmental power when they constitutionally centralized the control and management of all revenue collection and allocation of financial resources to the district, provincial, and county commissioners. That ultimately diminished any possibility for decentralized local governments to articulate and enforce their will on national leaders.

More than three-quarters of all individuals surveyed in Ethiopia, Zambia, South Africa, and Uganda (in that order of preponderance) were satisfied with their local municipal or district representatives. Surprisingly, about half of all Ethiopians and Ugandans surveyed strongly agreed that the legislature is weak and that parliament should be abolished. The same number of individuals in Ethiopia, Zambia, South Africa, and Uganda indicated that they would support a system of government where residents rule themselves at the municipal or district level, rather than empowering their elected representatives and having a central government rule on their behalf. Less than half of the individuals surveyed in Kenya, Burundi, Rwanda, and Tanzania (in that order of preponderance) preferred a decentralized system of government. The majority of citizens, more than 60 percent, strongly agreed that their respective central governments should guarantee equal political participation and contestation both at the national level and the local government or provincial levels.

Since the majority of citizens from all eight countries examined here (with the exception of Rwanda) strongly agreed that democracy is good for their country, they should demand moral leadership and more democratic accountability. It appears that Africans, especially those surveyed here, understand that their elected officials are selfish and their representatives do not attend to their basic needs. Citizens in these and other African countries should use various public forums and the mass media to actively question why their parliamentary and elected representatives fail to act on their behalf.

Citizens also answered questions about their pressing need for safeguarding the constitution against militarization. (See Chapter Seven for a detailed discussion of militarization.) Most likely, citizens from all eight countries want spirited and audacious politicians who can compete for political office and make bold decisions, without fear of reprisal from coercive and tyrannical state apparatuses. Although citizens generally believe that their votes count and the electoral process matters to them, their opinions do not necessarily translate into actions on polling day. Therefore, citizens should also follow up on their interests and convictions in ousting shoddy politicians in order to hold them, and the regime, accountable.

In some ESA countries, particularly Burundi, Ethiopia, Rwanda, and Uganda, government agents alter or modify voter registration lists and polling centers to deny voters the chance to elect opposition candidates. Kenyans and South Africans were less likely to report that the political process was not free of manipulation. In addition, with the exception of South Africans and Zambians, respondents indicated that their members of parliament (MPs) were weak and could not rein in presidential supremacy and autocracy of the government. Kenyans said that their MPs are the most disempowered, with Rwandese and Ugandans following closely behind.

Below are the tabulated results of citizen surveys in all eight ESA countries with an analysis of the results.

Liberal Democracy in ESA

A liberal notion of democracy requires regular free and fair elections under universal adult suffrage with an understanding of the separation of powers.[13] The core values of a liberal democratic society entail a commitment to fundamental human rights, equality for all citizens, rule of law, and other civil liberties.[14] The liberal model of democracy fills some critical gaps that are missing in conceptions of substantive democracy, particularly in ESA. For instance, a basic conceptualization of liberal democracy in most of these African countries is fundamentally understood to be about the exercise of civilian rights and the choice to participate freely in political campaigns. In the Western conception, however, liberal politics deals with individual interests and choices that are exercised under a neutral set of rules based on constitutionalism, and the protection of individuals from the state and each other.[15] During visits to Ethiopia, Rwanda, Uganda, and Zambia between 2008 and 2010, informal and formal conversations with a few members of parliament revealed telling evidence. They argued that their constitutions had provisions that could be accurately interpreted to infer liberal democracy. Some of these politicians said that their laws also provide for the protection of individuals from the denial of basic rights and

Table 3.3. Public opinion about procedural and substantive elements of democracy

	Burundi	Ethiopia	Kenya	Rwanda
I trust most election outcomes	6.02***	3.58*	4.71*	2.88***
My vote counts and it matters	5.21	3.21*	4.16	4.58
Democracy is good for our country	5.27	6.18	5.13	4.69*
Our democracy is good. No change	5.07	2.69*	5.44	2.32*
Our leaders attend to our basic needs	1.39	2.23	2.49	1.72
Elected officials are unselfish	3.09	2.66*	4.81*	3.65
Our elected leaders represent us well	5.28*	3.06*	5.16*	3.24*
Elected officials advocate equal justice	3.21	3.25	3.65	3.38
The gov't abides by the Constitution	4.96	4.55	5.04	4.82
Politicians contest without intimidation	3.25*	1.56***	4.35	4.92
In politics, it is the majority who rule	3.28	3.49	1.22***	1.98*
The military overrules the Constitution	6.23*	5.34	2.94***	5.08
MPs limit presidents' excessive power	2.25*	1.49	4.68***	1.98
To vote out shoddy politicians is vital	5.12*	6.02	6.62	6.88
Local governments serve citizens well	5.92	5.78	6.23	6.69***
Constitution should abolish parliament	2.56*	6.12***	1.95***	3.76

Notes:

- For mean differences between countries: * = p < .05; *** = p < .001
- The scores are based on a scale of 1 to 7 (1 = strongly disagree, 4 = neutral, 7 = strongly agree). Sample σ^2 explained = .73. All tests of significance were two-tailed with robust SEs.
- These are primary survey data collected by the author in 2007 and 2008–2009.

Table 3.4. Public opinion about procedural and substantive elements of democracy

	South Africa	Tanzania	Uganda	Zambia
I trust most election outcomes	6.12***	5.88*	3.64*	4.93***
My vote counts and it matters	5.81	5.11*	4.07	5.27
Democracy is good for our country	6.47	6.41	5.15*	5.89*
Our democracy is good. No change	5.04*	5.79*	2.16*	3.61*
Our leaders attend to our basic needs	1.47	2.19	1.75	2.42
Elected officials are unselfish	4.29	3.06*	3.38*	3.72
Our elected leaders represent us well	4.26*	3.11*	3.43*	3.48*
Elected officials advocate equal justice	3.83	3.81	3.04	3.25
The gov't abides by the Constitution	5.69*	4.98*	4.51*	4.95*
Politicians contest without intimidation	4.87*	3.76***	2.59***	3.14
In politics, it is the majority who rule	4.61*	3.29*	2.09***	4.11*
The military overrules the Constitution	2.40*	3.54	6.32*	3.31
MPs limit presidents' excessive power	5.01*	4.49*	2.12*	3.97***
To vote out shoddy politicians is vital	6.02*	6.13	6.58	6.21
Local governments serve citizens well	4.61*	6.01*	4.52*	4.69***
Constitution should abolish parliament	2.04*	2.01*	4.02*	3.06*

Notes:

- For mean differences between countries: * = p < .05; *** = p < .001
- The scores are based on a scale of 1 to 7 (1 = strongly disagree, 4 = neutral, 7 = strongly agree). Sample σ^2 explained = .73. All tests of significance were two-tailed with robust SEs.
- These are primary survey data collected by the author in 2007 and 2008–2009.

maltreatment, as well as for universal education, public health care, or legal representation.

Quintessentially, the governments and regimes of all ESA countries also claim to safeguard constitutionalism and the protection of individuals from the state.

Respondents in Rwanda, as shown in Tables 3.3 and 3.4, were least likely to trust election outcomes, with Ethiopia and Uganda displaying almost similar numbers of respondents who somewhat disagreed that they trust elections. Burundians, South Africans, and Tanzanians were much more trusting of election outcomes, while Kenyans felt that they could only somewhat trust the outcomes. In spite of harboring distrust of the election results, Rwandese somewhat agreed that their elections matter, although it should be noted that a considerable number of respondents could neither agree nor disagree with the idea that their votes count. Public opinion data on the question of trusting election outcomes statistically differ significantly across the eight countries.

Ethiopians displayed the most cynical attitude towards the power of the ballot box, while South Africans were the most optimistic. A cynical or indifferent attitude toward the electoral process, however, did not affect public opinion on ineffective leadership. Regardless of their opinions and attitudes towards the reliability of the electoral process, the majority of the respondents either agreed or strongly agreed that it was vital to vote out shoddy politicians. This sentiment was apparent in data from all eight countries. Tables 3.3 and 3.4 show that the desire of citizens to vote out shoddy politicians does not statistically differ significantly between countries. From this survey of public attitudes, it can be argued that public expectations have now reached a stage where citizens are demanding that their politicians enact transformative democratic strategies to deliver social justice and create opportunities for individual liberty. When such basic rights are not met, citizens become agitated with their elected officials and feel the urgency of rooting out ineffective politicians.

As shown in Tables 3.5 and 3.6, Ethiopia and Tanzania represent the extreme ends of the public opinion spectrum with regard to perspectives on the electoral system. For instance, Ethiopians were the least likely to trust the electoral process, while Tanzanians were the most likely. Due to the high level of distrust exhibited by Ethiopians, it is not surprising that they were also the most likely to perceive their government as authoritarian and to believe that the president is a dictator.

Curiously, in spite of their skepticism of the electoral process, the majority of Ethiopians either agreed or strongly agreed that presidential elections are fair and that state institutions are trustworthy. Tanzanians, in contrast, expressed the highest level of trust in the electoral process and were more likely to believe that their government functions effectively as compared to other Eastern African countries. They also agreed with the notion that state institutions can be trusted. Tanzanians were also the least likely to believe that their president is a dictator. One plausible explanation for these sentiments from Tanzanians is the regime's ability to enable the successful transfer of presidential power from the incumbent to a subordinate newcomer without fear of a *coup d'état*. Post-colonial Tanzania also has enjoyed forty years of relative internal peace and stability. There has been neither military coups nor civil wars, and the political situation is the least volatile of all East African countries.

It appears that the regimes in Zambia and Tanzania, which have allowed a smooth alternation of presidential power and government, have also engendered similar positive public attitudes. On the whole, Zambians tended to share similar perceptions as Tanzanians, with the only exception that Zambians did not believe presidential elections are fair. Kenyans and Ugandans tended to agree with Zambians on this issue. Ugandans and Kenyans present an interesting case, because while they were not as skeptical about the electoral process as were Ethiopians, a majority agreed that their government is authoritarian and that the president has some dictatorial characteristics. Although Ethiopians, Kenyans, and Ugandans agreed with the notion that the executive branch is guilty of abusing its power, they harbored much more positive agreement about the legislature. A possible explanation for this is that the executive branches of these governments have not fully transitioned from neopatrimonial systems that enable presidential supremacy to benefit their political party to a democracy that abides by the separation of powers. However, their legislatures effectively and competitively function as multiparty systems. For example, Ethiopians, Kenyans, and Ugandans were the most likely to agree or strongly agree that their country enjoys fair legislative elections. Ugandans, as well as South Africans, Tanzanians, and Zambians, also agreed, for the most part, that their governments function effectively.

Zambians displayed somewhat similar attitudes toward the electoral system as did Ugandans, even though they were much more trusting of the electoral process than Ugandans and other Eastern Africans. Just like Kenyans and Ugandans, South Africans and Zambians had much more faith in the legislative

Table 3.5. Comparison of the electoral system and existing democratic governance

	Ethiopia	Kenya	Tanzania	Uganda
Trust the electoral process	3.43*	5.41*	6.39*	4.25***
Gov't functions effectively	4.81	5.23	5.54*	5.11
Fair presidential elections	5.41*	3.91*	5.41*	3.72*
Fair legislative elections	4.38***	5.92	5.94	6.33*
Gov't is authoritarian	5.83***	3.74***	3.25*	5.44***
President is a dictator	6.69***	3.19***	2.25***	4.58***
Trust our state institutions	5.14	5.21*	5.76	4.75

Table 3.6. Comparison of the electoral system and existing democratic governance

	Burundi	Rwanda	S. Africa	Zambia
Trust the electoral process	5.94	5.25*	6.09*	6.18
Gov't functions effectively	4.62*	4.47	5.07*	4.76
Fair presidential elections	5.89*	4.63*	5.78***	3.89*
Fair legislative elections	5.28*	4.88*	6.06*	6.09*
Gov't is authoritarian	3.32*	5.74***	3.06***	4.75***
President is a dictator	2.74***	4.88***	2.64***	3.29***
Trust our state institutions	4.39	4.41*	4.32	4.19

Notes:

- For mean differences between countries: * = $p < .05$; *** = $p < .001$
- The scores are based on a scale of 1 to 7 (1 = strongly disagree, 4 = neutral, 7 = strongly agree). Sample σ^2 explained = .76. All tests of significance were two-tailed with robust SEs.
- These are primary survey data collected by the author in 2007 and 2008–2009
- The four countries in Table 3.5 are placed together here to represent the Eastern region.
- The four countries in Table 3.6 are placed together here to represent the Southern region, although Rwanda and Burundi are geographically in south-central Africa.

branch than in the executive branch of government. They were also less likely to characterize their government as authoritarian or their president as dictatorial. The latter have regimes that transformed their political systems into pluralistic open societies, away from those that were predominantly controlled through a state party system and subjugated particular groups of people. These latter regimes have also transitioned from centralized state institutions to decentralized local or provincial governments within the rule of law. These regimes also provide relatively efficient delivery of public services.

The data also show that Burundians and South Africans were confident about the fairness of the electoral process for both the executive and the legislative branches and that they were the least likely to perceive their government as authoritarian. Burundi has experienced violent ethnic conflicts and state collapse over the last two decades. Therefore it is quite surprising that Burundians still had a lot of confidence in their regime. Burundians exhibited similar public attitudes toward their government and politics as did South Africans in all areas, and they were the most likely to believe that their presidential elections are fair. A likely explanation is the mere fact that the current (2010–2011) Burundian government is presided over by the ethnic Hutu majority. Rwandese, while reluctant to characterize their electoral process as unfair, either agreed or strongly agreed that the government is authoritarian and that the president is a dictator. Similarly, a likely explanation is the mere fact that the current (2010–2011) Rwandese population is dominated by the ethnic Hutu majority, but its government and military are presided over by the Tutsi minority.

Of all those surveyed, Rwandese and Burundians had the greatest number of respondents who do not trust their governments, while Tanzanians and South Africans were the most trusting. Over half of the Rwandese and over a third of the Burundian respondents felt that their government was untrustworthy. This was in stark contrast to the 85 percent of Tanzanians and nearly 70 percent of South Africans who felt that their government was deserving of their trust. Citizens in the four remaining countries were more likely to trust rather than distrust their governments, but their endorsements were not as strong as those in Tanzania and South Africa. For example, 60 percent of Ethiopians and Kenyans placed trust in the government, with less than 60 percent of Ugandans and Zambians expressing similar support. The support and trust in government could be a result of nation-building efforts that aim to promote a consensus-oriented political culture, which embraces economic opportunity, social development, and the spirit of national unity.

In early 2007 through late 2009, I was constantly reminded by some of my hosts in public and private institutions in Kenya, Rwanda, Uganda, and Zambia about the causes of public agitation over the lack of tangible political goods. These factors included rampant corruption, high and growing unemployment levels, poverty, socioeconomic inequality, and the deterioration of public services such as universal primary and secondary education, and public health.

Chapter Summary

Even though Rwanda has the largest number of women in the legislative assembly, making it a global leader in this area, civil organizations from across East Africa have accused the ruling RPF of using women parliamentarians as rubber stamps for tightening President Paul Kagame's grip on power. Countries like Burundi and Rwanda still lack independent and vigilant human rights bodies that can play a watchdog role. Conclusions about which democratization processes work best for citizens of the ESA in their respective constituencies will be made in the next chapter after an examination of the waves of democratization in the ESA. However, tentative conclusions can be drawn about the powerful opinions gathered from the survey data and secondary sources on models of democracy and the democratization process.

For the most part, respondents from all eight countries indicated that democracy was a positive force in their countries, but not all agreed with the assumption that their democratic system was sound. Ethiopians, Rwandese, and Ugandans strongly disagreed with this notion, and some respondents told our field research assistants (or wrote on their individual survey questionnaires) that they desired change in the type of democracy that currently exists. Zambians displayed a somewhat more neutral attitude on this particular issue. The rest did not agree that imminent change is necessary in the type of democracy—as they implicitly assume and recognize it—in their respective countries. Statistically significant differences in public opinion exist on that issue across all eight countries.

Considering that Africans in the eight countries generally want democracy to take root and flourish, it is perhaps not surprising that they are highly critical of national leaders who do not share their political vision. Take for example the empirical findings in Tables 3.3 and 3.4. Very few respondents across all eight countries agreed or strongly agreed that their political leaders attend to their basic needs—whatever they assumed those needs to be. Kenyans and South Africans, however, were the least likely to regard their political leaders as selfish, while the majority of citizens in other ESA countries agreed or strongly agreed that their political leadership is somewhat self-serving. In Eastern Africa, the Burundian and Kenyan respondents were the most likely to agree that their elected officials are representing constituents well. However, their responses also indicate a lukewarm endorsement at best for other similar indicators. Public sentiment on that issue produced statistically significant differences across all eight countries.

In addition, ESA citizens do not feel that the system of checks and balances operates optimally. South African MPs were found to be the most successful in limiting presidential excess, while Ethiopians and Rwandese indicated that their MPs were abysmally failing to fulfill their responsibilities. Although most ESA citizens consider their MPs to be ineffective, they do not agree that constitutional power should be invoked to abolish parliaments or their legislative assemblies. Ethiopians were the exception to that question, but even they did not strongly agree or overwhelmingly agree in favor of such political action.

Regardless of the model of democracy and the level of democratization, Tanzania's ruling CCM party, as well as Uganda's ruling Movement party, still display presidential supremacy over their party agendas and their interests take precedence over parliamentary, judicial, and constituency interests. Empirical and anecdotal evidence[16] show how some of these countries, such as South Africa, Tanzania, and Zambia, have achieved comparatively remarkable gains in procedural and liberal democracy. Other ESA countries, however, namely Burundi, Ethiopia, Kenya, and Uganda, have recently experienced erosions in their democratization. Such erosion can delay efforts of empowering civil society, and citizens, to hold state leaders accountable to the rule of law and the enforcement of democratic obligations. As outlined in Tables 3.3 and 3.4, all respondents in ESA agreed that their leaders could do a better job of advocating for equal justice.

Democratization in these developing countries, including South Africa, should carry on the mantle of establishing a civilized citizenry and majority working-class society, which are by-products of economic development. For liberal democratic elements and substantive democracy to blossom in ESA, Africans must struggle to first achieve economic development and individual fiscal prosperity as much as their elites struggle for national power. These governments can achieve a sustainable democratic system leading to liberal substantive democracy if and only if economically empowered and well-informed citizens can challenge the domestic structure of authoritarian rule and the legitimacy of their regimes. These are all important elements of the democratization process that many Africans wish for themselves.

In the next chapter, insights underlying democratization and substantive democratic rule in ESA are examined from three central questions, with the intention of rigorously testing public opinion concerning the legitimacy of ESA regimes and the rule of law. Are citizens satisfied with their governments as legitimate? Do citizens regard their governments as competent enough to fulfill their democratic obligations in implementing what is acceptable for the collective needs of all citizens, regardless of their gender, social class, ethnicity, or political ideology? Are citizens in ESA satisfied with their governments' efforts to guarantee the rule of law and ensure that the needs and aspirations of citizens are fulfilled? Answers to these questions are extremely important to the stability and eventual consolidation of democratic rule in ESA. Chapter Four answers them by assessing the patterns of public opinion that emerge from the survey of average citizens.

Chapter Four

Rule of Law and Regime Legitimacy

In order to more fully understand democratization, this chapter presents an analysis of public opinion concerning the rule of law and the legitimacy of the regimes in eight Eastern and Southern African (ESA) countries. In most of ESA, state actors and law enforcement institutions refer to the rule of law in terms of constitutionalism, a well-functioning judicial system, and a respected or sufficient legal policy.[1] A well-functioning judicial system strikes the deepest, tormented part of many African journalists' hearts and souls; many of them have suffered at the hands of contradictory interpretations of libel and sedition laws in ESA.

Rule of Law

As a universal benchmark, the rule of law implies that governments in ESA are held accountable for all their actions and are bound by rules that prevent them from rendering individual efforts useless or inept by extemporized action.[2] This simply means that societies under the rule of law have sufficient individual liberties and citizens enjoy equal rights, equal protection, and equal privileges from the state. ESA leaders do not address or consider contemporary political events, respect for civil and political rights, and other political virtues as fundamental elements of the rule of law.[3] In most cases, the characterization of the rule of law by most state actors is so lax that it allows contradictory interpretations of the law between the enforcement agencies and the judiciary. The rule of law in ESA should prescribe a government of laws, not of men and women.[4]

The challenge facing ESA is that the majority of citizens in rural parts of Burundi, Ethiopia, Kenya, Rwanda, South Africa, Tanzania, Uganda, and Zambia do not have access to the courts. In Burundi and Rwanda, for example, the judiciary is still dominated by the minority Tutsi ethnic groups in both countries and is believed to be subjugating the majority Hutu ethnic population. In countries such as Ethiopia, Tanzania, and Uganda, the regimes have not endorsed autonomous oversight, active participation of civil society, and vigilant human rights commissions to ensure state transparency and accountability to the public.[5] In South Africa, Tanzania, Uganda, and Zambia, the unilateralism and supremacy of political parties such as the ANC, CCM, and NRM have threatened the primacy and preservation of constitutionalism.[6] The rule of law cannot take root unless these countries empower autonomous oversight institutions to protect human rights violations, enforce good governance, and promote civil liberties.

The rule of law works in conjunction with other models of democracy to ensure political rights, instruments of accountability, and civil liberties; thus, it leads to the political equality of all citizens. O'Donnell writes:

> Without a vigorous rule of law, defended by an independent judiciary, rights are not safe and the equality and dignity of all citizens are at risk. Only under a democratic rule of law will the various agencies such as the electoral, societal, and horizontal accountability function effectively, without obstruction and intimidation from powerful state actors.[7]

Everyone is entitled to equal treatment in society. An independent judiciary, media, and an informed and engaged civil society are crucial to achieving the rule of law. Many journalists working in ESA have not enjoyed these legal rights and privileges. The rule of law shares the following sense of universal values or purposes: It serves to protect people against anarchy, allows people to plan their affairs with confidence because they know the legal consequences of their actions, and protects people from the arbitrary exercise of power by public officials.[8] The rule of law links basic democratic ideas to legal doctrines or constitutionalism, with principles of governance conducted according to law. Societies in ESA are more likely to be stable democracies and achieve fast economic growth if the government safeguards the rule of law. Mahoney and Deutsch, for instance, argue that respect for the rule of law contributes to international order.[9] Weak states, especially those in Africa that have adopted the rule of law in the past two decades, have attained some level of societal pacification during institution building. The ESA nations ought to uphold the rule of law if they desire to attain pacification and sustainable democracy.

The rule of law guarantees that a regime's power and influence are legitimately exercised in accordance with openly disclosed rules and acts that are enforced on established procedure.[10] The rule of law is not only the enforcement of legal norms, as it also connotes the principle of the supremacy of legal procedure, which is fundamental for any civil order and a basic requirement for democratic consolidation.[11] This standard provides established measures for any regime and allows the state to rule by laws that govern everyone equally. In the case of ESA, the rule of law ought to be instituted to safeguard citizens against arbitrary governance through legislation, constitutional provisions, relevant treaties, and an independent judiciary. The rule of law can be qualitatively defined in two fundamental ways: formal and substantive. Formal conceptualization emphasizes the universality of enacted laws, which are created through some kind of democratic process.[12] Formal laws require accessibility and a transparent mechanism for legal and political change. They follow the general constitutional principles protecting human rights, but their protection and enforcement emanate from the ordinary legal process as deemed appropriate by the political regime and the legal institutions. The vulnerabilities of this formal (minimalist) law in the ESA transitioning democracies are tendencies towards injustice, especially the discriminatory treatment of people based on ethnicity, caste, gender, political affiliation, or religion, as discussed in Chapter Two.

The substantive rule of law emphasizes mandatory legal equality, justice, freedom, and political and economic rights. Substantive normative values include respect for individual or minority rights. The legal system in ESA needs the rule of law, which underscores an infrastructure of justice for the universal human good. Examples of a proper legal infrastructure include a decorous legislative authority to make laws without undue influence from the executive and military branches, judges from diverse ethno-political backgrounds to interpret the law, and a professional, better-remunerated judicial service that would guarantee its integrity and independence. All of these issues are major challenges for the rule of law in the eight ESA countries.

A constitutional law scholar for East Africa argues that the rule of law requires governmental commitment to safeguard and respect the outcome of legal rules.[13] Countries in the East African Community (Burundi, Ethiopia, Kenya,

Rwanda, Tanzania, and Uganda) are constitutionally obliged to enforce the orderly and non-violent resolution of political conflicts. Scholarship in the past decade shows how the legal system in Sub-Saharan Africa is set up and also demonstrates that the type of regime determines how the rule of law is promoted and preserved.[14] The transition to democratic rule and the stability of Africa's volatile states depend on a strong and vigilant civil society, citizen participation, adherence to constitutionalism, and the rule of law.

Prior to a court appearance or release in Burundi, Kenya, Rwanda, Tanzania, and Uganda, for example, the police regularly detain suspects beyond the constitutional limit of 48 hours.[15] The Human Rights Watch reports of 2006 and 2007 state that torture in Uganda had become a common occurrence under Museveni's rule. In Burundi and Kenya, the Human Rights Watch reports of 2005, 2007, and 2008 cite several incidents of tortured suspects.

Of particular note is a 2005 annual report that found widespread use of excessive force on civilians by the Kenyan police during arrests and while in detention. In Kenya, hundreds of ordinary citizens were killed, and thousands displaced, during outbreaks of political violence throughout the general presidential and parliamentary elections.[16] In 2005, Ethiopia's government carried out an operation to crack down on political protests and opposition. During that operation, about 200 citizens died at the hands of the police. Hundreds more were detained in Addis Ababa prisons and police cells for weeks without any charges. Their alleged crimes were protesting election malpractices and vote rigging during the elections.

Tanzania has also suffered similar episodes of political violence during and soon after the last two parliamentary and presidential elections. The 2000 demonstrations in Zanzibar and on the mainland, protesting the election results, resulted in the deaths of at least forty civilians. Throughout the remainder of 2000, several bombs and arson attacks rocked government buildings, including the Electoral Commission offices on the northern island of Pemba. At least forty-nine people were arrested that year, including opposition politicians who spent several weeks in detention without prosecution or trial. Some of the politicians were released on police bond after spending several weeks in detention without seeing a defense attorney. These political clashes were between the CCM party and the Civic United Front (CUF).

In Burundi, just as in post-conflict Ethiopia and Rwanda, the formal structures of the rule of law collapsed. However, there have been efforts to establish a justice and human rights system for the majority of citizens in rural communities who are faced with an influx of returning internally displaced persons (IDPs). Just as in Rwanda, Belgian colonial rulers in Burundi treated the minority Tutsi ethnic groups as superior to the Hutu majority, and they politically empowered them to subjugate the Hutu majority when the country gained independence in 1962. Burundian governments during the past forty years, motivated by ethnic sectarianism in the context of changing regimes, have engaged in large-scale human rights abuses, execution of opponents, and wanton destruction of civilians.

> In late 2000, during my tenure as an international journalist in Eastern Africa, I spoke with an advocate, Jean Pierre Mwambutsa, in the town of Gitega, Burundi, about his country's policy of transitional justice. He said that the major problem he saw with then president Pierre Buyoya's transitional justice was the incapacitation of an independent judiciary. He mentioned the constant mobility of political prisoners and rebel fighters from one detention center to another in the 1990s, even when these suspects did not commit the alleged crimes. It became very difficult for paralegals, lawyers, judges, and magistrates to set up fair trials or even to process case files and interview witnesses because the suspects constantly moved from one province to another.

> Meanwhile, when my cameraman, Ibrahim Mugwanya, and I last interviewed then president Pierre Buyoya in 1999, he told us that he had established a formidable judicial system to build peace and reconciliation between Hutus and Tutsis, in a wider effort to promote the rule of law. These adjudication processes were popularly known as the *bashingantahe*. Its judicial role was to find an amicable solution to a dispute between warring parties, where there was no established infrastructure for the courts of law.

In the Federal Democratic Republic of Ethiopia, one of the major challenges of constitutional governance is the lack of civil advocacy and independent human rights groups, which can build effective civic pressure towards political reconciliation and democratic rule. In the 1990s and 2000s, habitual uprisings and civil protests at universities and vocational institutions in Addis Ababa usually ended up in state executions or arbitrary arrests of protestors who are prosecuted in the courts of law without even the semblance of a fair trial.[17]

For decades in the late twentieth century, Ethiopia was engulfed in a major civil conflict regarding the secession of Eritrea, which sought to secure autonomy as a sovereign country. It is important to note that the Ethiopian federal constitution matches the constitution of the former Soviet Union on the question of secession. Eritreans recognized that the Ethiopian constitution gave copious promises of self-determination in their effort to gain independence for its ethnic provinces. However, when gigantic provinces such as Eritrea demanded to secede from Ethiopia, the Ethiopian government responded with ruthless force.[18] Human rights abuses and other violations occurred because of Ethiopia's parochial aggravation of ethnic consciousness.[19]

Although the Eritreans and other subjugated groups in Ethiopia demanded to secede, the federal government's actions were contrary and extreme based on its constitutional responsibilities. The regime curtailed and abolished ordinary rights and freedoms of the Eritrean people and other ethnic groups. This, incidentally, reinforced and justified Eritrean demands for secession.

In Kenya during the late 1980s and throughout the 1990s, there were reports of government repression, torture, and detention without trial of civilians who were regularly picked up by police from their homes. During the second and third multiparty elections, opposition supporters suffered constant episodes of politically motivated human rights violations at the hands of KANU politicians.[20] During this period, dozens of Kenyans were killed and hundreds arrested in episodes of ethnic clashes and political violence.

Many of the cases investigating those violent deaths remained unsolved and international human rights advocates who attempted to file these cases in the courts of law were threatened with deportation. For example, two well-known human rights activists, Wangari Maathai and Kivutha Kibwana, were briefly detained in 2001 by former president Daniel Moi. Former president Moi's regime in the 1980s and 1990s regularly used the practice of detention of suspects without trial.[21] Two years after their detention, Maathai and Kibwana joined the cabinet in President Mwai Kibaki's new government, but such detentions continued undeterred. President Kibaki used security operatives from 2005 to 2008 to shut down the media and to detain journalists.

Unlike EAC founding members Kenya, Tanzania, and Uganda, which trace their colonial past to Britain, Rwanda's colonial history goes back to Germany and later Belgium, the latter of which influenced its Francophone backdrop. Rwanda's ethnic composition, politics, history, culture, and economy are quite similar to Burundi's. In both countries, for instance, colonial rulers treated the minority Tutsi ethnic groups as superior to the Hutus and politically empowered them to subjugate the Hutu majority.[22] Because of its past legacy of political violence caused by ethnic divisions, Rwanda is still struggling to establish the rule of law. Is democracy feasible in this environment dominated by identity politics? According to Anastasia Mukamwiru, a local politician from Kigali, the ethnic polarization and superior power of the minority Tutsi, who are fearful and suspicious of the powerless Hutu majority, make the rule of law difficult to realize.

Mukamwiru illustrated the challenge with an example. The RPF leader, Major General Paul Kagame, became vice president in late 1994 when the RPF took power. In 2000, he assumed the presidency after the resignation of President Pasteur Bizimungu, a prominent Hutu moderate politician. "That resignation is believed to have been stage-managed by the RPF government," Mukamwiru said. The president's resignation triggered protests in subsequent weeks from leading Hutu politicians and members of parliament after Bizimungu accused Tutsi legislators of selectively persecuting Hutu politicians. Since then, President Kagame has been accused by human rights groups of condemning his opponents for instigating ethnic anxieties. His RPF government has suspended political party activities and forcibly co-opted political opponents into his party. Kagame held Rwanda's first presidential elections since the genocide in 2003 and received 95 percent of the vote. He again won the second presidential elections in 2010 by over 90 percent of the vote. A similar overwhelming vote total for the incumbent is also regularly witnessed in Tanzania's presidential elections, where the CCM dominates both national and provincial politics.

During the past two election cycles in 2000 and 2005 in Tanzania, the military police arbitrarily arrested citizens believed to be antagonists of the ruling CCM and held them for several days until after the elections.[23] In the late 1990s, Tanzanians became agitated by the increased arrest of human rights activists and some journalists on weak charges of being idle and disorderly. The regime's performance along with ESA countries is reflected in Table 4.1. The disintegration of civil order and collapse of the rule of law increased political dissatisfaction, political violence, and insecurity.[24] Press reports alleged that President Benjamin Mkapa's government ignored the administration of justice based on status-quo patronage. The CCM party enjoyed police protection from prosecution when atrocities were committed in association with their political activities.[25]

When some CCM bureaucrats faced criminal charges for extrajudicial killings and corruption, they were set free by state prosecutors due to lack of evidence. One prominent case among a myriad of examples occurred during the 2001 general elections on the Tanzanian island of Pemba when armed security forces massacred more than thirty opposition demonstrators who demanded

Table 4.1. Comparison of the rule of law—Indicators for emerging democracies

INDICATORS	Ethiopia	Kenya	Tanza-nia	Uganda
Preserve the rule of law	4.3	5.6	5.4	5.2
Guard judicial independence	4.4	5.7	6.1	4.6
Defend human rights	5.9	6.9	6.6	7.1
Respect for physical rights	6.1	4.7	3.6	7.3
Protect civil liberties	4.9	4.5	3.8	5.1
Promote political rights	4.7	4.4	4.3	5.1
Foster women's political rights	4.9	5.0	5.0	6.4
	Burundi	**Rwanda**	**S. Africa**	**Zambia**
Preserve the rule of law	4.4	4.7	7.7	5.9
Guard judicial independence	4.7	4.2	7.9	4.6
Defend human rights	5.9	6.9	6.8	7.1
Respect for physical rights	6.1	6.1	5.3	6.9
Protect civil liberties	4.8	4.9	5.9	6.2
Promote political rights	4.8	4.5	5.5	5.4
Foster women's political rights	5.2	7.0	6.1	5.9

Notes:
- The scores in Table 4.1 are based on a scale of 0 to 10, in which the weakest performance equals 0 and the strongest equals 10.
- These are 2007–2008 aggregate data drawn from a variety of sources including *Freedom House Index*, *Economist Intelligence Unit* (democracy index), *Ibrahim Index of African Governance*, and *The Africa Barometer*.

new presidential elections. Human Rights NGOs gathered eyewitness testimonies about these extrajudicial killings, but the government never pressed charges.

The Ugandan government came under increased criticism in the 1990s and 2000s from the Uganda Law Society and other advocacy and human rights groups for the political instability instigated by its police and the military. Press reports and election observers charged that the police and the Ugandan military forcibly disperse opposition campaign rallies, beat up and detain followers, and sometimes charge the entourage of opposition leaders with treason.[26] The 2006 Uganda Human Rights report, for instance, documents that the government also targeted political dissent and imprisoned critics of the regime on terrorism charges. The military also violated the political rights and freedoms of citizens by suppressing voices of the opposition, thus creating conditions of insecurity for civilians who attempted to freely engage in the electoral process.[27]

The EAC countries are required by Article 7(2) of the East African Treaty to abide by the rule of law and preserve human rights principles. Given the past aberration of principles of good governance and the rule of law in all eight African countries, it seemed unclear how these nations will in future promote constitutionalism and democratic rule. As Table 4.2 illustrates, all eight ESA countries are perceived in a negative light by citizens they govern on the questions of power and authority.

The challenges for improving the rule of law in ESA in general seem to be affected by the pace and scope of democratic rule. In light of the looming but contested political federation of the EAC, Kamanyi outlined the following necessities for the restoration of the rule of law in Eastern Africa and throughout ESA:

> In the arena of the rule of law, much is left to be desired when it comes to understanding and respecting the fact that an individual is innocent until proven guilty; the right not to be imprisoned without trial; and that all individuals regardless of their status enjoy the same rights before the law, or that nobody is above the law. The independence of the judiciary needs to be further secured in the partner states with regard to the terms and conditions surrounding the appointment of judges that would shield them from undue and improper personal and political pressure. Dismissal by the executive undermines the institution of the judiciary. Judges must be protected against unwarranted removal. The integrity of the judicial system must be protected and accorded control over its own procedural and administrative affairs.[28]

It may be difficult for these nations to achieve good governance that is safeguarded by the rule of law without fostering the intellectual and moral qualities of citizens. The success of the rule of law and overall democratization may in part depend upon the civic knowledge of the citizenry in terms of understanding their rights, how they are represented by their elected representatives in government, and the democratic effectiveness of the legislative assembly.

Table 4.2. Comparison of the rule of law—Indicators for the ESA countries

INDICATORS	Ethiopia	Kenya	Tanzania	Uganda
Judiciary and courts are independent	2.42*	4.06*	4.17*	3.96*
Government protects human rights	2.61*	4.12***	5.13***	3.89***
President uses excessive authority	6.23***	5.82*	5.19	6.19***
Parliament limits presidents' power	2.48*	3.16*	2.45***	3.21*
Our president is above the law	6.23	5.89	5.22*	6.51
Our government is authoritarian	6.32	5.25*	4.98	6.04
	Burundi	**Rwanda**	**S. Africa**	**Zambia**
Judiciary and courts are independent	3.31*	4.77	4.49*	4.43***
Government protects human rights	3.31*	4.11***	4.86***	3.92*
President uses excessive authority	5.12***	6.91***	2.29*	5.34***
Parliament limits presidents' power	2.35*	2.42*	4.26*	3.97***
Our president is above the law	5.41	6.04*	5.28	5.59
Our government is authoritarian	5.15*	6.06*	4.22*	4.73***

Notes:
- For mean differences between provinces: * = p < .05; *** = p < .001. Sample σ^2 explained = .74 across ESA. All tests of significance were two-tailed with robust SEs.
- The scores are based on a 1 to 7 scale: (1 = strongly disagree, 4 = neutral, 7 = strongly agree).
- These are primary survey data collected by the author in 2007 and 2008–2009.

In order to achieve good democratic governance, the governments in ESA should strengthen and ensure autonomy for the following institutions so that they can then advocate for transparency and accountability: the national assembly, the judiciary, the electoral commission, the media, law enforcement agencies, the auditor general's office, and civil society. However, at some point in the 1990s, the governments of all eight countries undermined most of those independent institutions with constitutional amendments that stifled national debate over the rule of law and other human rights issues.[29] For example, in Ethiopia, Rwanda, Tanzania, and Zambia, the head of state may, on the advice of one of those institutions, issue a presidential decree that either annuls the law or becomes a law that trumps some constitutional provision.

Realistically, it becomes extremely hard for some of these countries to monitor state compliance with the rule of law, as well as constitutionally protect fundamental human rights. This is particularly true of Burundi, Ethiopia, Rwanda, and Uganda, which have state-controlled local human rights bodies and less autonomous civil societies. Moreover, it is unlikely that the judiciary in all eight countries, being exclusively appointed by the executive, will challenge the regime in relation to its violation of the rule of law. Institutions like the judiciary, most of the news media in some of these countries, the auditor general, and the parliament may feel subjugated by the supremacy of the presidency. Attempting to expose violations perpetrated by the regime will be difficult since the government appoints or internally nominates who runs for public office. This is what breeds the presidential supremacy that diminishes democratic rule.

Regime Legitimacy

A regime can be defined as a governing body that determines who can share political power and who is at the center of leadership, and how that relates to the overall structure of the citizenry.[30] This section examines how ESA regimes use the democratization process and the media to enhance their legitimacy. The term *legitimacy* in this book refers to the notion of popular consent and validation of social trust by those who are custodians of the people's rights and well-being. The term *regime legitimacy*, then, refers to how a group of political decision makers gain the right to exercise authority and how they perform the basic governmental functions required by the collective needs and mutual interests of society. A legitimate regime is one whose members attain consent from citizens that existing political institutions are the most appropriate ones.[31] Regime legitimacy is the bedrock of democratic rule, in which a regime functions in established roles and acts according to accepted rules as expressed in the constitution.

Therefore, the rule of law and regime legitimacy go hand in hand. The governments in ESA can live up to their democratic responsibilities and gain greater legitimacy by ensuring that public goods and services are effectively delivered, law and order are maintained, and justice is effectively administered.

Data collected in 2007 show how well ESA regimes maintain law and order in their countries: South Africa lags significantly behind Tanzania, but slightly behind Kenya and Zambia. Perhaps this is due to its statistically high rate of crime. Accordingly, fewer Burundians than any other ESA country either agree or somewhat agree that their regime maintains law and order. African scholars of constitutional governance provide the following ten indices for state accountability, which fulfill the needs and aspirations of citizens and are also necessary for these countries to achieve legitimacy for good democratic governance:[32]

1. Respect for the rule of law by all the actors in the political process
2. Independence and capacity of the judiciary
3. Legally binding instruments to ensure unfettered press freedom, and the right to freedom of speech and expression
4. Mechanisms for self-regulation and external oversight of the activities of the executive and legislative bodies
5. Mechanisms to allow oversight and active participation of civil society to ensure state transparency and accountability to the public
6. Mechanisms to provide economic liberalization so that the private sector can participate in decision making
7. The extension of decentralized structures in market policy decision making
8. Gender and ethnicity representation in all spheres of decision making
9. Effective delivery mechanisms to service the poor
10. Independence of the legislature in drafting and enacting relevant legislation

The legitimacy of ESA regimes cannot be equated fully with enhanced consensus and the ability to sustain society's expectations for human rights protection. The culture of human rights demands that the legitimacy of a regime be determined by whether or not the government respects human rights and behaves in accordance with its precepts.[33] Several ESA countries have yet to meet these criteria. In most of Africa, regime legitimacy is based also on the implicit assumption that political leaders are responsible for providing economic opportunities to citizens so that they may provide for their families free from civil strife and unrest.

When political leaders behave in a responsible manner by caring for economically marginalized groups, and when they do not engage in geopolitical nepotism or tribalistic favoritism, they sustain their political legitimacy and stabilize the broader polity.[34] Research on political identity shows that in Eastern Africa, for example, state actors erode their legitimacy if they violate public expectations by engaging in nepotism. However, in some African societies, including South Africa and Zambia, political leaders tend to appoint their relatives and reward elite supporters from the same geopolitical ethnic regions in order to consolidate political ties.[35] In certain situations, some of those leaders look for qualified bureaucrats outside of such in-groups in an effort to appease international donors and the opposition.

Zambia's major challenge is the lack of non-political prosecutors. During former president Kenneth Kaunda's reign in the 1980s and Frederick Chiluba's presidency in the 1990s, prosecutors almost never prosecuted corruption cases involving public officials or state graft. Prosecution of state officials in Zambia was never an option in dealing with past human rights violations and graft because the courts' role in establishing the rule of law was handicapped by the regime.[36] The state amassed wealth through kickbacks but never promoted reconstruction, economic development, or the long-term stability of social programs such as education and the infrastructure.[37] In fact, former freedom fighter and president Kenneth Kaunda was widely quoted in 1988 on national television as saying, "Ambition never comes to an end."

Regime legitimacy is important to substantive liberal democracy in ESA because it encapsulates both substantive and procedural legitimacy. The term *procedural legitimacy* refers to either the democratic process of electing parliamentarians with input from other autonomous state institutions or the way citizens expect a government to conduct its business. The latter has to be accomplished through consultation with constituents in order to achieve legitimacy and ensure political activities are conducted to benefit citizens.

Public opinion data gathered in 2007 and 2008 clearly show that few citizens in ESA view their regimes as legitimate. As Table 4.3 below illustrates, none of the eight ESA countries can claim that public attitudes are on their side when citizens are asked, "Does our regime safeguard freedom of speech and expression?" The table also ranks the eight ESA nations based on citizen agreement with the statement: "The regime is legitimate."

Table 4.3. Public opinion about legitimacy and safeguarding freedom of expression

ESA Countries	The regime is legitimate μ and (s.d.)	We have free speech & expression μ and (s.d.)
Burundi	3.10 (1.573)*	3.04 (1.524)*
Ethiopia	3.27 (1.752)*	3.25 (1.657)
Kenya	4.12 (1.752)***	3.86 (1.709)*
Rwanda	3.07 (1.543)*	2.99 (1.541)*
S. Africa	5.06 (1.534)*	4.51 (1.674)***
Tanzania	4.60 (1.753)***	3.81 (1.856)
Uganda	3.61 (2.089)*	3.93 (2.085)***
Zambia	4.19 (1.711)***	3.79 (1.680)*

Notes:
- Respondents were asked to agree or disagree with the statements: "The regime is legitimate" and "We have freedom of speech and expression."
- For mean differences between provinces: $* = p < .05$; $*** = p < .001$. Sample σ^2 explained $= .76$ across ESA. All tests of significance were two-tailed with robust SEs.
- The scores are based on a scale of 1 to 7 (1 = strongly disagree, 4 = neutral, 7 = strongly agree).
- These are primary survey data collected by the author in 2007 and 2008–2009.

Legitimacy is also defined in terms of how procedures and directives at the national level are recognized by the masses. When ESA citizens evaluate the legitimacy of their regimes on political affairs, government actions are assessed based on accepted indiscriminate norms. According to Hayward and Dumbuya, government decisions are regarded as binding even when they are not the desired courses of action, so long as they are bound by the established rule of law.[38] If a regime is to enjoy both procedural and substantive legitimacy in the multi-ethnic ESA nations, it must operate under democratic rules that guarantee political accommodation for all its citizens. Nations that respect the rule of law also defend the judiciary, respect minorities, and recognize the independence of congress (parliament) and diversity in opinion. This is the genesis of attaining legitimacy both at the institutional level and at the national (presidential) level. The regimes must not only have policies that empower all ethnic groups with some share of state representation through constitutional protection and decree, but they ought to act upon these policies to guarantee their implementation.

Elections add value to the notion of regime accountability, while building trust in the state's institutional purpose. Regime legitimacy necessitates the acquisition of power through free and fair elections, in addition to the unconstrained political contestation for all political institutions. Earlier studies show that some African countries have used the democratic transition as a way to gain political control and consolidate the regime, while at the same time providing limited political space for opposition parties and the interests of civil society.[39]

During the 1990s in Ethiopia, Kenya, South Africa, Uganda, and Zambia, opposition politicians regularly and consistently accused the speakers of parliament in each country of excessive patronage toward the presidency and for the use of arbitrary power in pursuance of the presidents' agendas. This showed a lack of autonomy and created a tainted image for those august bodies. In addition, there are constant opposition charges of large-scale corruption in the ESA governments as well as a lack of transparency and accountability. A weak and patronized legislative body cannot hold public officials accountable; and in ESA countries, the executive branch currently exercises too much power over the legislature and the judiciary.

This leads to setbacks in the legitimacy of regimes in ESA and validation of the hegemony of their executive branches over other state institutions and civil society. For example, there are ongoing civic education programs for East Africans conducted by international NGOs such as DENIVA and the International Republican Institute (IRI). This information is also disseminated through the news media, which educate the electorate about the value of political legitimacy. Therefore, citizens who access this knowledge learn that the legitimacy of a regime can be determined by factors that they can easily observe and evaluate. For instance, citizens can observe and evaluate whether the manner in which state actors come to power (through free and fair elections) is acceptable and legal under applicable laws that are enforced by an independent electoral commission.

On FM radio networks throughout the ESA countries, political talk-show debates commonly assert that citizens should rise up and judge the regime by the degree to which political leaders, and all public service institutions, deliver on their promises and their ability to manage citizen expectations.[40] This validates regime legitimacy in ESA's democratization process, since it encourages all geopolitical constituents to judge the acceptability of the ruling elite and of the state institutions and its policies. This is still a challenge for most of Africa, however, because the ruling state actors can still contrive, even within the constraints of democratization, to manipulate the constitution and consolidate their political power and legitimacy.[41]

Regime Legitimacy under Multiparty Politics

Political parties are indispensable fixtures of democracies, and their liberty and mobilization in Africa are a measure of a regime's democratic strength. Research from Africa and elsewhere shows that political parties are one of the most important instruments of democratization.[42] Political parties in Africa are an integral part of governance and enhance the quality of democracy and political accountability in a polity by augmenting the representation of different groups and views.[43] They play a major role in facilitating citizen expression of dissenting views and contribute to democratic legitimacy and the development of a responsible state. Political parties are essential for establishing sustainable democratic rule in Africa because political participation and democratic competition can be maintained through fragmentation in diverse societies.[44]

In the EAC for instance, the wave of democratization has been facilitated by frequent elections in which political parties and civil society mobilize citizens to participate in democracy, particularly in local constituencies. In African politics, elections and parties invigorate political contestation and alignments through voting, from local to the state or national elections. This is a trend considered similar to Western voting electoral processes.[45] Regular elections contribute to the strengthening of party politics by imposing regime validation and legitimacy, and should continue to undercut regime hegemony—with its neopatrimonial tendencies—through electoral competition and mass mobilization.[46] Despite these positive trends, several setbacks emerge in the way Eastern African regimes, as well as those in South Africa and Zambia, claim legitimacy.

First, the news media report that their governments have not fully opened up political space for the opposition to contest freely in national elections. Regularly following current political events, especially in Burundi, Ethiopia, Kenya, Rwanda, Tanzania, Uganda, and Zambia, reveals constant reports about pockets of protests, civil disobedience, and police clashing with the opposition at political rallies. Such media reports are anecdotal evidence that there is still reason to doubt the "overwhelming mandate to govern" that most of these regimes claim in their rhetoric. In multi-ethnic (geopolitical) nations throughout ESA, attaining legitimacy becomes more complicated because the electorate expects the distribution of political power to be equitable within all state institutions, including the president's appointees to cabinet.[47]

Some African leaders who claim to have popular national legitimacy use a simple majority of support, which they systematically orchestrate using ethnic identity and regional sectarianism.[48] As discussed in Chapter Two, this political tactic of regional sectarianism is a pre-colonial legacy used to "divide and rule" the natives who were culturally and politically loyal to their kings and traditional chiefs.[49] East African states cannot pass the mantle of responsibility based solely on a theory that a national election outcome determines regime legitimacy because regional sectarianism determines which individuals, political parties, and politicians receive the best political goods from state leaders. Also, each ESA country is composed of provinces with individuals who speak different languages, have clans and ethnicities, and support a range of political beliefs and political parties.

Building political legitimacy associated with majority rule in some of Africa's multi-ethnic states results in repudiating the reality of ethnic diversity and the legitimacy of plurality.[50] In such circumstances, the rule of one dominant group leads to unjust treatment of other powerless ethnicities. For example, former president Milton Obote's reign orchestrated the military empowerment of Northern Ugandans, mainly the Langi and the Acholi, who misused their military power by arbitrarily arresting citizens and looting their personal property. Obote was ousted in a 1985 coup by his own military. Former Kenyan president Daniel Toroitich arap Moi filled key government positions with his ethnic lineage, the Kalenjin, while other groups, particularly the Kikuyu and the Luo, criticized his actions and lamented the practice, but without much success. In both cases, the Moi regime and the second Obote government claimed political legitimacy, yet they subjugated ethnic groups from different provinces. Some governments in Eastern Africa with substantive legitimacy engaged in ethnic tyranny and genocide. For example, the government of Burundi orchestrated the massacre of its Hutu citizens in 1972, and the Rwandan government coordinated the butchery of Tutsi citizens and moderate Hutus in 1994. In South Africa throughout the twentieth century, the apartheid regimes under the leadership of white South Africans are still memorable for the recent history of oppression, segregation, and subjugation.

Another dilemma related to the legitimacy of ESA regimes is the lack of political accommodation for the opposition and denial of equal political contestation to other political parties. Much of the research on African political leadership from the early 1970s until the early 1990s has consistently shown that presidential hegemony denies legitimacy to organized political competition. In order to achieve legitimacy, Tanzania's ruling party, the CCM, has sustained its monopolistic influence on the governing state institutions and encouraged political patronage. Proponents of CCM politics have argued that this dominant party has facilitated the control of ethnic cleavages without incurring a risk of internal discord, which could provoke ethno-regional instability.

Rubongoya's assumption (as a political scientist) is that African states, which enforce questionable authority and disregard the rules of power by stifling political contestation and mass mobilization, lose their legitimacy.[51] Meanwhile, some regimes in Africa still enforce hegemony by stripping autonomy from other state institutions, such as the judiciary and the state auditor, while state patronage and clientelism become part of the political game.[52] Consequently, equality, a moderate level of liberty, political competition, a strong civic tradition, and the safeguard of the rule of law are necessary ingredients of democratic rule.

Chapter Summary

In summary, this chapter highlights the urgent need for rebuilding the rule of law in ESA because without it the governments and their state institutions will continue to be perceived as illegitimate. The challenge is that there is still no political motivation from ESA governments to effectively manage the socio-economic and political expectations of citizens or to strategically recognize and service citizens' needs and aspirations through institutional and legal reform. Major priorities in countries such as Burundi, Rwanda, Tanzania, and Zambia are providing the necessary infrastructure to guarantee judicial independence. This is being done through transparency in the appointments of autonomous institutional leaders to secure tenure, as well as with improved conditions of governance. In countries like Burundi, Rwanda, South Africa, and Tanzania, statutory instruments such as the Truth and Reconciliation commissions were established, following the dark periods of heinous violation of human rights in those countries, which provided a legal and institutional framework for national healing.

Ndulo said:

> Good governance consists above all else in its effect in nurturing and promoting the best qualities in the people—the habits of obedience to government as the constituted authority, its laws and its interposition in the settlement of disputes and the redress of grievances; the habits of integrity, probity, fairness, self-restraint, and discipline in the conduct of social relations and public affairs; the spirit of enterprise, hard work, self-reliance and inventiveness in the pursuits and activities of life, and the quality of public-spiritedness and patriotism in matters affecting the interests of the community.[53]

As Ndulo rightly argued, authority can be legitimate if there is an established legal and institutional framework that is implemented and safeguarded in accordance with accepted institutional criteria, processes, and procedures. Although these instruments have not eradicated the negative vision of justice and the rule of law in ESA, they have been a positive and necessary step in the right direction. To strengthen the rule of law even further in ESA, governments should open up political space to allow opposition political contestation, for citizens to seek legal counsel and redress, and public discourse without undue influence, or any limitation on free speech and expression.

Chapter 5

Media Policies and Regulation

The previous chapter posits that the governments in Eastern and Southern Africa (ESA) can achieve sustainable democratization and work toward liberal substantive democracy, if—and only if—economically empowered and well-informed citizens can challenge the domestic structure of authoritarian rule. This chapter proceeds with the assumption that successful democratization can be achieved if the media empower and provide an outlet of discourse for civil society—non-governmental organizations (NGOs), for example—to advocate and market their cause to the masses. When such media discourse within the public sphere is unimpeded and fairly mediated from civil society to the general public without challenge from authority, it creates a significant and independent influence for accountability on ESA regimes. Therefore, civil society and rule of law intervention on behalf of society that creates unfettered media, unhindered speech, and political expression is necessary for a democratic society.

Lippman explained in the early twentieth century that the media are critically important public educators of democratic governance because they build an informed, responsible, and active citizenry, who can demand the establishment of viable regimes and the rule of law.[1] The rule of law can be sustained if institutions such as NGOs, human rights activists, legal and bar associations, and the news and mass media internalize these rules and inculcate them into the everyday behavior and expectation of citizens. In building the rule of law, the news media ought to demand the legitimacy of legal institutions and the regimes themselves, as well as serve as a watchdog on the administration of justice. Unfortunately, however, media laws in Burundi, Ethiopia, Kenya, Rwanda, South Africa, Tanzania, Uganda, and Zambia have not been conducive for building the rule of law and advocating good governance. The regimes in those democratizing countries place too high a burden on the media through stringent communication policies and free speech regulations. This chapter first discusses what the term *media policy* broadly entails and then how it should be changed in order to foster democratization.

Comparing Media Policies

The term *media policy* refers to regulations and policy making that concern the function of the mass media and guide decisions of the authorities. State actors or government bureaucrats usually enforce media policy. Policy making in the media environment can be imposed via content, structure, or infrastructure. In ESA, media policy is understood in this context to regulate the following:

a. What the press reports as news or deliberates on current affairs talk shows (content).
b. Ownership of the media: regulation of the relationship between media owners and government authorities, as well as the market (structure).
c. Regulations concerning control of the airwaves, and matters of technical infrastructure and technological development (infrastructure).

The universal conception of an ideal media policy, which respects the rule of law and is grounded in democratic governance, would provide absolute protection for freedom of expression. Every citizen should have the right to freedom of thought and expression; the right to seek out, investigate, and disseminate information, regardless of the affairs of state; and the right to freely speak, write in print, or deliver information in any form. Governments must provide an enabling environment for citizens of all professions or social strata, enabling them to deliver their thoughts and expression through any mass medium without obstruction.

In the United States, for example, the First Amendment to the Constitution provides protection for political, economic, and social discourse, whether in face-to-face speech, broadcast speech, or writing in press, periodicals, and pamphlets. Also protected are other forms of communication such as picketing, marching, and distribution of political or religious pamphlets to publicly assembled audiences; door-to-door solicitation; and other forms of assembly. Policy making for the media in the United States also occurs legislatively, such as through the Freedom of Information Act (FOIA) that allows access to government records. Such constitutional protection and legislation are nonexistent in ESA countries. FOIA provides access to records of all federal agencies, such as the CIA, the FBI, and the Department of Defense, in the executive branch, unless the records fall within one of nine categories of exempt information. U.S. president Barack Obama on his second day as president in 2009 issued presidential executive orders that the White House was "committed to creating an unprecedented level of openness in government ... to ensure the public trust and establish a system of transparency, public participation, and collaboration."

In Europe's media policy systems, the right to information and freedom of expression are weighed against an individual's right of privacy and reputation.[2] Europe's contemporary media policies are shaped by two historical events: the French and Russian revolutions. In the eighteenth century, the French Revolution gave rise to liberal ideas about freedom that questioned the state's intervention in freedom of expression. English philosophers John Stuart Mill and John Locke approached the problems of the day by asserting a liberal conception of the press. Mill and Locke argued that a press free from censure was essential to the nature of a free state and any restraints upon publication would destroy liberty.

Governments typically create the communication space within which all public and decision-making discourse takes place. A government determines the kinds of information that will be disseminated to inform those discourses that are not detrimental to the safety of the broader polity and citizenry. When a government sets policy that guides media institutions, it also provides other monitoring institutions and processes within which discourse takes place. A government, therefore, offers many of the tools used to implement policy decisions directed at other types of information processes that are mediated within the public sphere.[3]

The next section provides an overview of how regimes in the eight ESA countries set policy that guides their media institutions.

Burundi

The government dominates Burundi's media industry. It owns *Le Renouveau*, the country's only daily newspaper, as well as the only national television station and sole national radio station—*Radio-Télévision Nationale du Burundi* (RTNB).

There are four to six privately owned and independent weekly newspapers, but some are intermittent. They are generally restricted to the Bujumbura area because of financial and infrastructure constraints.

The ownership of local, private radio stations tends to be highly concentrated, and a few independent stations, such as *Radio Publique Africaine* (RPA), sometimes provide diverse and balanced coverage. However, more than a dozen RPA journalists have either been roughed up, beaten, and arrested or have faced constant harassment and interrogations from police and other security agencies. RPA also has been closed down by the National Communication Council (CNC — a French acronym) numerous times between 2000 and 2010, during municipal, parliamentary, and presidential elections. The arrests of RPA journalists and numerous temporary closures of the station usually stem from allegations of politically biased reporting or suspected violation of Burundi's Secret Information Act or other press-gagging laws.

In November 2007, for example, RPA journalists Serge Nibize and Domitile Kiramvu reported a coup plot and were imprisoned and later acquitted on charges of violating the Secret Information Act. In late 2007, journalist Mathias Manirakiza, director of *Radio Isanganiro,* was detained for the third time in five years on charges of authorizing his station to broadcast information capable of breaching national security. There are endless stories like these about the intimidation, harassment, and detention of journalists in Burundi and other ESA countries.

No major government restrictions on Internet access exist in Burundi. Conversely, the CNC has banned dozens of websites from posting documents or other statements by political organizations that disseminate hate or violence, despite the reality that less than 1 percent of Burundi's population accessed the Internet in 2007, due to economic and infrastructure limitations.

Although Burundi's constitution provides for freedom of expression, this right is rarely respected in practice. According to Freedom House 2009 and the World Press Freedom Review of 2008, much of the current media legislation is vague about the offenses for which a journalist may be charged. For example, the 1997 Press Law forbids the dissemination of "information inciting civil disobedience or serving as propaganda for enemies of the Burundian nation during a time of war." The 2003 Media Law also provides for harsh fines and prison terms of up to five years for the dissemination of information that insults the president. In 2006, legislation was proposed that would more accurately define the responsibilities and limitations of journalists, but the law never materialized. A watered-down version of the legislation was passed in early 2009.

Burundi's media environment is not conducive for the promotion of the rule of law and democratic governance because authorities ruthlessly crack down on media outlets critical of government policies.[4] The regime also continues to dominate the media agenda and does not tolerate criticism of the president or other national leaders in the ruling party. In 2006, the Committee to Protect Journalists (CPJ) ranked Burundi as Africa's third leading jailer of journalists. In 2009, it was among the top ten, while Eritrea and Ethiopia ranked one and two.

Internet access is not yet restricted or monitored by the Burundi government, but it was only available to less than 1 percent in 2007 and 2 percent of the population in 2010.

Ethiopia

The Ethiopian Constitution guarantees freedom of the press, but that right is often restricted in reality. Security organizations and state authorities frequently invoke the 1992 Press Law to prosecute or intimidate journalists who are critical of government misconduct. The 1992 law deals with libel, false and offensive information, and incitement of ethnic hatred. Dozens of journalists have been detained and arrested without trial for several weeks using the 1992 Press Law.[5] In many instances, court cases continue for years. Independent journalists often have multiple charges pending against them, except for those who self-regulate by steering away from investigative political stories. Unlike in some of the other ESA countries, the Ethiopian government has cracked down on international journalists who exposed the regime's wrath against dissidents and protestors. In May 2004, for example, when three *New York Times* journalists reported on the Ogaden conflict, they were arrested and detained for five days in the eastern town of Degehabur. In addition, two Eritrean journalists from Eri-TV, who were reportedly arrested in 2005 by Ethiopian forces in Mogadishu, the capital city of Somalia, continue to be held at an undisclosed location in Ethiopia.

Since 2000, access to foreign broadcasts has been restricted occasionally. However, international correspondents and Ethiopian journalists working for foreign news organizations have generally operated with fewer restrictions than their local counterparts. In 2007, the Ethiopian government jammed the transmission signals of *Deutsch Welle* radio and Voice of America. Faced with an increasingly restricted print and broadcast media environment, many citizens turned to the Internet for information, but the government responded accordingly. By the end of 2009, the Ethiopian Telecommunications Corporation remained the only Internet service provider, enabling the government to monitor the e-mails of organizations and individuals. Other than allegations from opposition politicians, however, no concrete evidence exists that the regime actually engaged in e-mail snooping. Nevertheless, the government blocked access to some websites and blogs, particularly news websites run by members of the Ethiopian Diaspora who were critical of the regime. Owing to a poor telecommunications infrastructure, Internet access was still limited primarily to the major urban areas by late 2009. Internet access is not yet restricted or monitored by the Ethiopian government, but less than 5 percent of the population in 2010 regularly used the Internet. Its popularity is growing with the abundance of privately run Internet cafés.

A 2006 World Press Freedom Report about Ethiopia indicated that efforts to revive independent media were repeatedly hampered after a government crackdown in which dozens of journalists and opposition politicians were jailed or exiled. The report disclosed that in 2005, two publishers' applications for media licenses were rejected by the government even though the Ministry of Information said that all legal requirements for the licenses had been fulfilled. The Charities and Societies Proclamation, a law criminalizing certain human rights protection activities, also caused alarm in 2005 and 2006. Violators faced penalties of up to five years in prison. Although the law bans censorship of private media and detention of journalists suspected of law infringement in certain circumstances, it allows prosecutors to impound publishing materials prior to publication. The law provides for the creation of an agency with wide discretion to regulate civil organizations in Ethiopia. Cases of libel and defamation saw increased fines and were prosecuted as criminal offenses with imprisonment under the penal code.

The government was particularly aggressive in response to coverage of opposition politicians and celebrities. Tewdros Kassahun, a singer and outspoken government critic, was imprisoned on hit and run charges. *Enku* magazine's publisher and editor, Alemayehu Mahtemework, and three other staff members were arrested and 10,000 copies of the magazine were seized after they published a cover story on Kassahun. Two other editors were also prosecuted simply for writing about the singer. Amare Aregawi, the editor-in-chief of the *Reporter*, Ethiopia's leading independent newspaper, was imprisoned in connection with published stories addressing criticisms about the management of a brewery linked to the government. The charges were quickly dismissed. A few months later, Aregawi was attacked by two assailants, who struck him on the back of the head. He lost consciousness and required medical treatment, but the two men were soon apprehended. Local sources believe the attack was connected to his work at the *Reporter.*

Kenya

Throughout the 1990s, veteran independent Kenyan journalists lamented the absence of favorable media laws and policy, a predicament that undermined media freedom and independence.[6] In 2004, the Kibaki government attempted to introduce new laws that would require stronger regulation of the news media. Because the government charges high registration fees, investors find it difficult to buy new media titles that would create an independent press in the newspaper and magazine sector.[7] The Kenyan government's Ministry of Information and Communications established a state regulatory body called the Communications Commission of Kenya (CCK) through a 1998 act of parliament. The CCK deals with licensing, regulation, and coordination of telecommunication, TV, and radio communication frequencies and equipment. Investors are required to purchase a bond of about USD 15,000 to license a newspaper. High registration fees serve as a gag on alternative print media that the government finds suspicious.

In March 2006, Minister of Internal Security John Michuki sanctioned raids on the *Standard* newspaper and the offices of KTN-TV for publishing and broadcasting news stories that undermined the legitimacy of Kibaki's regime. Four journalists from those news organizations were detained and interrogated without trial. In both Moi's era and Kibaki's first term in office, journalists were imprisoned for trivial offenses whenever the political elite were exposed in money-laundering schemes and corruption.[8] In 2007, the CCK attempted to introduce legislation that would require all journalists practicing in Kenya, including editorial management, to register with the state. According to the Kenya Union of Journalists (KUJ) and the Kenya Institute of Mass Communication (KIMC), there are an estimated 2,200 local and international journalists who work in the country. In order to counter the CCK's power, not-for-profit organizations like the Media Council of Kenya lobby for press freedom and media self-regulation.

The constitution of Kenya does not explicitly guarantee freedom of the press, as outlined in Section 79. That provision also fails to guarantee freedom of speech, instead establishing an ambiguous right to freedom of expression.[9] The regime employs different laws to curtail the independent critical media. Press freedom in Kenya faces a major challenge. In certain instances the Official Secrets Act is used, while other journalists with similar charges are prosecuted under the penal code or criminal libel statutes.

The Kenyan Parliament passed a government-sponsored media law in 2007, the Kenya Media Law, after months of bitter debate between parliamentarians and media representatives. The bill authorized the creation of a statutory media council to replace the voluntary and self-regulatory council that had existed since 2002. However, the bill maintained archaic, discriminatory laws on the statute books, according to prominent Kenyan journalists Joseph Odindo of *The Daily Nation* and Isaac Mwangi of *The East African* newspaper, who denounced the bill at journalism workshops. Media policies in Kenya enforce accreditation of reporters by defining a journalist as someone who holds a degree or higher diploma in mass communication from a nationally recognized college and mandating that practitioners register with the Media Council. The Media Council enforces other policies that screen or impose limits on media ownership, among other restrictive provisions. It also imposes a levy on all media and collects an annual practicing or registration fee on all journalists.

One of the major legal challenges for media in Kenya, and throughout Africa, is the way in which law enforcement officials interpret some of the statutes. For instance, in Kenya the police still enforce the colonial-era offense of "misprision of treason," which occurs when a journalist is alleged to have committed an offense by possessing knowledge of the actual or intended commission of a treasonous act. Law enforcement personnel in Kenya can also interpret misprision of treason as the broadcasting (radio, TV, or Internet) or the publication (gutter press, newspapers, or magazine) of a treasonous expression without immediately informing the authorities about it. Journalists can also be charged with this offense by inciting disaffection with the government through public utterances or the press.[10]

Internet access is not yet restricted or monitored by the Kenyan government, but it was available to less than 6 percent of the population in 2010.

Rwanda

In the early 1960s, the Rwandan and Burundian governments imposed stiffer regulations on national broadcasting and state newspapers that focused their coverage on educational information about health care delivery, morality, national peace, and food security.[11] That was before the early 1990s when the media in both countries were used to fuel sectarianism, dividing the population along ethnic lines. At that time, the news media broadcast instructions to the Hutu majority about how to engage in the ethnic cleansing of more than a half million Tutsis.[12] The media heavily involved were RTLM and ORINFOR. RTLM was owned and controlled by associates of the Hutu president, Juvénale Habyarimana, and ORINFOR was owned by the Rwandan government.

The Rwandan Patriotic Front (RPF), which overthrew Habyarimana's government to end the genocide, faced an enormous challenge in its attempt to rehabilitate the national media. Major General Paul Kagame, who has presided over Rwanda since the 1994 genocide, has gradually reformed the public and private press.[13] The government secured funds from international agencies, such as the IMF, UNESCO, and others, to renovate and rebuild newsroom equipment and train young journalists. The Kagame government passed a media law in July 2002 that established a High Press Council to guarantee freedom of the press. This body regulates electronic broadcasting and censors the press under the pretense of preventing a repeat of the hate speech rampant in 1994.[14] The first privately owned independent radio station was established in 2004, but all private media face government restrictions and exercise self-censorship. Some proprietors of the so-called privately owned media are members of the governing council with close ties to the presidency.

According to Freedom House, Rwanda has recorded some improvements in political rights and civil liberties since the 1994 genocide, but "authorities continued to restrict the media in 2007 through the illegal imprisonment of critical journalists and the harassment of independent outlets."[15] The media are still tightly controlled by the regime, despite a 2002 media law that outlaws press censorship. Libel remains a criminal offense, and there are no laws guaranteeing access to information. Freedom House reported that in 2007, the Minister of Information, Louise Mushikiwabo, arbitrarily revoked the license of the *Weekly Post* newspaper. This happened just three days after the first edition of the *Weekly Post* hit the newsstands, despite laws requiring a court order for such a move.

Many critics have been alarmed by the government's harsh restrictions and intimidation whenever Rwandese journalists investigate corruption, authoritarianism, and abuse of public office.[16] Seventeen well-known journalists have been incarcerated in the past ten years—some without trial—on charges and allegations of treason, inciting genocide, and hate speech. Many young journalists have disappeared without a trace. Rwanda lacks a daily independent newspaper. Some topics are forbidden, such as the military, the justice department, State House, and any tyrannical acts committed by the ruling RPF. The risk of going to prison poses the greatest threat to independent journalists.

In January 2010, for example, authorities arrested the editor of the *Umurabyo* newspaper, Agnes Nkusi-Uwimana, charging her with divisionism and discrimination following the publication of an article that was critical of the RPF. Nkusi-Uwimana was incarcerated for a year and fined approximately USD 760 on charges of being a threat to state security. Also in 2010, a magistrate convicted three journalists who work with the privately owned weekly *Umuseso*: editor Charles Kabonero, acting editor-in-chief Didas Gasana, and reporter Richard Kayigamba. They were charged with invading the privacy of Cabinet Affairs minister Protais Musoni and Kigali mayor Aisa Kirabo Kacyira, under Rwanda's 1977 penal code and 2009 Media Law. *Umuseso* is known for its critical coverage of the regime, but the government has also used the criminal defamation law to muzzle the independent press and other journalists critical of the regime.

A few independent newspapers face financial constraints that prohibit them from running a daily paper. The state-run *New Times* is the only daily newspaper. Just like the other East African nations, the Rwandan government does not advertise with independent media, which criticizes the regime and its government.

Internet access is not yet restricted or monitored by the Rwandan government, but it was only available to less than 2 percent of the population in 2010.

South Africa

In the last 30 years, successive South African governments have permitted the existence of a relatively free independent press with private ownership. However, the government still owns and controls SABC, the national radio and television station. SABC is a commercial public service enterprise. Regardless of the apparent government ownership and control of SABC—plus other media that are partly owned or heavily invested in private media by African National Congress (ANC) politicians—public service broadcasting in South Africa offers the freest and most professionally run news organization in Africa.[17] The government has also taken major steps toward institutionalizing independent broadcasting and divesting its control of media corporations.

Just like other ESA countries, South Africa has major challenges in its enforcement of media policies. An examination of two specific laws reveals both positive and negative outcomes. Section 32 of the South African Constitution gives the public the right to access state records or any information in the government's possession. However, that law is trumped by other legislative policies and decrees that hinder the ability of journalists to gain access to public state records. A specific example is the enforcement of the 2002 Promotion of Access to Information Act, which requires that the general public—including journalists—request special permission from concerned parties and other bureaucratic channels in order to access official records of the South African cabinet, provincial administrators, and members of parliament.[18] The policy still exists and is dynamically enforced.

In 2007, the *Sunday Times* published several articles reporting that Minister of Health Tshabalala Msimang needed a liver transplant because of alcoholism. The *Sunday Times* claimed that she jumped transplant queues in the neighboring country of Botswana because of her connections to the health sector in the region. When Minister Msimang complained about the *Sunday Times* stories and pronounced them as quack journalism, the high court in Johannesburg took on the case with vigor. In early 2010, the high court ordered the newspaper to return copies of the minister's records and to pay legal fees and damages. Numerous other incidents of a similar nature could be recounted.

Other prohibitive media laws, such as the 2001 Promotion of Equality and Prevention of Unfair Discrimination Act 4, curtail a fully autonomous journalistic enterprise in South Africa.[19] Its purpose is to impede and eliminate unfair discrimination, but it also thwarts and punishes hate speech. An extremist broadcaster, such as American radio political commentator Rush Limbaugh or Fox News TV commentator Glenn Beck, would not see the light of day in today's South Africa. Sections 10 and 12 of that act make illegal any broadcasting or publishing that could reasonably be construed to demonstrate a clear intention to be hurtful, promote hatred on any basis, or cause harm. The South African government does not mandate the licensing of journalists before they can practice. However, journalists register and enjoy membership benefits in various self-regulatory media advocacy groups, such as the Media Workers Association of South Africa (MWASA).

Some media advocacy bodies enforce policies that favor the ANC ruling party and the regime. More than 100 statutes, many of which date back to the apartheid era, still regulate the publication or disclosure of information.[20] Those who do not abide by these self-regulating bodies suffer the wrath of the regime, often in the courts of law. In early 2007, for example, renowned SABC radio journalist John Perlman claimed on the air that SABC had inadvertently banned outspoken critics of Thabo Mbeki's government and regime. He later resigned suddenly without explaining why. Ensuing press reports suggested that media advocacy groups were responsible for the demise of John Perlman. In the same year, leading activists from civil society and political actors, such as the Congress of South African Trade Unions (COSATU) and the Freedom of Expression Institute (FXI), accused the government of harassing independent journalists and radio talk show commentators. They also accused Mbeki's regime of denying critics a platform for political expression on the state-owned SABC.

Almost a decade has passed since President Nelson Mandela relinquished power and opened the way for easy transitions in the top executive job under post-apartheid South Africa. Media freedom and expression, however, are becoming toxic at every turn in national elections. The 2009 presidential elections were marred by the harassment of political journalists who questioned ANC's supremacy and exposed its internal wrangling. The atmosphere was so bad that the relationship between the government and the news media deteriorated even further, prompting SABC news executives, including Phil Molefe, to say publicly that its political press corps had received numerous threats from some unnamed politicians and their representatives. They charged that SABC was expected to tow the line with some incumbent politicians and state actors within the ANC, and sternly ordered that SABC was to report favorably on their political manifestos and campaigns. According to several press reports from various major newspapers and broadcast outlets, including SABC, the media had not witnessed so much intimidation since the country's first post-apartheid democratic elections in 1994.

Regardless of these setbacks, which are minimal compared to media challenges in other ESA countries, there is still an effort by the South African government to safeguard SABC's independence. One of the roles of the Media Development and Diversity Agency (MDDA) is to encourage the development of free public expression and dialogue in programming, in the interest and welfare of the general public. MDDA was created in 2002 by legislation. Agencies like MDDA have encouraged ownership and control of media by historically disadvantaged communities and cultural groups. For now, the media in South Africa have much to celebrate compared to media in other ESA countries. But for the foreseeable future, the media are becoming more restricted than ever before, even after the Independent Communications Authority of South Africa (ICASA) legislation was passed in 2000. In fact, the controversial ICASA Amendment Bill of 2005 still exists, which effectively gives the Minister of Communications power to hire and fire councilors, a move many South African journalists frown upon. It could further hamper this emerging democracy's efforts to move toward the rule of law with open governance, state transparency, and political accountability.

Internet access is not yet restricted but it is monitored by the South African government. It was only available to less than 15 percent of the population in 2008.

Tanzania

When Tanzania attained independence almost forty years ago, former revolutionary leader and father of the nation, President Julius Nyerere, instituted a policy that press freedom was guaranteed only if the national media produced content that reflected the values of socialist consensus and respected decisions reached by the regime as well as popular political mandates.[21] At that time, media in Tanzania were totally owned by the government. From the 1960s through the 1990s, the regime expected the media to help with national development. Then president Nyerere announced through the Arusha Declaration of 1967 that with *Ujamaa*, his concept that formed the basis of his social and economic development policies, the national press had to propagate and promote the spirit of collectivism as the principle for organizing Tanzanian society.[22] During that time, the state-owned Tanzania Broadcasting Corporation (TBC) featured daily programs on *Ujamaa* that propagated the intrinsic worth of African socialism, brotherhood, and nationhood.[23] Radio and television program producers were all mandated to focus their broadcasts primarily on the national development agenda of *Ujamaa* and its political indoctrination.[24]

Since the early 1960s, journalists who exposed abuse of public office by national leaders were prosecuted by those leaders under the 1962 Regions and Regional Commissioners Act and the Area Commissioner Act of 1962.[25] Those acts still give regional bureaucrats in Tanzania the power to arrest and detain journalists if they suspect a breach of peace or disturbance of public tranquility.[26] The Prisons Act of 1967 impedes journalists in their investigation and reporting on the conditions of prisoners, even those detained for days or months without due process. For journalists to avoid repercussions, they have to meet the expectations of the Tanzanian government to educate citizens about entrepreneurship and contribute to a shared national consciousness, identity, and continuity. The Tanzanian government also expects all media (radio, television, and newspapers) to publish content that caters to state ideas about culture, the arts, and education.

Other legal impediments in Tanzania also prohibit journalists from playing a watchdog role toward public officials. For instance, the 1995 Revenue Authority Act and the 1995 Public Leadership Code of Ethics protect the public holdings of state actors and their personal wealth. This legislation makes it difficult for journalists to expose corruption and tax evasion. Furthermore, the 1989 Civil Service Act forbids government employees from disclosing government information in their possession without the express consent of a cabinet minister or his or her deputy. Finally, publication of information about illegal conduct or poor performance of a national leader or senior government official is not protected by the absolute privilege standard.[27] The burden of proof lies with journalists to prove their innocence on charges of publishing false and malicious information, rather than with plaintiffs to prove guilt.[28]

The government made an unprecedented move at a critical time of comparatively smooth election cycles and a fairly libertarian regime when it adopted the 2003 Tanzania Communications Regulatory Authority Act. Legal scholars in Arusha and Dodoma have concluded that the law breaches the right to freedom of expression in several important respects. For instance, Article 19 empowers state actors and authorities to interpret or amend the Tanzanian Constitution when such action is done in the service of national security and sovereignty. Such loose policies negate other constitutional guarantees of freedom of expression. Clearly, Article 19 somewhat negates the amended Article 18 of the Tanzanian Constitution. Article 18 stipulates that every person has the right to freedom of opinion and expression. It also gives the right to seek and disseminate information and the right to be informed about various events of importance to society.

In 2008, Tanzania tabled a bill on a freedom of information law and the media services bill after President Jakaya Kikwete published a decree on the same matter. The decree contains changes to defamation and sedition laws that are more favorable to journalists but requires that the Media Standards Board license all journalists. The board is appointed by the government and includes members of the CCM party. However, changes that were believed to be favorable to journalists did not help in a high-profile incident that involved the presidency and a possible coup. Journalists from various media outlets, including editors and reporters, took to the streets to protest a four-month ban on an independent weekly, *Mwana Halisi*, which the government had accused of fomenting sedition. The skirmish emanated from a report of an attempted coup to oust President Jakaya Kikwete. A year later, in 2009, the same independent *Mwana Halisi* was ordered to pay damages of USD 2.25 million in a civil defamation lawsuit filed by Rostam Aziz, a member of parliament, who accused the newspaper of linking him to corrupt dealings involving government business contracts.

The Minister of Information, Capt. George Mkuchika, defended government actions in 2009 as a warning to other media to steer clear of unfounded controversial and "unethical" stories. But journalists surprised the regime with a three-day protest. The media reported in their editorials that Tanzanian journalists were united against oppression of any media professionals or entity and cautioned that they were united with other media advocacy groups to fight against government interference into their work.

Internet access is not yet restricted or monitored by the Tanzanian government, and it was accessible to less than 3 percent of the population in 2008.

Uganda

The 1995 Ugandan Constitution states in Article 29(1) that media personnel have a right to freedom of speech and expression. In all, media in Uganda are regulated by the Press and Journalists Act of 1995, the Electronic Media Act of 1996, and the Access to Information Act of 2005. The Ugandan government established a Media Council in 1997, through the Press and Journalists Act of 1995, to regulate the media and license journalists with practicing certificates. These certificates are exclusively issued to university degree holders by the National Institute of Journalists of Uganda (NIJU), a statutory association of journalists. The government equates the registration of media personnel with the professionalization of journalism in Uganda. According to the Media Council, practicing journalists without degrees are not considered professional journalists, and their work cannot be protected even if it is published in a recognized media outlet. The Media Council has the power to suspend newspapers, reprimand journalists, restrict information, and adjudicate disputes between the state and the news media.[29]

Another law presenting a major challenge to the Ugandan media is Section 50(1) of the Penal Code Act, which states that anyone who publishes statements deemed false, or which may cause public fear, alarm, and disturbance, is guilty of a misdemeanor. Under this law, several Ugandan print and radio journalists have faced criminal charges for allegedly printing materials the government deemed seditious.[30] Also, the Ugandan Penal Code was amended in 1998 to include the offense of sectarianism, forbidding publication or expression of information that evokes contempt, alienation, or disaffection of others based on ethnicity. Since the Ugandan government passed the Anti-terrorism Act in 2002, more than 120 politicians and independent local journalists have been charged with engaging in or supporting terrorism.[31] The 2002 Anti-terrorism Act presents journalists with a daunting challenge for the following two reasons. First, it defines any act of violence or threat of violence as a terrorist act and has been used against political opponents and journalists.[32] Second, it effectively outlaws coverage of people and organizations declared as terrorists.

Whenever violence between political parties breaks out, journalists get caught up in the middle of the conflict. In 2010, for example, a spasm of violence engulfed journalists during a power struggle between the Uganda government and the Kingdom of Buganda. Relations became strained over ownership of land in the Buganda Kingdom and the government that currently occupies it. During a scuffle in the spring of 2010, police blocked the Bugandan monarch from visiting a town on territory where the kingdom owns land. Local media, such as the *Daily Monitor* newspapers and several FM radio stations, covered the stories comprehensively and exposed how government security agents killed dozens of residents and arrested more than 600 bystanders. As a result, the state-run Uganda Broadcasting Council shut down radio stations and halted political debates and commentary on that issue. The government banned live talk radio, called *ebimeeza* in the vernacular language, from debating those incidents out of fear that state officials would not be able to control the messages.

In a separate stringent measure, the Ugandan army raided the Central Broadcasting Services (CBS) radio at night, then seized and dismantled its transmission equipment. The Buganda Kingdom owns CBS, which had previously enjoyed immunity from state interference because of its ownership and connection to the King of Buganda. However, its unique role as a government watchdog and relentless criticism of the president's misdeeds landed the station and the kingdom into trouble with the government. Some journalists from CBS said that government policies and warnings have created constant fear among other radio employers. Many CBS journalists cannot find jobs at other stations, and they blame this predicament squarely on government actions and intimidation tactics. Two journalists from other privately owned radio stations confided that their stations were under surveillance and had been instructed by some government officials not to hire media personnel from the banned stations. Nevertheless, those journalists intimated that the government crackdown on watchdog independent media has emboldened them to continue exposing its archaic laws and authoritarianism.

In 2010, the Uganda government tabled a bill to amend the Press and Journalists Statute ahead of the 2011 presidential elections. The bill proposes that in order to operate in Uganda, newspapers must register with and receive a license from the Media Council. The bill seeks to restrict foreign ownership of the media. It criminalizes the publication of information that is deemed prejudicial to national security, stability, unity, or economic interests. Independent media advocacy groups, such as the Uganda Journalists Safety Committee (UJSC) and the Uganda Journalists Union (UJU), argued that the bill would wipe out critical and independent scribes and media establishments. The *Monitor* newspaper, which is privately owned by a foreign media conglomerate, enumerated its fears in an editorial:

> This Bill is more than an attack on press freedom. It is an attack on our collective right, as Ugandans, to the truth and to the information we need to be free and self-governing. We appeal to all Ugandans to oppose this attempt to control free speech and to erode our right to know.[33]

Internet access is not yet restricted or monitored by the government, and it was only available to less than 3 percent of the population in 2010.

Zambia

Zambian journalists, and the country's media in general, have been prone to harassment, threats, and physical harm. The Penal Code, which is a relic of the colonial era, criminalizes journalistic attempts to expose presidential autocracy as defamation or sedition. Section 53 of the code empowers the presidency to censor publications that it considers contrary to the public interest, while the State Security Act classifies official documents as national security. The laws have a chilling effect on the media, rendering them unsure about how far to go in seeking out and disseminating information. Moore argued that a gap existed between the ideology of humanism and its actual practice in Zambia. The Zambian government under the reign of Kaunda established the philosophy of humanism.[34] It is the government expectation that the press will promote and advance the ideas of traditional African communal values in the larger context of nation building.

This gap also extended to the press:

> Zambia has publicly claimed the existence of a free press. But, the reality of the situation is that the media are owned by the government, to serve the government. There are no guarantees of press freedom in the constitution and, generally, individual provisions of freedom of expression do not seem to apply to the press.[35]

In 1996, for example, three top independent journalists and editors, Fred M'membe, Bright Mwape, and Lucy Sichone, were sentenced to indefinite imprisonment by the parliament and the president's office for probing into businesses operating out of the vice president's office. A week after their incarceration, the High Court of Zambia released the three journalists, declaring in a ruling that the detentions were illegal. Parliament fought back with an appeal, and the vice president's office swung into action and re-arrested them on a different charge.[36] From 2003 to 2008, the Media Institute of Southern Africa Zambia (MISA) documented ninety-nine incidents of physical attacks on journalists, including beatings with batons and verbal hostility from police and other security agents.

The lack of press freedom can be traced back to the colonial era and the United National Independent Party's (UNIP) attempts to model Zambia's political and economic organizations on those of the former Soviet Union. According to Moore, "Political pluralism and an independent press were shunned and regarded as luxuries, which a country whose priority was first and foremost social and economic development, could not afford to enjoy."[37] The two national dailies, the *Times of Zambia* and the *Zambia Daily Mail*, came under party and government control, respectively, for their failure to achieve the goals of humanism. From 1975 to 1983, a protracted struggle for press freedom ensued between the government and the newspapers. Newspaper editors called for the right to publish without government interference, while UNIP politicians wanted coverage that portrayed the party only in a positive light. Ultimately, the regime under President Kaunda was successful in imposing its limited version of press freedom. Radio and television fared no better during this period, and state ownership and control of Zambia National Broadcasting Corporation (ZNBC) continues today.

During this era the *National Mirror*, established by an interdenominational organization of Christian churches in 1972, was the only alternative voice to the government-controlled press. The paper's coverage of corruption and its policy of equal access to any group, including the government, made it the most credible news medium in the country during the 1980s. Repressive media policies contributed to the deterioration of newspaper coverage, but journalists also lacked proper training and professional standards. In the 1980s, there were two forms of censorship: pre-production censorship imposed by government and self-censorship by journalists who feared retaliation.[38]

It is evident that in Zambia none of the existing media genres—print, radio, or television—are free of state interference. State-owned radio and television have dominated the country's airwaves for over three decades, while privately owned broadcast stations offer little investigative coverage that would hold the regime and state institutions accountable. Of the three media types, radio has the broadest reach. The state-owned ZNBC is the only national broadcaster, and *Radio Phoenix*, a privately owned station, broadcasts in four provinces. When the government liberalized the media sector under the Zambian National Broadcasting Act in 2008, the number of radio stations increased to thirty-four.[39] Within the last decade, Zambia's Roman Catholic Church has emerged as a dominant radio proprietor, with fourteen stations. Many other investment moguls and politicians who own community radio stations and privately owned commercial radio stations have followed the Church's lead. The state-owned ZNBC continues to propagate the government's agenda and an elite political perspective, while the new privately owned radio stations provide more diverse programming.[40]

In contrast to the radio sector, growth in the television sector has been hampered by high startup costs and the state bureaucratic practice of delaying the issuance of licenses. Television is the least accessible medium, but it is subject to the greatest amount of state regulation. ZNBC monopolizes the broadcast industry with the broadest coverage, but it is closely monitored by the government. The other two competitors are the Christian Trinity Broadcasting Network (TBN) and Muvi Television. TBN has little political content, while Muvi Television's reach is limited to Lusaka, the capital city. In Zambia there are three national daily newspapers, four national weeklies, two regional weeklies, and one local weekly. While newspapers are the easiest to launch, they are

not easily sustained in part because of the inability to attract advertising revenue.[41] The privately owned *Post* newspaper enjoys the largest readership, followed by the state-owned *Times of Zambia* and the *Zambia Daily Mail*. One of the
main challenges to newspapers is a lack of reliable printing presses. Just like
broadcast media, the journalistic independence of newspapers is hampered by
their owners. The state-owned newspapers tend to be in favor of the ruling
party, while the privately owned media tend to give more space to opposition
political parties.[42]

Internet access is not yet restricted or monitored by the Zambian government, and it was accessible to less than 5 percent of the population in 2010.

Media Policy Indicators in ESA

Several ESA countries now have bills that institute media councils. Some
Media Councils are self-regulatory bodies that were set up by associations of
journalists in Africa to advocate for quality local news and mediate any misun-
derstandings with either law enforcement agencies or with media proprietors.
But in some countries, these councils are set up by the governments to prevent
what they consider erroneous and libelous information. Most of their enforce-
able policies and functions include, but are not limited to, the indicators shown
in Table 5.1. Not surprisingly, Ethiopia received low ratings from citizens' indicators in Table 5.1 for its protection of media freedom. It might be expected
that South Africans would be more open to the idea that laws regulating media
are necessary since their country has few mechanisms for government interference. In light of the vibrant and successful commercial independent media in
South Africa, anecdotal evidence points to the recognition within state-run media, such as SABC, that professionalism is viewed as necessary for journalists'
survival. However, this anecdotal evidence does not seem to have made South
Africans more open to the idea of government regulation.

Two East African nations also have press laws that purport to strengthen
the autonomy of the media and improve media professionalism. In fact, the
media councils of Kenya and Uganda claim that their laws simply ensure media
autonomy from government interference. The qualitative meta-narrative of
statutory acts as shown in Table 5.1 is consistent with the results from survey
research across ESA. This plausibly explains why Kenya and Tanzania are the
only countries that rate "fairly" in the qualitative meta-narrative as well as
among respondents on the question, "Does the government promote ethical
standards among journalists?"

Interestingly, the data in the table also reveal that all ESA nations rate "fairly" on the issue, "An independent body advocates for the rights and privileges of journalists in the performance of their duties," regardless of how little freedom journalists have to practice journalism. In contrast, the meta-narrative of only two countries—Zambia and South Africa—selected "fairly" on the issue of "independent bodies arbitrate disputes between the government and the media."

Public Attitudes about Press Freedom

Hopefully, governments in ESA are aware that a free press is a pillar and purveyor of state accountability, and legitimizes regimes with the seal of good governance in any democratic society. Nevertheless, state leaders are suppressing this pillar of a democratic state. It is an assault on the collective right of citizens to information that is necessary for them to make rational decisions about governance, self-determination, and political choice. Given this background, how do citizens perceive the media, and the regimes, in light of their countries, media policies?

Respondents in all ESA countries somewhat disagreed with the idea that laws regulating media are necessary. Ethiopians strongly disagreed that the media, whether privately owned or state owned, should be regulated by the state. This may be because, as some independent Ethiopian journalists confirmed in Addis Ababa in late 2008, Ethiopians have openly experienced archaic laws being used to restrict press freedom. Ethiopia is the only country in ESA that has scored high on all indicators of state restriction of the press.

Citizens from all of the ESA countries agreed that there is a threat in government control, and either somewhat disagreed or disagreed with the proposition that laws regulating media are necessary. The governments of ESA sometimes license broadcast outlets and newspapers as a means of controlling these media. Yet at that same time, some ESA governments allow independent advocacy bodies to operate in order to satisfy agitators of media reform, while they carefully prevent these bodies from wielding real power to influence political and social change. Independent advocacy bodies are free to offer their opinions, but their rhetoric is weakened by the lack of authority to prompt mass mobilization and peaceful protest. As shown in Table 5.2, nowhere did respondents strongly agree that the press is holding leaders accountable. Citizens of Burundi, Ethiopia, and Rwanda somewhat disagreed while citizens of Kenya

Table 5.1: Qualitative rankings of media policy indicators in Eastern and Southern Africa

INDICATORS	ETH	KEN	TZ	UGA	BRD	RWA	RSA	ZBA
Government protects media independence and freedom	Poor	Fair	Fair	Fair	Poor	Poor	Fair	Fair
Government promotes ethical standards among all journalists (private sector or civil employees)	Poor	Fair	Fair	Poor	Poor	Poor	Poor	Poor
An independent body arbitrates disputes between the government and the media	Poor	Poor	Poor	Poor	Poor	Poor	Fair	Fair
An independent body advocates for the rights and privileges of journalists in the performance of their duties	Fair	Fair	Fair	Fair	Fair	Fair	Fair	Fair
Laws protect the rights and privileges of journalists against frivolous "seditious and libelous" charges	Poor	Poor	Poor	Poor	Poor	Poor	Fair	Poor

(Table 5.1—continued)

Government licenses broadcast media or newspapers (renewal based on cordial relations)	At hand	At hand	At hand	At hand	At hand	At hand	At hand	At hand
Government regularly licenses professional journalists	At hand	None	At hand	At hand	None	At hand	None	None
Government enforces journalists' employment criteria	At hand	None	None	At hand	None	None	None	None
Government maintains a registry of journalists	At hand	At hand	At hand	At hand	At hand	None	At hand	None
Government reserves some adverts for state media	At hand	None	At hand	At hand	At hand	None	None	At hand
Government enforces restrictions on area coverage or the establishment of national private media	At hand	None	At hand	At hand	At hand	At hand	None	At hand

Notes:

- The results in Table 5.1 are based on a qualitative meta-narrative of statutory acts, legislative media bills, and media self-regulatory decrees from ESA countries.
- The meta-narrative is based on legal or policy documents produced between 2000 and 2010, drawn from a variety of sources including *Parliament Hansard, Media Bills, Media Advocacy Reports, and Media Council Constitutions.*

and Uganda barely disagreed or were unsure whether the press holds leaders accountable.

Citizens of Tanzania, South Africa, and Zambia somewhat agreed. Chapter Eight goes into detail and explores why these variations exist in public opinion across and between the eight ESA countries. It is worth noting here that all ESA countries, except for South Africa, received a poor rating for the protection of the rights and privileges of journalists against frivolous charges of sedition and libel.

This is the most consistent way that journalists go unprotected in ESA. Existing literature supports the idea that sedition and libel charges have proven to be effective tools for government prosecution of journalists, using atrocious but legal actions. These data collected in 2007, 2008, and 2009 reveal that the public does not support these actions against the press.

Public opinion between countries also varies in response to whether private media are free from state control. South Africans agreed that private media are free from state control. It is imperative to highlight that the South African government does not openly restrict journalists by licensing and registering them or restricting privately owned media. But the South African media face the general licensing of broadcast media and newspapers, which has the potential for state abuse. Burundians, Kenyans, Tanzanians, and Zambians somewhat agreed that private media are free from state control; Ugandans and Rwandese were unsure; and Ethiopians somewhat disagreed. As enumerated in the preceding sections of this chapter, it seems obvious why Ethiopians disagreed with that proposition more than citizens in other countries. Surprisingly, Burundians somewhat agreed that their private media are free from state control—yet the only argument they have is that the Burundian government does not regularly license individual journalists. Few respondents may have even been aware of that fact. Perhaps a few persistent adversarial press outlets may make a big difference in public opinion towards state control of the relatively weak private media.

Respondents from across all ESA countries disagreed or somewhat disagreed that state media are free of state control, except for South Africans, who were ambivalent. It is notable that South Africans cannot say that state media are free of state control. First, this contrasts with their opinion of the private media, which South Africans agreed are free of state control. Second, the SABC has been singled out as an exemplar of a fairly independent state-owned broadcaster. But citizens are unsure of its autonomy from government influence. In Zambia, respondents disagreed that state-owned media are free from

Table 5.2. Rule of law indicators for press freedom in ESA

INDICATORS	ETA	KEN	TZ	UGA	BRD	RWA	SAF	ZBA
Laws regulating media are necessary	2.38*	3.21	3.27	3.18*	2.68	2.92*	3.11	3.19
The press holds leaders accountable	2.58*	4.11***	4.86*	3.92*	3.03*	2.89*	4.08*	4.19*
Private media free from state control	3.48***	5.13*	4.82***	3.72*	4.86***	3.92***	6.12***	5.26*
State media free from state control	2.39	2.88*	2.92	2.51	3.09	2.19*	3.67	2.18*

Notes:

- For mean differences between provinces: * = $p < .05$; *** = $p < .001$.
- All tests of significance were two-tailed with robust standard errors. Since data were designed for HLM, each variable and model passed a link test and SEs were adjusted to account for correlation within provinces.
- The scores are based on a 1 to 7 scale: (1 = strongly disagree, 4 = neutral, 7 = strongly agree).
- These are primary survey data collected in 2007 and 2008–2009.

state control—as did Ethiopians and Rwandese. On the issue of media independence, the press and religious institutions are the most vigilant and influential voices in civil society in most of Africa.

Chapter Summary

In a democratic society, institutional frameworks such as the independent media (given the existence of press freedom) help to advocate for the rule of law. The media have a major responsibility to scrutinize state institutions, hold public servants accountable, and encourage healthy and informed debates about good governance. Public opinion from across all ESA countries indicates that state leaders and bureaucrats have not exercised political authority to safeguard and respect the autonomy and functioning of a free press.

Although all forms of media are important, radio still remains the most pervasive medium in ESA, and is easily accessible to groups underexposed to media, such as rural and illiterate populations. Its role is especially crucial to strengthening social change for democratic consolidation and legitimacy in democratizing ESA. A push for participatory community radio has emerged as a popular solution to patriarchal media ownership and government control of both state-owned and some commercial media. The next chapter explicates whether the radio ownership environment can advance participatory discourse through community radio and other genres in a way that can effect social change.

Chapter Six

Radio, Media Infrastructure, and Social Change

Since the 1990s, struggles with democratization and economic liberalization have placed serious demands and hopes on radio in Eastern and Southern Africa (ESA). My earlier research[1] and that of others[2] found that in urban and rural areas in ESA, radio has been the dominant medium, as well as the most accessible source of public affairs information and news. Radio is regarded in Africa as a medium that narrows the knowledge gap on current affairs and as an outlet for sociopolitical expression.[3] Radio continues to provide information from a variety of perspectives. It still creates free and open public debate. For these reasons, it is befitting to dedicate a chapter here to radio and democratization. How does radio perform to educate citizens about living in a democratic society? Does it create opportunities for participation? Does radio change an individual's interaction with information and with the government to promote and enhance social change?

Although all forms of media are important, radio's accessibility to groups underexposed to media, such as rural and illiterate populations, has made it especially crucial to strengthening social change for democratic consolidation and legitimacy. African media scholars argue that control and ownership have generated a major debate about the effectiveness of radio in meeting those goals.[4] While governments and organizations such as the Media Institute of Southern

Africa (MISA) assumed that media liberalization would automatically create media pluralism and improve debate, scholars such as Barker and Nassanga assert that liberalization has simply replaced the monopolistic government control of broadcasting with monopolistic commercial control.[5] Compounding the problem, those in control of commercial companies are the same people who control the government. A push for participatory community radio has emerged as a popular solution to the top-down and often untrustworthy nature of government-controlled and commercial media. However, community radio stations in ESA are often hobbled by their dependence on NGO nonprofits and a lack of training. The question is whether community radio airs diverse voices and pays attention to the needs of the marginalized in order to achieve democratic social change. There is a danger with government influence and big donor assistance, making the focus of information content on funded or sponsored radio suspect.

The debate about the utility of radio for social change has opened up immensely since the 1980s and early 1990s when complete state control of media existed. For example, political rights on alternative media were denied on some unsubstantiated grounds of national stability, and economic and governmental development. From 2007 to 2009, some government officials in ESA countries argued that it makes sense for governments to have control of a media channel in order to inform and mobilize citizens for development.[6] ESA governments, however, need not have a monopoly on media, particularly alternative media. Similarly, emerging from the period before media liberalization is Kasoma's proposal for media cooperatives. He observed that, in Sub-Saharan Africa in the late 1980s, few privately owned radio stations existed, and they were shrinking in number, while the state-owned ones were expanding.[7] Kasoma advocated for media that are owned directly by citizens and communities. Participatory media are a solution to government-controlled media and should be seen as a possible catalyst for social change and citizen empowerment.

Well-intentioned development projects that were under the control of government or international nonprofits also provoked calls for an increase in participatory media. Radio has long been used for development purposes, because, as Opoku-Mensah explained, "Early development communications theorists believed that mere exposure to radio messages was enough to cause social changes that would lead to development." Nassanga considered these efforts historically unsuccessful, mainly because of the philosophy behind them. She explained:

During this period, views on media's role were influenced by the "bullet" theory advanced at the time, which saw the media as being all powerful, since it was believed that for every message sent through the media, there had to be a reaction ...Thus, during the 1960s and 1970s, there was much emphasis on media expansion as a way of encouraging psychological orientation that would lead to adoption of new/modern ideas and development changes.[8]

Radio and Development

Information and knowledge in and of themselves were believed to generate desired social development. Apparently, support and creation of knowledge and the economic well-being of society have always been the hallmark of developed countries. Influenced by Rogers's diffusion of innovations model, the approach provoked rich countries to transfer knowledge to the poor in developing countries.[9] Some international investors and donor agencies saw local cultures as a barrier to development in the ESA developing countries. Making tangible investments into community media as a venue for educating, advancing, and empowering poor communities was not a priority. Radio in particular took a while to attract investors as a vehicle to positive social change to empower the citizenry in rural communities.

Meanwhile, neglecting two-way communication in media policy left many rural ESA communities alienated. The infrastructure enabled media to send messages only from capital cities to the periphery, and feedback from local communities was minimal. Most media have clearly targeted markets that are concentrated in urban areas or major cities, and their content at times seems irrelevant to rural residents. It is important to note that rural residents are sometimes considerably misinformed.

If the goal is social change, perhaps the most counterproductive consequence in the early days was that the diffusion approach had communicated innovations down the social structure, but left the structure of dependence intact.[10] Hence, the most prominent discussions about radio and media in general now revolve around participation, and often, in the process, transform the idea of what development can be.

The World Bank Institute's Development Education Program provides a traditional definition of development as a qualitative change and restructuring in a country's economy in connection with technological and social progress.[11] This traditional definition is materially oriented, which is perhaps what encouraged the diffusion approaches to development. The need to overcome the structure of dependence encouraged the emergence of a more holistic view of development, one in which participation plays a leading role.

In his plea to not sacrifice political and civic rights in the name of economic and social rights to development, Ansah suggested a wider idea of development in which human development is a crucial aspect, and where economic and human rights guarantee each other.[12] In this mode, participation is crucial and there is a positive correlation between the right to express one's ideas in an open debate and the contribution to the development efforts of the nation.

Though participation is central to the idea of development, it is also about having the right to take part in social, political, and other informative debates. Many students of participatory and community media see participation in media production as much more thorough and profound. Dialogue and context are seen as key to communication for development. They often defend the right to free speech, which is necessary to development and democratization. Many scholars also understand participation as transformative, an all-engaged process that allows people to take control of their lives and communities.[13] Manyozo expanded the concept of participatory and rural/community radio so that it "no longer refers just to a broadcasting approach toward rural people, but, rather, refers to a local station that spiritually belongs to the people."[14] This conceptualization also justifies the essential reason that community radio enhances political emancipation and creates a platform for debate, exchange of ideas, and reactions to plans and projects. It also can accommodate people's ideas, and satisfy their spiritual and psychological well-being, much better than any other form of media.[15] Such an attitude regards public participation as more than just the right to speak one's opinion, but it is also seen as a transformative and empowering process.

Community Radio and Participation

Connecting to a member of a "marginalized" community in ESA is now both easier and harder than ever before. Media channels are quickly spreading to distant corners of ESA that were once unreachable. Consequently, people and organizations are also utilizing media at an accelerated pace. But when a person in a rural or urban region turns on the radio, he or she is unknowingly entering a complex world of competing ideologies and diametrically varied strategic objectives. Because of its unparalleled ability to overcome cultural or individual barriers (regardless of ethnicity, geographic location, gender, wealth, or literacy), community radio is becoming increasingly important as a key tool in reaching out to marginalized populations. With growing attention toward the importance of grassroots development approaches and indigenous participation in ESA, community media—particularly radio—are a vital ingredient in democratization and any effective development strategy.

Being knowledgeable about democracy is not always enough to connect the community to democracy. South Africans and Namibians show the greatest understanding of democracy among Southern Africans, but they are also the most pessimistic about democracy and show the least support for it. In the early 2000s, they were more likely than other Southern Africans to trust elected institutions and saw economics as more important than democratic processes. Kivikuru speculated:

> These intriguing results could perhaps be interpreted as that Africans who have lived under an indigenous authoritarian government (e.g. [Kamuzu] Banda, [Robert] Mugabe) have learned to attach an independent value to democracy [as opposed to instrumental] that has not yet been widely developed in Namibia or South Africa. Instead, ordinary people in these two countries are distressed about the slowness of change ... both South Africans and Namibians have the highest level of access to political information through the various forms of news media in the Sub-Saharan region, and they are significantly more informed than their neighbours when it comes to awareness of important national leaders. Yet they exhibit a low sense of citizen efficacy, though they retain a general sense of the efficacy of voting and elections.[16]

The reason that participation generates so much attention in Southern Africa is that the act of participating itself is seen as an inherently democratic act. Participation is different than the mere transmission of information about democracy because the act of participating teaches citizens more about living in a democratic society. Nassanga observed that the participatory process created total change. Audiences transformed from "docile and passive" into "a focused and engaged public, with many people talking fearlessly about corruption, poor governance, and other social concerns."[17]

Here is how Wanyeki articulated that theory:

> The nature of community media is participatory and the purpose of community media is development, "a process of public and private dialogue through which people define who they are, what they want and how they can get it." Community participation is thus seen as both a means to an end and an end in itself. The processes of media production, management and ownership are in themselves empowering, imbuing critical analytic skills and confidence about interpretations reached and solutions found.[18]

Participatory and community radio may be useful to democracy but might also serve other social goals. The functions and aims of community media are broader than promoting freedom of expression and association. Community media can broaden the role of traditional forms of communication, preserve indigenous knowledge, and close the information gap among peasants and the working blue-collar citizens. Many stations in ESA took on specific societal goals, such as cutting down on alcoholism and violence towards women[19] or fostering peace and development journalism.[20]

Community Radio as an Educator

Rural radio got its start in remote areas as an efficient way to provide education programs about farming and public health concerns. In places like Rwanda, many donors were invested in spreading cheap radios across the countryside for that purpose, and radio is still used to transmit practical information today. However, ideas about what information is important have expanded. Much of the focus on radio's current potential is on its ability to educate the people about democracy and their rights in a democracy. Some of the most striking anecdotes describe Ugandans learning information about their rights. When children hear on the radio that they have a right to an education, it compels them to ask their parents to send them to school. It has also helped adults claim their rights to defend themselves against abusive police.[21]

Many see a participatory element even in the educative role of radio. The developmental, environmental, and religious sectors of national agendas in some ESA countries have tended so far to achieve greater community participation in the ownership and management aspects of media than in the human rights and legal sectors.[22] The latter tended to address community participation only in the production aspects because although participants wanted to receive information, they did not feel confident in their ability to speak out in a two-way communication approach.

Donor Dependence

Radio, especially community radio, faces a number of challenges. There are four major areas of concern, the first being donor dependence. The obvious problem with dependence on charitable support is financial unsustainability—once funding stops, projects can be at risk of ending immediately. When funding is available only for certain aspects of their projects, stations have a shortage of independent and relevant programming. For example, Manyozo discussed the limited range of some stations in Africa:

> A former station manager for Dzimwe Community Radio in Katete, Malawi, acknowledges the failure of the station's broadcasters to visit remote communities and to research and produce programs, due to the lack of fuel to power the UNESCO-donated vehicle. As a result, broadcasters have tended to produce top-down programs, consisting of advice by experts living within the vicinity of the stations.[23]

Kivikuru also discussed the problems of dependence on NGO donors, especially because it is difficult for community radio stations to afford quality content. Most content is cheap and attainable, not necessarily the most relevant. The willingness to air whatever content is at hand may lead to questionable local control. Kivikuru noted:

> Many domestic producers receive funds from either domestic or international donors, willing to promote "good" causes such as health, HIV/AIDS prevention or refugees. These donors must be accountable to their home base. Accordingly, they put conditions on their support: their programmes should be broadcast within a particular time slot, or even on a particular date and time.[24]

Just as troubling as the financial instability are the negative effects of NGOs on participatory ethos, even when NGOs claim participation as a priority. Many attempts to involve the community in starting local stations were pitiful. The association of donor agencies with the allocation and administration of funds may well have impaired local initiatives to manage their own projects.

My friend Samuel Gummah, in Kampala, Uganda, is a victim of this donor problem. A European organization that I will not name here because of an ongoing legal battle (as of late 2010) came in to meet the logistical costs and capital needs of a community-oriented radio news agency called the Uganda Radio Network. The project was almost hijacked and Mr. Gummah almost lost all of his investments in the well-established network because the international donors pulled out and failed in their attempts to claim financial investments into the Uganda Radio Network.

Evaluating Impact

Another problem in the field, both for practitioners and researchers, is the lack of evaluation instruments to determine how well radio stations actually impact social change. Consequently, it is impossible to enforce development achievements of community media with inadequate research about its impact on the community. Practitioners with only anecdotal information operate on untested assumptions about the role of information and participation in development, as well as about the communities they are working with. The evaluation methods used to assess the role of community radio in the promotion of social change sometimes lack the sociocultural understanding of the community. The evaluation process of radio for social change ought to be self-managed and participatory.

Well-trained media personnel ensure that staffing and programming needs are being met, content seems relevant and of high quality, and community involvement in the initiative is strong and satisfying.[25] There is also inadequate information about community satisfaction with programming in many of ESA's community media. It is unclear whether programs respond effectively to the needs and interests of the community, and whether they are useful, effective, informative, and entertaining. If such goals can be assessed, then community media in the long run can lead to some of the desired basic social change in the community and empower citizens to make rational decisions pertaining to democratic governance.

Professionalism and Performance

Arguments have been made that the standards of journalism are low because 63 percent of working journalists only possess short-course training qualifications.[26] In Tanzania, for example, the nine journalism training schools are not adequately equipped with the necessary tools and suffer from a lack of investment. In addition, the private sector and even some of the media owners lack sufficient resources to support professional and editorial independence, thus impairing the quality of news reporting and writing.[27] Most journalists work as freelancers, earning USD 1.45 per published story or photograph. On average, freelancers earn about USD 30.00 per month, which is less than the Ministry of Labor's official minimum wage of USD 36.00. Most employed journalists work without contracts and earn an average USD 220.00 per month. In a national survey of 200 full-time employed Tanzanian journalists, 83 percent were regularly not paid on time at the end of the month.[28]

In Kenya, the standards of journalism are relatively better than in Tanzania and Uganda, but they are still universally low. Fifty percent of journalists in Kenya do not possess noteworthy journalism training qualifications.[29] The cost of one-year journalism certificates is high and unaffordable to many aspiring journalists. Although private training institutions may have better facilities than state institutions, some of them lack the modern media equipment and resources necessary to produce well-trained news reporters. There are about seven technical institutes and colleges in Kenya that offer basic and advanced media studies.[30]

Similar to the Tanzanian situation, most Kenyan media owners lack sufficient resources to support professional development of their scribes, hence impairing the quality of journalism.[31] Kenyan journalists receive better salaries than their Ugandan and Tanzanian counterparts. A 2006 newsletter from the Kenya Union of Journalists (KUJ) indicates that in 2000, the average salary for a full-time journalist in Kenya was USD 800 per month, yet the majority of those permanent employees worked without contracts and earned less than USD 450. Freelance reporters make up 75 percent of all journalists and earn an average USD 130 per month. Most of the freelance correspondents in Kenya live in upcountry towns or other provinces besides Nairobi and generate most of the content for radio news and newspapers.

There is evidence that media investors in FM radio stations are denied a frequency on partisan grounds, especially when the government is unhappy with the political inclination of the local investor.[32] Ethnic groups also started launching vernacular FM stations to broaden their political agendas. A recent example is Kass FM, a vernacular station that broadcasts in the Kalenjin, which is former president Moi's native ethnic language. When Mwai Kibaki, a Kikuyu, took over power, Kass FM had its frequency temporarily suspended, and the station was closed for a few weeks in 2006 for allegedly broadcasting anti-government messages. Kibaki's ethnic kinship then started two vernacular stations that broadcast primarily in Kikuyu, broadening their appeal and influence in the nation.

According to the National Institute of Journalists of Uganda (NIJU), Uganda has about 800 journalists who are fully employed, partially employed, or work as freelancers. NIJU executives reported in 2007 that an unscientific 2006 survey showed more unemployed journalists with a bachelor's degree than others who are employed in the media industry. The Uganda Journalists Union (UJU) estimates that over 2,500 journalists are registered and licensed by the government, as required by the Press and Journalists Act of 1995.

As in Kenya and Tanzania, both the state-owned media and the privately owned media organizations in Uganda lack sufficient capital and resources to support professional development of their journalists.[33] Broadcast stations pay exorbitant annual license fees, and their revenue from advertising spots is heavily taxed by government, forcing employers to hire low-wage and poorly trained workers.[34] It is commonly known that journalism institutes do not own or operate radio stations or run television stations. Broadcast media in Uganda tend to use interns or young and inexperienced journalists from these ill-equipped training institutions for on-the-job training.

Ugandan journalists receive slightly worse salaries than their Kenyan counterparts. According to NIJU, the average monthly gross salary in 2008 for full-time journalists was USD 680.00, yet the majority of permanently employed reporters had no contracts and earned less than USD 250.00. Freelance journalists in Uganda earn an average USD 2.50 per published news script or footage with text. On average, freelancers earn about USD 150.00 per month, which is equivalent to the average salary of a state-employed primary school (elementary) teacher.

In Ethiopia, according to the International Research and Exchanges Board's (IREX) Media Sustainability Index 2008, low salaries force many journalists to leave their jobs for positions with NGOs in industry communications, public relations, and other related fields. Journalism is a "benefit-free" position in Ethiopia, which means that journalists receive no housing or transportation allowances, and no health insurance or pensions unless they work for public media. Salaries vary as much as 50 percent among media outlets, with a few private newspapers paying much better than government outlets or other privately owned media. The average monthly gross salary in 2007 for full-time journalists was USD 485.00, yet the majority of permanently employed reporters had no contracts and earned less than USD 240.00. Freelance journalists in Ethiopia earn an average USD 2.40 per published news script or USD 3.90 per television video news package with text. On average, freelancers earn about USD 175.00 per month, which is almost equivalent to the average salary of a state-employed primary school (elementary) teacher. Low salaries have led to alleged sales of favorable articles to politicians and businessmen in exchange for cash or gifts.[35]

In South Africa, salaries are high enough to somewhat dissuade or at least limit the pressures of corruption, although some senior journalists still leave for jobs in better-paying industry communication fields.[36] The absence of senior mentors has had a negative effect on quality and balanced reporting. Female journalists are paid on average 25 percent less than male journalists.[37] The cost of investigative journalism has caused shallow reporting with little in-depth analysis. The lack of a journalists' union has also been cited as a reason for low-quality reporting. The average monthly gross salary in 2009 for full-time journalists was USD 1,040.00. Many journalists who work with small independent newspapers and weekly magazines had no employment contracts and earned less than USD 700.00. Freelance journalists in South Africa earn an average USD 5.75 per published news article.

Salaries for Zambian journalists are extremely low and vary depending on the media source. The salary range in 2008 hovered between USD 150.00 to 360.00 per month. While USD 150.00 per month would be high for those in community media, salaries in one private newspaper ranged from USD 1,000.00 to 1,500.00 a month. In a focus group study, some of the journalist sources in Lusaka said that the IREX-quoted journalism/media salary of USD 2,100.00 was an outlier. Focus group participants disclosed that payments and "brown envelope" freebies are commonly accepted in media circles. The IREX report also confirms this story-payment method to low-paid journalists. This hurts the media's credibility with certain segments of the Zambian population, who consider it a corrupt practice. The average monthly gross salary in 2008 for full-time journalists in Zambia was USD 650.00. Most of the permanently employed reporters do not have contracts and earn less than USD 300.00 per month. Freelance journalists in Zambia earn USD 3.90 per television video news package with text. On average, freelancers in Zambia earn about USD 160.00 per month or an average USD 2.40 per published news script. This is less than the average salary of a state-employed primary school (elementary) teacher.

Three institutions in Zambia offer college-level training in journalism and certificates, while many more professional development workshops take place throughout the year. Many untrained practitioners have entered the field recently, not just in Zambia but also in other ESA countries such as Burundi, Uganda, and Rwanda. Especially in community media, untrained volunteers have been widely hired to work as editorial or production assistants, but these volunteers tend to have little understanding of the ethical requirements of the field.[38]

Inadequate training opportunities are another major problem. Skills development is mostly done as in-house training but is sporadic and unsustainable. In-house skills training does not often address other needs beyond technical training, such as learning to do good, impartial investigative reporting.[39] Training is needed not only in obviously practical areas like financing, technology, and management, but also in journalistic standards and in ways to prevent further media marginalization. An important note about training is that coverage that meets more professional standards does not necessarily bring the political process closer to the people or get them more involved. For example, the South African media's coverage of the 2000 elections was, according to Kivikuru, a failure of professional responsibility.[40]

Figure 6.1. A radio journalist doubles up as a music producer and disc jockey. This journalist at the ZNBC FM Radio studio was preparing her talking points on a current affairs show on December 14, 2008. She briefly chatted with me about her work at the state-run FM station. Photo taken by Yusuf Kalyango in Lusaka, Zambia.

Government and Public Broadcasting

Another challenge for radio is the lack of national policies on communication for development.[41] Previous research shows that many African governments have technically created policies to promote media diversity but often overlook the participatory role in community media. "The challenge has been implementation of such policies, as lack of political will alongside weak and minority governments surviving through oppressive apparatuses have been unwilling to offer media the space designated to them in the policies."[42] Media regulation has in general focused on controlling the flow of information, rather than equalizing access to information and the means to produce that information. This is a role that media policies can play that has seldom been applied before in ESA. Commercial media have seen a little change, with recent pressures for privatization, but few concrete policy provisions have been made to support and develop community media.[43] Manyozo's belief that the government's role in media can be a positive one requires a perspective shift, given the oppressive history of state interference in media.

ESA governments should reconsider the public broadcasting model that would engender social change for economic growth development and create a debate over the importance of structure and ownership in radio and other community media. Some media liberalization efforts have brought negative impacts. But in opening up media space to non-governmental control, governments and reformers often acted on the assumption that media liberalization would produce media pluralism. They assumed that diverse democratic-encouraging media would emerge once liberation opened up private ownership of media. In reality, markets created monopolies in commercial radio, limiting the number of owners and thus the voices represented in public discussion.[44] Furthermore, the separation between "private" and "government" control in many countries is meaningless when the same elites still control both spheres. Much of the private sector in ESA was controlled by the state, either by blurring the lines between private and state companies or because companies were—and are still—owned by government ministers, their relatives, or important civil servants.

Even those in the private sector without direct connections to government may self-censor themselves to ensure that their advertising is not withdrawn. Opposition or marginalized voices continue to be silenced in such a system. When government interests control the market, both private and public media stick to safe positions. Content therefore tends to favor market power.[45]Aside from the conflict of interest in ownership, market forces have had a negative effect on the quality of broadcasting, especially for local material.

When a Ugandan business entrepreneur, Gordon Wavamunno, hired me in the mid-1990s to head the news and current affairs department of WBS Television, our major occupation then was to acquire foreign programming content to broadcast, which filled up about 60 percent of our 24-hour television programming. In other words, liberalization saw a sharp rise in imported content because of the economic limitations of producing locally and also because there was simply not enough local programming to match the capacity of new distribution systems.

For example, when Joy TV in Zimbabwe started broadcasting, it bought up all available independent Southern African productions but still ran out of material in just days. Producers orient programming toward well-off, urban audiences who are targeted by advertisers. In the early days of media liberalization, this also led to a reduction of programming orientated toward the poor and rural dwellers. If universal media access is to stand a chance, Barker recommends positive government regulation and subsidies, and even a reconsideration of the role for public broadcasters:

> Because historically the biggest problem with media quality has been the government using media as the voice of the ruling party, suppressing debate, and refusing access to different ethnic groups, some say that "supporting an increased role for public broadcasting may be seen as promoting a view based on the first world, mainly Western European context, where public broadcasters are mainly doing the right thing in terms of cultural pluralism." But the realities seem to bear out that competition in the sector doesn't itself promote pluralism ... it means the same basic commodity appearing in different markets and in a variety of packages.[46]

Persuading commercial sectors to serve less wealthy audiences requires financial incentives from civil society, foundations, and government, rather than from advertisers. To achieve pluralism in the commercial media requires anti-monopolization legislation and government enforcement of the same. ESA governments ought to limit mergers and small press acquisitions. That support should be redirected towards the public interest. Barker says that re-regulation often referred to as deregulation is a misnomer: "What is at stake is not so much the number of rules but the shift in their overall rationale away from a defense of the public interest (however that was conceived) and towards the promotion of corporate interests."[47]

This is a major problem with the current trend of media liberalization in ESA. Public broadcasting was a neglected opportunity—in some ESA countries, public media outlets were left with mega-bureaucracies when governments turned them into corporations. Kivikuru pointed out that no domestic democracy advocacy groups or foreign donors considered public service broadcasting as an opportune outlet for impacting social change.[48] Instead, these institutions were ignored and were considered as belonging to the past. The heft and reach of public broadcasters could make them valuable for accessibility and sustainability, particularly when community radio is not up to the job. Having a more national reach may also be useful for the kinds of actions that cannot adequately occur in community radio because of its small group organization. Any attempt to build a broad coalition for social change must move beyond the passive communication approach of agenda building (discussed at great length in Chapter Eight) to create an infrastructure that promotes and enables a broad, independent, liberally oriented and multimedia environment.

Figure 6.2. An outdated on-air analog production gallery at ZNBC in Lusaka. This executive producer was in one of the ZNBC Television post-production studios, communicating with two presenters of a current affairs show on December 17, 2008. He later told me that the government is still looking for funds to renovate the station and update studio equipment. Photo taken by Yusuf Kalyango in Lusaka, Zambia.

Ownership

The South Africa Broadcasting Corporation (SABC) is an example of a rehabilitated, politically independent public broadcaster. SABC exemplifies a public broadcaster, which functions as an independent medium. Many radio stations are seen as unique media that are solely community oriented with a desolate focus on grassroots communication. Private, public, and community radio ownerships can function independently but should serve the communities in ESA with one main goal of promoting social change for positive growth and human development.

It is difficult to have a litmus test for community-ness with respect to a focus on community involvement and a sense of ownership. Community media can evolve to play an equally important role as the well-funded commercial media, despite the limited finances, broader control or external influences, and lack of accountability to their citizenry. According to Opoku-Mensah:

> The crucial issue is not whether people have access to a radio station to express their opinions or personal messages, nor even whether some local people participate on a paid or volunteer basis in radio programming. What really matters is the institutional structure of the radio station. Who is in control? Is there a mechanism to make it accountable to those it serves?[49]

Kivikuru compared two forms of ownership structure to see if the differences also correlated with their impact on the quality of programming for the purposes of democracy. His case studies were community broadcasters in South Africa and their nonprofit content supplier Democracy Radio versus a public broadcaster in Namibia and its regular call-in shows known as *People's Parliament*. This is not a clear-cut competition between public and community broadcasting because the South African case was a mixed model. The community radios themselves were bottom-up media, but they were heavily connected to the donor NGO Democracy Radio, which had semi-public support. The South African case's mixed nature, however, may be a realistic reflection of the kinds of ownership at work. "Only very rarely is a community radio station born out of genuine communication needs; in most cases, it is established as an NGO activity because the activists behind it—outsiders or community members—know that this is a project that can get outside financing."[50] The two programs had different claims on the extent to which they could be considered grassroots or outlets for the people's voices.

There are also other media in ESA that have similar current affairs programs with a similarly translated title. The *People's Parliament* call-in shows in other ESA countries, such as Tanzania, Uganda, and Zambia, also allowed a great deal of spontaneity and freedom to speak. These current affairs shows also tended to deal with national and not local problems, and were somewhat limited by the small range of people who typically could afford to call in using their cell phones. They were also limited in the scope of their critique, as such programs tended to criticize the implementation of policies but rarely the overall political agenda. By comparison, Democracy Radio's use of people's voices in South Africa was limited to pre-selected sound bites, but it chose more daring subject matter and political opinion than did Namibia's *People's Parliament*.[51]

Kivikuru's study provides an enlightening contribution to this chapter. It documents that in the early 2000s, South Africa's community radio was by definition bottom-up, but it was intertwined with and influenced by its centralized support mechanisms. The Namibian *People's Parliament* was a part of national programming but turned out to be a forum to share popular voices from different levels of society. Both had successes and limitations in their ability to reach the grassroots, and reached places that would not be predicted simply by categorizing them as community or public. The important question is not about who owns the channels and sets the agenda for public debate, but what level of debate quality citizens should demand for democratization. What level of involvement and change are necessary?

Tables 6.1, 6.2, and 6.3 show that Eastern Africans somewhat agreed that radio talk shows on both community and privately owned FM stations have the ability to empower listeners to effect change on issues that are important to them. They agreed with the statement that current affairs and political issues increase their knowledge of good governance and improve their self-esteem to make rational decisions about government.

On the question of whether talk shows are a venue for political dissent, however, Kenyans and Ugandans were both generally noncommittal. Burundians, Tanzanians, and Zambians were less certain that current affairs talk shows are a venue for political dissent. South Africans and Zambians, in contrast, had the highest opinion of talk shows and said that they increase their knowledge of good governance and improve their self-esteem. By and large, respondents did not necessarily perceive political dissent to be closely related to social change on issues that are important to them. On the same question of whether radio talk shows are venues for political dissent, citizens across ESA were less certain. Their attitudes on the same question towards content in newspapers and on television stations varied significantly between countries and across regions within countries.

Respondents from Ethiopia had a higher positive opinion on the issue "radio talk shows on current affairs issues are a fitting venue for political dissent," than they did of the talk shows' ability to empower them to effect change on issues that are important to them. In fact, Burundians, Ethiopians, and Rwandese held the bottom three lowest opinions on the issue of being "empowered

Table 6.1. Attitudes towards current affairs programs on different types of radio

Provides information about economic and dev't opportunities	*Community* μ and (s.d.)	*Private* μ and (s.d.)	*State-owned* μ and (s.d.)
Burundi	5.47 (1.325)	5.13 (1.132)	4.59 (1.044)***
Ethiopia	5.18 (1.543)*	5.03 (1.220)*	4.53 (1.023)*
Kenya	5.61 (1.176)***	5.52 (1.129)*	4.89 (.812)*
Rwanda	4.07 (1.132)	4.08 (1.131)*	5.18 (1.095)***
S. Africa	5.97 (1.357)*	5.77 (1.238)***	5.17 (1.231)*
Tanzania	5.62 (1.158)***	5.44 (1.242)***	5.29 (1.326)***
Uganda	5.54 (1.233)*	5.48 (1.104)***	3.48 (1.323)
Zambia	5.68 (1.243)****	5.42 (1.127)***	5.43 (0.996)*

Notes:

- Respondents were asked to agree or disagree with the statement: Radio (community private, private, and state-owned) regularly provides information about economic opportunities and community development projects.
- For mean differences between provinces: * = $p < .05$; *** = $p < .001$. Sample σ^2 explained = .79 across ESA. All tests of significance were two-tailed with robust SEs.
- The scores are based on a scale of 1 to 7 (1 = strongly disagree, 4 = neutral, 7 = strongly agree).
- These are primary survey data collected by the author in 2007 and 2008–2009.

by community and privately owned radio stations to make change on issues that are important" to them. They held equally low attitudes toward the ability of radio talk shows to increase their knowledge of what it means to have good governance. On the issue of radio talk shows as a media venue for political dissent, the data show that even a relatively positive attitude is still close to uncertain.

Radio talk shows seem to be playing fairly different roles in each country, as public attitudes towards community radio and the ability of privately owned radio to impact social change wane across countries. Public attitudes towards radio talk shows in Burundi are relatively low on every measure. But in Zambia these attitudes a relatively quite high on self-esteem. In Ethiopia they are relatively high on political dissent. Given these outcomes, what are the prospects for media and social change in ESA that could lead to good governance and democratic consolidation?

Table 6.2. Attitudes towards current affairs programs on different types of radio

Does radio empower citizens for change?	Community μ and (s.d.)	Private μ and (s.d.)	State-owned μ and (s.d.)
Burundi	3.77 (1.148)*	3.83 (.897)*	3.57 (1.028)***
Ethiopia	3.48 (1.064)***	4.63 (1.203)	3.37 (1.093)
Kenya	4.33 (1.201)*	5.22 (1.011)***	2.38 (1.086)*
Rwanda	3.81 (.754)***	3.98 (.837)***	3.12 (.654)***
S. Africa	4.51 (1.131)*	5.39 (1.030)***	4.93 (1.030)***
Tanzania	4.18 (1.364)***	5.21 (1.102)*	3.99 (1.006)*
Uganda	4.04 (1.046)*	5.09 (1.014)***	1.53 (1.528)*
Zambia	3.99 (1.002)*	5.32 (1.007)***	2.62 (1.406)*

Notes:

- Respondents were asked to agree or disagree with the statement: News and other current affairs programs on community, private, and state radio stations in our region empower citizens to make change.
- For mean differences between provinces: * = $p < .05$; *** = $p < .001$. Sample σ^2 explained = .71 across ESA. All tests of significance were two-tailed with robust SEs.
- The scores are based on a scale of 1 to 7 (1 = strongly disagree, 4 = neutral, 7 = strongly agree).
- These are primary survey data collected by the author in 2007 and 2008–2009.

Prospects for Social Change

Although it seems democratic for popular political programs in Eastern and Southern Africa to allow citizens to voice their opinions through call-ins, it is important to pause and question their relevance to social change. Shows like *People's Parliament* and others across ESA are useful because they provide a platform for political discourse and feedback from criticized public figures. This *prima facie* creates an impression of mutual communication. One has to wonder, however, whether such productions work only to strengthen the existing power structures and national elites. For instance, some journalists contend, and the public opinion data from across ESA also reveal, that current affairs shows give an illusion of power not only to those who engage in discussion over the air-waves but also to those who only listen.

Table 6.3. Attitudes towards current affairs programs on different types of radio

A venue for all to express political dissent	*Community* μ and (s.d.)	*Private* μ and (s.d.)	*State-owned* μ and (s.d.)
Burundi	3.08 (1.671)	3.94 (1.007)*	3.49 (1.033)***
Ethiopia	3.89 (1.914)*	4.49 (1.124)*	3.41 (1.116)*
Kenya	4.11 (1.679)	5.42 (1.501)	2.39 (1.081)***
Rwanda	3.49 (2.501)	3.79 (.899)***	2.88 (1.164)
S. Africa	4.19 (1.798)*	5.98 (.894)***	4.83 (1.008)***
Tanzania	3.35 (1.613)	5.62 (1.304)*	3.47 (1.141)***
Uganda	3.76 (1.447)*	5.48 (1.084)***	2.09 (1.168)
Zambia	3.21 (1.617)*	5.50 (1.097)***	3.48 (1.177)*

Notes:

- Respondents were asked to agree or disagree with the statement: Radio is a venue for all interested people to express political dissent. The scores are based on a scale of 1 to 7 (1 = strongly disagree, 4 = neutral, 7 = strongly agree).
- For mean differences between provinces: * = $p < .05$; *** = $p < .001$. Sample σ^2 explained = .74 across ESA. All tests of significance were two-tailed with robust SEs.
- These are primary survey data collected by the author in 2007 and 2008–2009.

One question addressed whether citizens feel that their self-esteem is improved, and their participation strengthened, as a result of call-in current affairs shows. The majority of citizens agreed that their self-esteem is increased from such interactive shows. The data also support the idea that interactive shows about politics and governance create a feeling of empowerment and give a voice to the voiceless in society, both of which are important goals of participatory radio. Interestingly, a majority of focus group respondents said that the broadcast media are allowed to have interactive current affairs shows because governments and state leaders indoctrinate citizens to consider the rhetoric on radio and television as pure political comedy, and a form of entertainment. The power structures also allow broadcast media to operate freely, particularly privately owned radio and television, because they approach people as individuals and not as organized citizens. Consequently, the focus group participants concurred that this rhetoric is good for ratings but lacks the ability to mobilize citizens for social change toward good governance.

Take, for example, *Radio Isanganiro* in Burundi, Zami Public Connections in Ethiopia, *Radio Salus* of Rwanda, Monitor FM in Uganda, and *Radio Phoenix* in Zambia. They have popular current affairs talk shows, but many journalists and focus group respondents say that these stations do not impact political change through mass dissent or mass appeal. The structure of these stations has changed, whether they are owned by government or by private firms. Participants said that governmental and commercial influence in most of the broadcast media is still strong, despite their rhetoric and contribution to political debate. Even at the start of the liberalization phase of privately owned stations, government representatives were present to monitor political programs. In the early phases of the liberalization of FM radio stations, some Western donors also influenced political programs. Participants considered the situation with *Radio Phoenix* in Zambia to be particularly troubling. They argued that radio stations were remarkably responsive to Western priorities and likely to promote ideas that are in fashion with international agencies.[52]

The push for the kind of social change desired by Western donors may be important, but it diminishes the importance of media autonomy in the long run. Commercial, community, and public service radio stations may have a platform for public political discourse that impacts social change and state accountability, but such goals should be met without necessarily promoting the financiers' agenda. Focus groups across all eight ESA countries revealed that the agenda of the proprietors routinely cripples a station's advocacy for, and contribution to, good governance, state accountability, legitimacy, and the rule of law.

Chapter Summary

A few radio stations and television stations are not as independent as envisioned, and almost all are influenced by their sources of support—be it the government, advertisers, or even well-intentioned NGOs that advocate for participation. The impact of radio for social change is much more mixed and is difficult to completely and adequately explain here. It is important to note that the potential sources of control and bias in radio content do not always hold back stations from engaging in independent investigative journalism, unless the proprietors of these organizations are held in bondage to authoritarian or dictatorial governments.

However, proprietors sometimes hold stations back in unpredicted ways, particularly in the quality of programs. The challenge with radio journalism and current affairs programs is that they have not achieved the desired social change that citizens expect them to provide. It is still difficult for community journalists to prosper without the necessary journalism skills and adequate training. For example, how can untrained community journalists keep a local politician from evading answers? Community radio and other independent radio broadcasters must define and pursue their journalistic endeavors by protesting undue influence from their proprietors and dictatorial states, as equally as they detest the bad laws and media policies enforced by authoritarian or militaristic regimes. It would be difficult for ESA broadcasters to implement successful radio initiatives to bring about social change without first determining what support systems are either good or detrimental to meeting their overall objectives. The next puzzle to unravel is the issue of authoritarian or dictatorial governments vis-à-vis states that are ruled by military control and how this impacts media performance and democratization in ESA. That is the subject of the next chapter.

Chapter Seven

Media in Authoritarian and Militarized States

Why should we care about or study authoritarianism and militarization in the subfield of media and communications research? The answer to this question is quite straightforward. The underlying government intention to use the army to crush independent journalists and editors is often overlooked in the political debate surrounding state militarization. A number of previous media studies have ignored how such militarized and authoritarian regimes disrupt or thwart media content that exposes the destructive consequences of military leaders on substantive democracy. Understanding the determinants of a militarized state or militarized regime is important because today's governance choices by military presidents in Eastern and Southern Africa (ESA) usually determine tomorrow's decisions about how their regimes democratize. While a few media scholars have rightly pointed out the toll that authoritarian regimes have taken on media independence, many African scholars have not addressed the impact of Africa's militarized states on the autonomy of the privately owned and state-owned media.

This chapter reconstructs authoritarianism and dictatorship by examining whether they shape how regimes democratize. The latter part posits different theories of militarization of the state in Africa compared to other parts of the world, drawing from political science theorists and sociologists about the militarization of states by authoritarian governments.

Conceptualizing Authoritarianism

The notion of an authoritarian government is often used synonymously with non-democratic government. Such a broad application of the term makes it difficult to outline a theory of authoritarianism that is useful and coherent. It has led to disagreements over the role that totalitarianism, monarchy, and dictatorship play in authoritarianism.

Before exploring the varying and even contradicting definitions of authoritarianism, it is best to begin with two of the simplest definitions available. Although these definitions are relatively basic and do not include any information about the specific characteristics of an authoritarian regime, they are commonly employed in other definitions of the term.

1. "Government by arbitrary authority that ignores fundamental rights of individuals and rules through force rather than consent."[1]
2. "A state in which obedience to authority is favored as against liberty; and in which there is little control over the way in which authority is exercised." That is to say, there are next to no established restrictions on that authority.[2]

Many of the basic definitions of authoritarianism implicitly explain it in contrast to democracy. Democracy is present when "in some undefined sense, political power is ultimately in the hands of the whole adult population, and that no smaller group has the right to rule."[3] Democracy asserts "the right of a majority over any minority." The only time elite control will be tolerated is via "mass approval or especial emergency."[4] Governments that reject political power sharing through the legislative process and other forms of governance also reject pluralism.

Pluralism is defined here as "specific institutional arrangements for distributing and sharing governmental power."[5] If pluralism is an understanding of the way democracy can work in society, elitism is its opposite and is the way authoritarianism works. If democracy is defined by conferral of a bottom-to-top authority then authoritarianism is a top-to-bottom assertive pressure where the defined government needs no transfer of authority from its subjects. To understand authoritarianism as a whole is to understand this directionality of power and authority within a state. A forceful, downward direction of authority characterizes authoritarianism, but there are nuances in its embodiment. Insistence on a dichotomy between democracy and authoritarianism does not always hold up. A defining feature of modern authoritarian governments is that they claim commitment to democracy and may make democratic displays, although they remain dictatorial. Some academic literature characterizes the term *authoritarianism* not as the opposite of democracy, but as a way to describe a middle ground between democratic regimes and totalitarian regimes.[6] Authoritarianism should be understood as

> political systems with limited, not responsible, political pluralism, without elaborate and guiding ideology, but with distinctive mentalities, without extensive nor intensive political mobilization, except at some points in their development, and in which a leader or occasionally a small group exercises power within formally ill-defined limits, but actually quite predictable ones.[7]

Are Authoritarian Regimes Totalitarian?

Totalitarianism is not synonymous with authoritarianism. It is considered an extreme form of authoritarianism or a form entirely unto itself. Totalitarian states have an all-encompassing ideology because they completely ban pluralism and use terror to maintain power.[8] In ESA, former presidents Michel Micombero of Burundi, Mengistu Haile Mariam of Ethiopia, Juvénal Habyarimana of Rwanda, and Idi Amin Dada of Uganda were widely regarded as totalitarian leaders. Totalitarian regimes, such as these former ESA governments, share traits with authoritarianism by ruling through force and forbidding political competition. Such ruthless features are also classified as a form of authoritarianism. Totalitarian states are interested in having a strict reach into everyday life that authoritarianism rarely attempts. Authoritarian regimes of the past century often permitted a considerable degree of individual liberty so long as there was no threat to what the authorities regarded as law, order, and social stability.[9]

Linz[10] determined that limited political pluralism was the most distinctive feature of an authoritarian regime because democratic governments practiced unlimited pluralism, while totalitarian governments allowed for none at all. In the early stages of authoritarian regimes in ESA, political participation was very intense and sometimes controlled. In the 1950s through the 1960s, many ESA states were either still colonized or ruled by monarchies. Consequently, in regimes that were typically both totalitarian and authoritarian, political mobilization often arose as the exception rather than the rule. In ESA, colonial states such as Burundi, Kenya, Rwanda, Uganda, and Zambia had both authoritarian colonial rulers and totalitarian monarchies. At the same time, during the struggle for independence, many opposition groups who fought to remake society were harassed and treated as enemies of the established status quo. Totalitarian monarchies dissuaded their subjects from questioning traditional leaders and called for total obedience, while colonial regimes dissuaded the natives from exercising free choice and other freedoms that were essential to their independence.

Are All Authoritarian Regimes Dictatorships?

Evidently, there is some disagreement about whether totalitarianism and pre-modern political systems should be understood as authoritarian. Furthermore, it is also unclear whether dictatorship in ESA is an integral part of authoritarianism. Dictatorship is "a form of government in which one person has sole and complete political power."[11] In a dictatorship the political elite control policy making in governance, to the exclusion of all other people or groups. It is usually first established through force or fraud and is eventually maintained through the restriction of civil liberties, such as freedom of speech, freedom of the press, and freedom of assembly.[12] According to Brooker, the predominant modern form of a non-democratic regime is a dictatorship that nonetheless makes claims of commitment to democracy.[13] As previous chapters have revealed, the regimes of ESA nations from the 1950s through the early 1990s have had those characteristics. Accordingly, militarization of these states played a major role in their dictatorships.

It is largely agreed among scholars that dictatorship is a form of authoritarianism, and not the contrary.[14] Perhaps the biggest difference between authoritarianism and dictatorship is that authoritarianism is more widely applicable.[15] The term *authoritarianism* is not clear-cut and can be applied to monarchies and traditional forms of government as well as totalitarianism, whereas dictatorship generally cannot. A dictatorship concentrates power in one person or group of people with few or no restrictions on their rule. In ESA nations, authoritarian regimes of the past and present concentrate power and supremacy in one individual or political movement. In theory, Burch takes this idea further by considering totalitarianism to be an extreme form of dictatorship, and where totalitarianism combined with dictatorship are understood hierarchically as a more severe variation of authoritarianism.[16]

Other definitions split authoritarianism into two categories—dictatorships and totalitarian governments—making authoritarianism more of an umbrella term for regimes that monopolize power within the government.

Alternatively, in the past, Linz did not see dictatorship as a useful term for any well-established governments, whether authoritarian or totalitarian, because there are many different ways of concentrating power. Instead, he reserved the term *dictatorship* for an "interim crisis government that has not institutionalized itself and represents a break with the institutionalized rules about accession to and exercise of power of the preceding regime, be it democratic, traditional, or authoritarian."[17] Opposition politicians in all of the current governments in ESA have similar arguments concerning the ruling party or coalition parties and their regime types.

Even if the term *dictatorship* is extended to established regimes, a transitional dictatorship can also be an indicator of how governments that run authoritarian regimes came to power in the first place. The idea of a dictatorship as a transitional phenomenon is a relatively accurate description of many military dictatorships in the 1960s and 1970s, as well as in the new millennium. Brooker explicated the particular characteristics of military versus party dictatorships. Military dictatorships are regimes where members of the military also have political control of the country and are usually the result of a coup undertaken in the military's self-interest. Such regimes tend to not last as long as other dictatorships—about five years on average—because military usurpers often have limited goals and do not always even intend to stay in power for more than a few years.[18] Many African nations are an exception to this rule.

Sometimes military dictatorships transform into party dictatorships. Examples are Mexico in the 1940s, Castro's regime in Cuba, and the Baathist regime in Iraq.[19] In ESA, for instance, the Rwandan Patriotic Front is led by Major General Paul Kagame, who is also the head of state. The National Resistance Army in Uganda is led by Lieutenant General Yoweri Museveni, who is head of state. Each transformed his military-political institutions into political party institutions. Party dictatorships tend to be more ambitious. They usually enforce a regime whose main long-term political strategy or national agenda is just to stay in power. They also declare their political party to be the only official and permitted party in the country. Although studies of party dictatorships usually focus on fascist and communist regimes, they can come from many ideologies and approaches. The majority of party dictatorships have been in Africa.[20] Straying briefly from the focus on eight ESA nations, the following comparative case study demonstrates how the main long-term political strategy of both the Nigerian and Ugandan military regimes was to keep their military leader permanently in power. Moreover, the comparative case study provides an exemplar of how these problems are not just unique to ESA but are prevalent as well in some countries in other regions of Africa.

Figure 7.1. Formation of militarized states from 1992 to the present

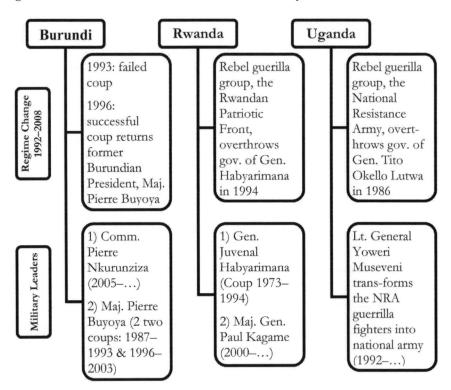

The Comparative Case of Nigeria and Uganda

What emerges in this case study of Nigeria and Uganda is that media exposure has been a powerful tool used by military states to promote their political agendas, using authoritarian tactics to appear to promote democratization. The goal was to determine whether the media in both countries acted as democratizing factors that would expose the military regimes that attempted to usurp and shape political space through dictatorial means. This is important because, as the latest wave of democratization sweeps across

Africa, a number of presidents—both military and civilian leaders—are trying to amend their national constitutions in order to eliminate political opponents or extend their stay in office beyond constitutional term limits. For example, President Sam Nujoma of Namibia in 1999 and President Frederick Chiluba of Zambia in 2001 attempted to abolish presidential term limits by using the democratic means of amending the constitution.[21] These attempts produced different outcomes. Nujoma succeeded in Namibia, and Chiluba failed in Zambia.

Both Uganda and Nigeria considered amendments to constitutional term limits. There was varying public awareness of such provisions. In early 2005, Ugandan president Yoweri Museveni successfully campaigned to change the constitution, abolishing the presidential term limit. In the Afrobarometer public opinion survey, only 40 percent of Ugandans correctly identified the constitutional two-term limit that was being contested and widely reported in the news at the time of the survey. In contrast, a similar amendment proposal, linked to Nigerian president Olusegun Obasanjo, failed in late 2005. In this case, 63 percent of Nigerians correctly identified the term limit. Afrobarometer is a publicly funded non-for-profit research organization, which conducts regular comparative public opinion surveys on democracy, market reform, and civil society in Africa.

During the first decade of Nigerian independence from its British colonizers, the country enjoyed an economic boom fueled by oil revenue.[22] Until the late 1970s, the Nigerian currency (the Naira) was stronger than the U.S. dollar and widely accepted in monetary transactions outside Africa. Since the late 1970s, ethnic tensions and north-south political disputes have disrupted these economic gains.[23] According to Young and other scholars, despotic military men plunged the federal union into military coups, mass violence, attempted secession, and civil war.[24] In late 1978, Nigeria attempted its first democratic transition to an elected government under civilian rule, but regional conflicts sparked by separatist politicians using the military continued to destabilize the country's nascent democracy.[25]The collapse of oil prices throughout the 1980s battered the already fragile economy, fueling inter-regional competition, breeding corruption at the state level, and instigating intense public discontent over inequality.[26]

Prior to the economic recession in 1979, General Olusegun Obasanjo took over a militarized state, but then oversaw a military transition to civilian rule and retired as head of state. He subsequently returned in 1999 as a civilian presidential candidate and won the election. His government still referred to him as General Obasanjo when he returned to politics, but he continued to oppose militarism as a form of government.[27] General Obasanjo raised the level of military professionalism, attempted to de-legitimize militarism, introduced a zero-tolerance policy toward perpetrators of military coups, and restored some democratic institutions.[28]

Despite these developments, the political landscape in Nigeria was still dominated by powerful authoritarian military leaders within government, and the president was surrounded by patronage networks at the grassroots, state, and federal levels of government. In 2005, Obasanjo favored a bill to amend the constitution, allowing both him and state governors to seek a third term. Nigeria's Senate rejected the bill in May 2006. The incentive for a third term was the lure of financial and other inducements for state governors.[29] According to press reports, Obasanjo gracefully accepted defeat and hailed the rejection of the bill as a victory for democracy. A March 2006 Afrobarometer survey reported that 84 percent of Nigerians agreed that the president should serve no more than the constitutionally prescribed two terms.

In a similar development, Uganda became well known in the 1970s when Idi Amin Dada, a British-trained army officer, assumed the presidency via a *coup d'état* and turned the country into a theater of political massacres and economic disaster, as well as a nightmare for Western diplomacy.[30] Amin established a dictatorship and ruled with absolute authority from 1971 to 1979. That was the beginning of a series of military dictatorships and authoritarianism that have plagued the country since the 1970s. Amin's successor, Milton Obote, used government troops to commit atrocities, while his military generals and Special Forces lieutenants plundered natural resources and state coffers at unprecedented levels.[31] Some scholars have argued that Obote's use of the military to destroy political opponents resulted in more brutality, devastation, and death than was recorded during Amin's rule.[32]

Uganda has gone through several political changes since the current president, Lieutenant General Yoweri Museveni, and his National Resistance Army (NRA) overthrew the Obote government in 1986. In the late 1980s and 1990s, Museveni outlawed most activities related to political parties. Electing party leaders and cadres, operating division offices, and holding rallies and member conferences were all banned. The 2001 presidential victory of Lt. Gen. Museveni also meant that his stay in power was constrained by the constitutional limit of two terms of five years each, albeit within the single-party political system. In his efforts to get around this constraint, Museveni reversed his doctrine of the single-party system in favor of multi party politics, against which he had initially campaigned. The price for this reversal, however, was elimination of term limits. He succeeded in securing the passage of a resolution in favor of a national referendum seeking to amend the constitution and lift the presidential term limit. Museveni aggressively secured support for the referendum by using the power of his dictatorship and the influence of his military patronage and his presidential supremacy, as well as the maneuvering of parliamentary proceedings.[33]

Meanwhile, there was opposition to this ploy, which was met with the considerable weight of Museveni's hegemonic presidency. Longtime political activists and opposition politicians saw the 2005 referendum as a smoke screen for keeping him in power.[34] The president became more dictatorial and hostile toward the news media and others who opposed his plan. The independent media in Uganda, just like that in Nigeria, debated the issue and publicly supported the opposition by calling on voters and parliament to reject the president's efforts.

The referendum was subsequently supported by the voters. By this act they allowed multiparty competition to resume, while Museveni earned the right to contest the presidency as many times as he wishes. The lesson here is either that the Ugandan electorate simply ignores the agenda espoused by the media or that there is simply no relationship between media exposure and the public's attitudes toward the issue of military dictatorship and democracy.

Another important question is how to measure participation within an authoritative militarized state. Therkildsen observed that Ugandans exercised their democratic right by boycotting a referendum in the major cities and trading centers, but not in rural regions.[35] City dwellers and the educated class understandably have more access to the mass media and are more engaged in public affairs than those in rural and agrarian areas. However, defining political participation as just taking to the streets is difficult when there is real fear that the military might be deployed on those streets and public squares. Bratton and Lambright argued that Ugandan voters expressed disapproval of Museveni's regime by staying away from the polls.[36] As reflected in Table 7.1, in the Ugandan sense of political participation, a democratic course of action can be a process of inactivity for those who do not wish to reinstate a military or an authoritarian regime to power. Perhaps that abstention from a political rally or a voting place may represent a positive act of protest, and hence political participation, in situations where the government is known for deployment of military forces on the streets to destabilize and dismantle civilian dissent.

Since military leaders have long governed Uganda and Nigeria, Afrobarometer data showed that 83 percent of Ugandans and 73 percent of Nigerians were interested in politics. However, two-thirds of Ugandans and Nigerians also stated that politics and government sometimes seem so complicated that one cannot really understand what is going on in militarized states. In Nigeria, 84 percent were satisfied with democracy and 83 percent of respondents said political parties are necessary, while a similar number reject one-man military rule. In contrast, only 53 percent of Ugandans felt the same way about the need for political parties and one-man rule. Descriptive results from the Afrobarometer survey data looked at democratic variables regarding the support for a multiparty democracy, as opposed to a single-party system. Overall, media exposure in both Nigeria and Uganda plays a significant role in the formation of attitudes towards democracy and enhances political participation.

The issue at hand in this comparative case study is largely the presidential two-term limits that produced different results between the military-led regimes of Nigeria and Uganda. Why did Lt. Gen. Museveni succeed in amending the constitution and get re-elected for a third term in Uganda in early 2006, while Gen. Obasanjo failed to lift the term limits in Nigeria and so relinquished the presidency in early 2007? The survey data as illustrated in Table 7.3 support the premise that greater media control by proprietors and government in Nigeria and Uganda leads citizens to express negative attitudes towards democracy. Uganda's military and authoritarian regime of the 1990s still owned the biggest national newspaper in the country, and presidential appointees and state patrons still own 60 percent of the private radio stations.[37]

Although some independent newspapers try to expose graft and nepotism in state institutions, the state-owned media in Uganda do not mount investigations of state failure because of military influence and interference, military tribunals or kangaroo courts, and wrongdoing within government. Consequently, the state-owned media have acted as a government mouthpiece by presenting the official state position on all accusations levied against the political elite.[38]

Moreover, media personnel are threatened and sometimes whisked away by plainclothes military and policemen if they expose the atrocities of the Uganda People's Defence Forces (UPDF) on the news.[39] The stifling of the media in

Table 7.1. Principal components of public attitudes and political participation

Dependent Variable	Components	Extraction	KMO
	Uganda		
	Satisfied with democracy	.493	
Attitudes towards	*Political parties necessary*	.530	.671
democracy	*Democracy worth having*	.721	
	Term limits for president	.128	
	Into activism, protests, debates	.598	
Political participation	*Freedom for all to vote*	.619	.712
	Close to a political party	.416	
	Discuss politics	.537	
	Nigeria		
	Satisfied with democracy	.474	
Attitudes towards	*Political parties necessary*	.746	.631
democracy	*Democracy worth having*	.645	
	Term limits for president	.031	
	Into activism, protests, debates	.781	
Political participation	*Freedom for all to vote*	.621	.751
	Close to a political party	.418	
	Discuss politics	.651	

Notes:
- In this model, Varimax rotation method with Kaiser Normalization was used for the principal component analysis to extract components for the Eigen solution. This model predicts 62.3% of the cumulative variance.
- *Data source*: The 2004 Afrobarometer. Raw data (in this model) were run by this author.

both Nigeria and Uganda by past military regimes and authoritarian governments—sometimes using the constitution to prohibit the freedom and autonomy of non-military institutions—has had repercussions on how Nigerians and Ugandans use the media and participate in governance and politics.

Media institutionalization and control by owners in military states have created exclusion and marginalization of citizens who cannot hold the media and government accountable.

In Nigeria, however, other former political leaders from other established political parties also own some nationally respected media. For example, President Umaru Musa Yar'Adua is a part-owner of the independent *Reporter* newspaper and some FM stations. These media, which are owned and operated by strong opposition politicians such as Nigerian senators and governors, vigorously represented their interests by building a political agenda and national consensus against General Obasanjo's third presidential term. More pointedly, independent media such as the *Vanguard* and *Guardian* newspapers—whose former owners had political interests different from Obasanjo's regime—took a leading role in opposing the third-term amendment bid, which was eventually blocked.[40]

Table 7.2. OLS—Comparison of media exposure in Nigeria and Uganda

Predictors	Uganda *Coeff. &SE*	Nigeria *Coeff. &SE*
	Model 1	
Exposure to radio news	.087* (.025)	.046* (.023)
Exposure to television news	.031 (.019)	.019 (.020)
Exposure to newspaper content	.077*** (.020)	-.060*** (.018)
Public affairs discourse	-.037 (.035)	-.033 (.019)
	Model 2	
Exposure to radio news	.101*** (.025)	.197*** (.036)
Exposure to television news	-.074*** (.019)	-.154*** (.030)
Exposure to newspaper content	.002 (.020)	.013 (.028)
Public affairs discourse	.198*** (.035)	.167*** (.030)
N = 1643 *Model 1* →	Adj. R^2 = .048	Adj. R^2 = .041
Model 2 →	Adj. R^2 = .057	Adj. R^2 = .062

Notes:
- Model 1 shows predictors of media exposure on attitudes towards democracy.
- Model 2 shows predictors of media exposure on political participation.
- The asterisk (*) indicates a statistical significance at .05 and the asterisks (***) denote significance at .001 alpha level.

- The figures in parenthesis indicate Standard Errors.
- *Data source*: The 2004 Afrobarometer. Raw data (in this model) were run by this author.

This explanation clarifies why the media did not appear to have a significant role in influencing Ugandans to denounce the presidential bid to abolish term limits; yet in Nigeria, the third term limit was blocked. The close relationship between media proprietors and state actors has compromised the independence of the press in Uganda. It has also limited media influence on the public regarding key issues of democratization, such as the rejection of presidential term limits. But in Nigeria, media ownership by powerful opposition politicians contributed to the resilience of its press, and influenced public opinion and national debate to reject the bill that would have allowed a third term.

Hybrid Regimes in ESA

It seems that authoritarianism in ESA, and all across Africa, can best be described as a paradigm because of the increasing existence of hybrid regimes. Many previous and current regimes, especially modern military regimes, in some of these states maintain the guise of democracy and pluralism. This creates a problem for democratic consolidation. Authoritarianism and democracy run in opposite directions because of the ways in which state actors utilize power and authority. Elections are far from sufficient to establish democracy because they "have been an instrument of authoritarian control as well as a means of democratic governance."[41] There are several categorizations of hybrid regimes, which can be called semi-authoritarian, electoral authoritarian, and competitive authoritarian. These categorizations of hybrid regimes overlap closely but may vary in the specific ways that they are democratic and non-democratic. In ESA, countries with past militarized authoritarian regimes faced much more complicated problems around their hybrid regimes than did non-militarized states such as Kenya, Tanzania, and Zambia.

Semi-authoritarian is often used as a catch-all term for hybrid regimes. Semi-authoritarian regimes tend to have a lack of consistency in guaranteeing civil and political liberties; and "it is their regard for some of these liberties that distinguish them from authoritarian regimes."[42] Common versions of semi-authoritarianism include electoral authoritarian regimes, which conduct regular multiparty elections at all levels of government but then negate some basic democratic standards. Similarly, in competitive authoritarian regimes, formal democratic procedures such as elections are viewed as the principal way of gaining authority, but incumbents violate the rules so often that the regime fails to meet the minimum standards for democracy. Framing hybrid regimes as diminished forms of democracy is dangerous because it reflects a bias towards democratization. Hybrid regimes are a diminished form of authoritarianism because hybrid governments are not necessarily heading towards democracy.[43]

Schedler believed that authoritarian regimes of the 1990s and 2000s resemble democracies much more than their predecessors, and they elude the classic categories of one-party, military, or personal dictatorship. They manage to get elections right but "fail to institutionalize other vital dimensions of democratic constitutionalism, such as the rule of law, political accountability, bureaucratic integrity, and public deliberation."[44] As soon as any aspect of the election process is compromised, however, the regime can only be considered electoral authoritarian, and not compliant with minimal democratic norms.

Schedler built upon Dahl's concept of a democratic chain of choice to develop seven requirements, *all* of which must be fulfilled to count as democratic. Otherwise all the other elements are compromised. The seven requirements for democracy are empowerment, free supply of alternatives, free and informed demand, universal inclusion, insulation (a secret ballot), integrity of vote counting, and irreversibility.[45] These parameters of democracy can be used for better comparisons of authoritarian regimes.

Dictatorships and Maintaining Power

It is also worth considering some of the methods used by dictatorships and authoritarian regimes to stay in power. As mentioned earlier, authoritarian regimes are the embodiment of elitism, whether or not the ruling elite acknowledge their absolute position of authority. Many dictators, such as General Idi Amin of Uganda and Lt. Colonel Mengistu Haile Mariam of Ethiopia, acknowledged their right to rule through elitism. Their claims reflect an early argument of Pareto that the process of political leadership yields superiors and therefore rulers, refuting the notion of equality in leadership and power.[46] Such dictators are conspicuous elitists.

Magalhães also identified a traditional approach to claiming dictatorship. Such an approach maintains prevailing societal forces like class structure, while proceeding with new forces for change. By contrast, a conservative dictator establishes authority by referring to history and tradition rather than to the future and the modernization of the nation.[47] Some regimes are "hegemonic when the domination of one actor is taken for granted and unchallenged by these over whom it holds sway."[48] This is the case in most of Africa and elsewhere in non-democratic states. For example, Stepan looked at relationships between the governing and society that sustain authoritarianism and dictatorship. He studied the power dynamics in South American and Southeast Asian authoritarian regimes. And he identified five main parties that affect the hegemony of the regime: the core group of regime supporters, the coercive apparatus that maintains the regime in power, passive supporters, active opponents, and passive opponents.[49]

Figure 7.2. Authoritarian, dictatorships, and hybrid regimes—1992 and beyond (Burundi, Rwanda, and Uganda)

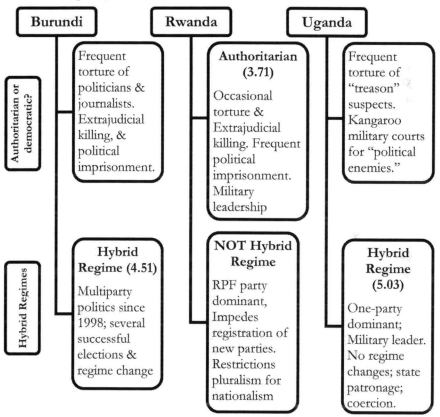

Notes:
For additional information: *The Economist* Democracy Index 2008. Based on a scale of 0 to 10, a score of 8 to 10 indicates "democratic," a score of 6 to 7.9 indicates "flawed democracy," a score of 4 to 5.9 indicates "hybrid regime," and a score below 4 indicates an "authoritarian regime." Frequency of torture, extrajudicial killing, political im-

prisonment, and disappearance are based on The Cingranelli-Richards Human Rights Dataset (CIRI) in 2008. (Principal Investigators: David L. Cingranelli and David L. Richards; URL: http://www.humanrightsdata.org)

Figure 7.3. Authoritarian, dictatorships, and hybrid regimes—1992 and beyond (Kenya, Nigeria, and Ethiopia)

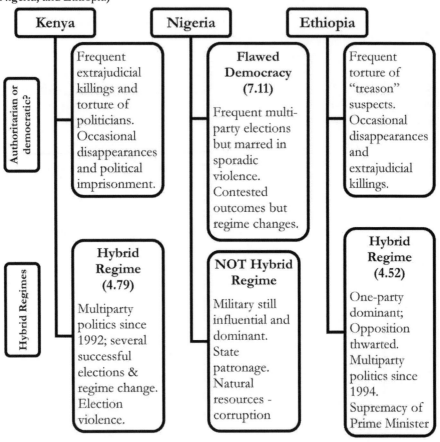

Notes:

For additional information: *The Economist* Democracy Index 2008. Based on a scale of 0 to 10, a score of 8 to 10 indicates "democratic," a score of 6 to 7.9 indicates "flawed democracy," a score of 4 to 5.9 indicates "hybrid regime," and a score below 4 indicates an "authoritarian regime." Frequency of torture, extrajudicial killing, political imprisonment, and disappearance are based on The Cingranelli-Richards Human Rights Dataset (CIRI) in 2008. (Principal Investigators: David L. Cingranelli and David L. Richards; URL: http://www.humanrightsdata.org)

Figure 7.4. Authoritarian, dictatorships, and hybrid regimes—1992 and beyond (S. Africa, Tanzania, and Zambia)

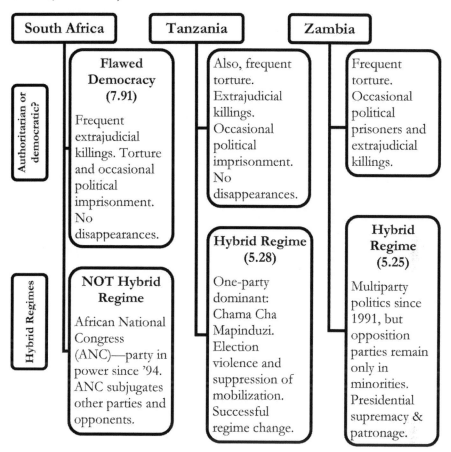

Notes:

For additional information: *The Economist* Democracy Index 2008. Based on a scale of 0 to 10, a score of 8 to 10 indicates "democratic," a score of 6 to 7.9 indicates "flawed democracy," a score of 4 to 5.9 indicates "hybrid regime," and a score below 4 indicates an "authoritarian regime." Frequency of torture, extrajudicial killing, political imprisonment, and disappearance are based on The Cingranelli-Richards Human Rights Dataset (CIRI) in 2008. (Principal Investigators: David L. Cingranelli and David L. Richards; URL: http://www.humanrightsdata.org)

When it is strongest, a regime is able to silence opposition through fear. As a regime begins to demonstrate inefficiency in maintaining social order and the status quo, many of its core supporters begin to fragment, and the opposition is able "to undertake a broad array of activities to pressure the regime and publicly state their case for change."[50] Dahl's theory is also applicable in the African political experience: "The likelihood that a government will tolerate an opposition increases as the expected costs of suppression increase."[51] Stepan's model is a more nuanced look at the internal political dynamics of authoritarianism and dictatorship, and can be used to understand how regimes in ESA and across Africa maintain control over a state.

Understanding Militarization

Like authoritarianism, *militarization* and *militarism* are broad terms, and there are differences in understanding their role in politics. Militarization refers to a more tangible and institutional process. It is a multidimensional process through which military coups and regimes, authoritarian government, patriarchy, powerful military apparatuses, repressive state apparatuses, war and armed conflict, rising military spending and arms imports, and external intervention become dynamically linked to each other and to capital accumulation for national hegemony.[52]

In Africa, the role of the military in nation building and in maintaining order was explored from widely different perspectives over the last half century. Pye and Klare viewed the military as precursors to African modernization and allies against the spread of communism.[53] Some viewed the military as "a modernizing and stabilizing source of organizational strength in society, a last stand-by reserve which could be called in, or could take over, to prevent subversion or a total collapse of the political order."[54]

African scholars later abandoned notions of the military as protector of order by recognizing the disorder and malignancy of many African military regimes. The military in Africa was then viewed more as a source of strife and grievance than of control. Luckham called it a structuralist illusion to say that the military and militarized states were somehow separate from the society in which they originated and separate especially from their pre-colonial power dynamics.[55] This view merely rationalized the exercise of violence in the hands of warlords and military cliques far beyond the state.

The military is not a self-sufficient institution. Militarization in many countries in post-colonial Africa lacked "the basic facets of social integration" that are visible in other nations such as Cuba, Argentina, or Ecuador.[56] The armed forces are characterized by the same diversity and rifts of language, region, and ethnicity that are present in the rest of society.

Militarization in Africa, as opposed to other continents, is often studied as a post-colonial phenomenon. The Scramble for Africa took place before and during the beginning of the twentieth century when many European nations laid claim on African territories by drawing up boundaries, establishing colonies, and extracting the region's resources. In 1941, the Atlantic Charter called for autonomy for imperial colonies, and the move towards independence in Africa gained momentum. Early observers of the process saw the new African armies and police forces "as part of an 'institutional transfer' of Western paradigms of governance."[57] But as former colonies worked to establish themselves, it became clear that the military and the state were not as cohesively linked as most believed.

Following the militarization of the African states, there were three types of military intervention. In the first type, the military was relatively hands-off and uninvolved in politics. This type was particularly visible during Africa's post-independence period when the armed forces were separate from the political arena in some countries. The second type of military involvement was the rebellion stemming from anger with European officers and colonialist African political leaders. The rebellions were aimed at forcing colonial governments to adopt certain policies, such as higher pay or pension policies. The third type of military involvement was the *coup d'état*, which brought the military fully into politics.[58]

Coups d'état have a long history on the African continent, with the first taking place in Sudan in 1958. According to Onwumechili, more than sixty military coups had taken place on the continent by 1990.[59] A military *coup d'état* occurs when a country's armed forces abruptly seize control of the civilian government. In Africa, *coups d'état* are often regarded synonymously with militarization.

In 1985, as a young teenager, I witnessed my first coup when General Tito Okello Lutwa led a successful *coup d'état* and toppled his boss, Dr. Apollo Milton Obote. We lived in a flat (apartment complex) in the middle of Kampala, the capital city, where we witnessed massive looting of commercial goods and muggings in the city. I saw two soldiers break into a warehouse with hand grenades on Wilson Street and load their army truck with large cartons of commercial goods. The soldiers fired shots into the air to disperse us before they set the store ablaze with paraffin. This type of looting by defeated soldiers of Obote's government was widespread in the city and lasted two days.

One interpretation of coups is that they are purely internal affairs; another interpretation considers them internal affairs but points out the influence of European and American military training or education on many officers.[60] However, a third take on military coups is that foreign interests in some cases desire political change and therefore encourage or influence the armed forces of another country. Foreign powers have sometimes clearly been participants in coups in Africa, although their possible influence does not fundamentally change the concept of a coup.[61] The varying nature of foreign involvement highlights the wide spectrum of military force used in Africa and the difficulty in isolating coups from other forms of military force and conflicts. Luckham argued that militarization was an inherently international process. A 2008 *Foreign Policy in Focus* analysis argued that the United States' military intervention in Africa, also known as Africa Command or AFRICOM, may be unfavorable to the interests of African nations. Feffer explained that AFRICOM was intended to build "partner capacity" with Africa but believed that the new structure was really designed to secure oil resources for the United States, engage in counterterrorism, and roll back Chinese influence.[62]

The Southern African Development Community (SADC) called on Africa to avoid the presence of foreign forces on its soil because an influx of foreign troops could disrupt relations between African countries. Instead of implementing AFRICOM to further the United States' own interests, Feffer suggested that Washington politicians should work to boost education, jobs, and health care in Africa.

Media under Siege?

In conclusion, this chapter discusses how citizens believe military leaders use authoritarian tactics to change their constitutions and allow unlimited presidential terms. Table 7.3 bears out these attitudes. Media should be able to act as arbiters, disseminating information that empowers the public to make rational decisions that promote democracy and enhance participation. This function has been diminished by authoritarian government influence and censorship both in Nigeria and Uganda. Most news organizations in Africa served the state, not the public, and the outcome was that news and editorial support for democracy were weak because political messages were merely government mouthpieces. In the 1980s, for example, the National Party of Nigeria (NPN) benefited from favorable editorial content and promotional coverage provided by the Concord Group of newspapers, particularly the *National Concord*.[63] This continued in the 1990s. The *National Concord* represented the interests of its owner, former Nigerian president Moshood Abiola. Both Nigerian state-controlled newspapers and some independent national newspapers engaged in political party partisanship throughout the 1990s. The state-owned *Daily Times* and the independent *Guardian* were prominently involved.

The independent *Guardian* newspaper was renowned and touted as the flagship of Nigerian journalism and press accountability. But its owner, Alex Ibru, later accepted a cabinet-ministerial appointment in the mid-1990s, which compromised the independence of his newspapers.[64] When he was Minister of Internal Affairs, Ibru's two newspapers, including the *Guardian*, were shut down by the military government of General Sani Abacha. Instead of protesting or resigning, Ibru apologized to the government for any offensive reports from his newspapers. Subsequently, there was an attempted assassination of Ibru when he was fired as cabinet minister. The co-opting of private media owners into the military state and the muzzling of the free press continued in Nigeria throughout the 1990s.[65] Meanwhile, radio and television were not considered credible sources of information throughout the 1980s and 1990s. The independence of Nigerian newspapers and electronic media was also compromised because proprietors depended on the state for acquisition and the ability to accumulate wealth.[66] Because of military influence, the media failed to draw attention to government failures and was incapable of transforming Nigeria into a stable democracy.

The state-owned press in Uganda, in particular the *New Vision* newspaper, was susceptible to external manipulation from both political and military leaders. Independent newspapers like the *Daily Monitor* were highly regarded and provided the most politically balanced and detailed information on politics and the democratic process. However, results indicated that fewer people read newspapers in Uganda than do those who listen to radio or watch television. The stifling of the media by the regimes, using constitutional provisions that prohibit the freedom and autonomy of political journalists, has had repercussions on how Nigerians and Ugandans use the media. Government control in Uganda ranges from providing media proprietors with attractive investment incentives to placing advertisements from state parastatals in exchange for the use of media to build political agendas.[67] Although some independent newspapers try to expose graft and nepotism in state institutions such as the military, the state-owned media do not mount investigations of state failure, injustice, or warmongering.

Table 7.3. OLS—Attitudes towards democracy in Nigeria and Uganda

Predictors	Uganda *Coeff. &SE*	Nigeria *Coeff. &SE*
Satisfied with democracy	.217*** (.040)	-.163*** (.039)
Political parties necessary	-.115*** (.029)	.057 (.031)
Presidential term limits necessary	-.034 (.036)	-.010 (.039)
Democracy worth having	.020 (.028)	-.066* (.030)
Military overrules the constitution ✓	.93*** (.016)	
Government is authoritarian ✓	-.101*** (.019)	
President is a dictator ✓	.84* (.022)	
N = 1643Model 1→ N = 481✓	Adj. R² = .037	Adj. R² = .019

Notes:
- The asterisk (*) indicates a statistical significance at .05 and the asterisks (***) denote significance at .001 alpha level.
- The figures in parenthesis indicate Standard Errors.
- The symbol ✓ indicates original data collected by the author in 2007.
- Secondary data without a symbol ✓ are from Afrobarometer in 2004.
- Raw data (in this model) from Afrobarometer were run by this author.

This comparative case study of Nigeria and Uganda shows that regardless of media advocacy that rejects dictatorships and authoritarian rule, greater media control by proprietors and military governments leads citizens to express negative attitudes towards democracy. It also indicates that the majority of citizens would most likely give in to the wishes of their military governments. What emerges here is that the role of media in militarized states is diminished by the enormity of presidential and military supremacy. The press has been a powerful tool for agenda building on behalf of authoritarian governments, not only in Uganda and Nigeria but also in other ESA countries. The next chapter discusses the politics of agenda building in greater depth, and how the media set or do not set national agendas.

Chapter Eight

Politics and the Media Agenda

One of the main reasons for examining media performance in the democratizing states of Eastern and Southern Africa (ESA) is to determine which communication process offers the strongest influence on public attitudes towards democratic rule. Two different communication processes are purposefully used here: the agenda setting and the agenda building processes. The survey questionnaire used to gather public opinion in the ESA nations was designed to gauge media influence (agenda setting) and government influence (agenda building) at the individual and provincial levels. The individual level simply refers to each ESA citizen who responded to the survey questionnaire.

It is important to examine media performance at the individual level and province level because of the nature of politics, and the tendency of political elites to use ethno-regional sectarianism to coerce and shape public attitudes. Many political elites in Africa use ethnicity and geopolitical sectarianism as a source of political mobilization to either influence the state or to gain power.[1] This chapter examines how the media performed under such a political culture, and how the media informed and educated citizens whose opinions were probably shaped by other intervening factors such as the regime type, ethnicity, social economic status, and the prevailing rule of law. Earlier research and case studies were unable to provide this type of empirical evidence of either media influence or government influence on public attitudes in ESA.

The purpose here is to examine whether citizens believe that their politicians use the media to promote ethno-political isolationism and other political hyperbole to influence favorable attitudes. Does sectarian politicking lead to ethno-political conflicts? How do the newspapers cover them? How do citizens respond to a statement, such as, "Politicians use the media to incite violence and ethnic hatred"? What attitudes do citizens hold toward the president regarding regional sectarianism? To what extent do the media influence public attitudes towards regime legitimacy in each ESA nation? Does the government in each ESA nation have a greater influence than the news media on public attitudes toward democratic rule? For a graphic illustration of these concepts, see Figure 8.1.

Agenda Setting and Agenda Building

How citizens of the ESA learn about important issues of democratic rule and economic development continues to be an important question in agenda setting research. How the media perform and influence citizen attitudes on issues of democratic rule is also an important agenda setting inquiry. Do governments of ESA build the public agenda through media messages? Or is it exclusively the media that set the public agenda? In the last twenty years, evidence from single-nation studies in Africa has demonstrated volatility and instability in democratic rule, which suppresses press freedom and media performance. These cases have been highlighted in previous chapters. However, no known research has tested the agenda building and agenda setting functions in Africa.

The first level of agenda setting is the idea that the media acquaint information seekers and consumers with the salient issues, and the media shape how these audience members think about those issues. The second level of agenda setting suggests that the media influence how people think by attaching added meaning to the news presented. However, these concepts are based on Western media researchers' understanding of the influence of state actors on the media and the impact of media on public thinking and discourse. In semi-authoritarian regimes in ESA, the African media's depiction of state actors may not be related to public perceptions of leaders, regime legitimacy, and the rule of law unless the media's description of the issues and the participants also includes important factors such as patronage, regional alignment or political identity, social status, or even media ownership.

Agenda Setting as a Media Influence

One of the main tasks of the news media in any society is to inform the public about important issues. Public enlightenment about the relative importance of issues through news coverage in the media is a function of agenda setting.[2] Agenda setting is the idea that a person's media exposure to an issue in news content will generate an opinion about that issue.[3] The theory is public about important issues. Public enlightenment about the relative importance of issues through news coverage in the media is a function of agenda central to the role of the news media in the formation of public opinion and public attitudes. Agenda setting studies have reaffirmed the influence of the media on the public's attitude towards issues, even in areas outside the United States.[4] However, until now, this theory had not yet been widely tested in ESA.

In their seminal study, McCombs and Shaw[5] established that the positioning and prominence of a story influences the public's ordering of priorities on news issues. The study established the power of media messages on voter perception of issues during elections.[6] After four decades of evolution, agenda setting by the media has now reached a new level, whereby the public expresses concern on issues, which then receive extensive media coverage. This was demonstrated in the United States during the extensive press coverage that followed the September 11, 2001, terrorist attacks.[7]

What eventually becomes the public agenda is not the exclusive domain of the news media, however; it is also the domain of government. Recent studies have shown that when individuals are highly interested in national issues, it is more likely there will be a strong agenda setting effect.[8]

The media exert tremendous influence over citizens in political discourse, but agenda setting cannot occur without exposure to the news media.[9] Media exposure serves as a catalyst for the agenda setting process.[10]

Agenda Building as a Government Influence

Most of the literature on Africa shows that the media provide political leaders with an outlet for their agendas, as opposed to independently reporting without interference from state leaders.[11] Furthermore, during parliamentary and presidential elections, the media in Africa have the ability to reinforce the policies of state actors by expanding their outreach to uninterested observers or reluctant participants.[12]

Figure 8.1. Agenda setting and agenda building during democratization in ESA

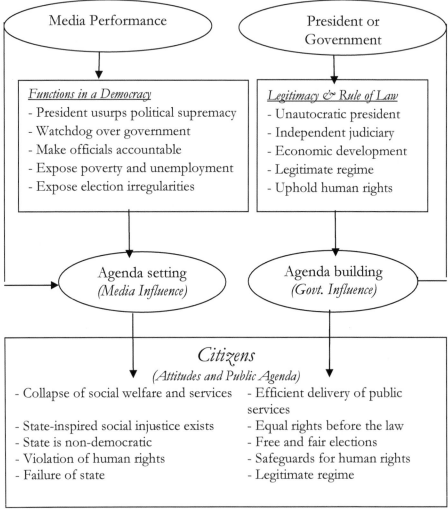

Notes:

Figure 8.1 is a schematic typology of how agenda setting and agenda building are measured in terms of media performance, regime legitimacy, and the rule of law. The arrows show the influence of the media and the influence of government on citizens in Eastern and Southern Africa. It is also a representation of attitudes of citizens towards the media and the regime.

Likewise in the United States, as succinctly stated by Scheufele, "Spokesmen and spin masters play an important role in promoting issues and symbols and establishing a feedback loop to media coverage, to increase issue coverage or at least to keep the issue alive."[13]

Media influence, or agenda setting, does not function in isolation. Elite individuals or institutions contribute their own issues that build an agenda for public discourse.[14] For that reason, media influence can be examined as both an independent and dependent variable. In other words, it is a dependent variable for picking up an issue and an independent variable for creating issues and keeping them alive. Based on that understanding, it is probable that if the issues that get onto the media agenda are controlled or "orchestrated" by external sources, it is then plausible that agenda building could have an impact on the public agenda in East Africa. That proposition has yet to be tested. As McCombs has stated, "There is a vast wealth of research on the impact of mass media content on the public agenda and considerably less attention to the variety of influences shaping the media agenda."[15]

Many Western scholars have increasingly placed more attention on news sources and real-world events as key determinants,[16] although it can certainly be argued that media ownership, the rule of law, and regime type shape the selection of issues in media and public agendas. Individuals and institutions in power build sociopolitical ideas that they can propagate through the press, and then the press imparts them as salient issues of interest to the public.[17]

In a widely cited agenda building study, Behr and Iyengar combined trend data from three national surveys with a content analysis of the *CBS Evening News* to determine the influence of the media on the audience agenda.[18] The data they assessed also included presidential speeches to the nation on a number of issues. Interestingly, they found an agenda building function where presidential speeches increased coverage of issues on *CBS Evening News*. But they also established that real-world conditions and events had minimal influence on television coverage of the same issues. This suggests a relationship in which the media interact with external forces, such as the president, to create their agenda and to influence the public agenda. Berkowitz also concluded that policy makers and other elite members of civil society dominate the agenda building process, especially on television newscasts. He found that television journalists, more than print journalists, relied heavily on routine news events such as press conferences and comments from the elite as their primary news sources.[19]

A strong argument about agenda building effects can be made regarding coverage of medical stories, since most health journalists are not trained in the health and medical field. In a survey of health reporters, Tanner found that journalists relied heavily on health sources in the community, particularly medical doctors, to select issues of importance.[20] She attributed this agenda building effect to the reporters' lack of formal training in health and medicine, coupled with the technical nature of health and medical topics. More than 60 percent of respondents agreed that health sources often affect the health content that airs on TV. This agenda building effect in health and medicine could be similar to a situation in ESA, where the majority of freelance journalists, who comprise 75 percent of all practicing journalists, lack formal training in covering politics economics, and public affairs.

In emerging democracies like those in ESA, one would expect government sources to influence both media content and the public political discourse, just as health sources often affect the health content that airs on TV. In most developing states in Africa, democracy is seen as an incentive for outgoing dictators because it allows them to manipulate the electorate and legitimately compete for political power. State actors can achieve this aim by building an agenda of legitimacy through socioeconomic incentives, and thus maximize their absolutist tendencies. Therefore, to many authoritarian leaders, democratic transition is not an end in itself but merely a means to build an agenda of absolutism that will maximize their ability to cling to political power. In a situation where many untrained journalists are still learning about the values of democratic rule, these agenda building efforts could be very effective. According to Weiler, ESA presidents and their lieutenants have sustained legitimacy and political power by taking advantage of a lack of understanding by citizens of their political rights to participatory democracy.[21]

The discussion in the next few pages of this chapter contains some simplified statistical analysis and technical information. If you are not technically minded, please proceed to the "Determinants of Issue Salience" section in this chapter, p. 182, for a summary and discussion of the results.

The following analysis of the agenda building and agenda setting framework was conducted with two assumptions: (1) the media do not perform their obligations with a clearly defined agenda regarding broad issues like democratization, and (2) the media are not equally accessible to everyone in all provinces within each ESA country. Prior to conducting this research, the assumption was that the African media's influence on public attitudes could be undermined by regional variations in political experiences with their respective central governments and that public opinion in ESA could be shaped by regional alignment, ethnicity, political identity, and other factors enumerated in earlier chapters.

Comparing the EAC with SADC

The survey data across all eight countries show that the media in the East African Community (EAC) statistically influence public attitudes when issues of regime legitimacy are raised. The media in the Southern African Development Community (SADC) also statistically influence public attitudes on issues of regime legitimacy. But there are interesting differences. When gender is taken into account, the outcome of public attitudes on issues of regime legitimacy for East Africans is significant within and across all five provinces of each country in the EAC. Interestingly, the outcome of public attitudes on issues of regime legitimacy is significant within and across all five provinces in South Africa and Zambia when social class and education are considered. There is no statistical difference in public attitudes on issues of regime legitimacy in SADC when gender differences are considered.

Education is not a significant predictor of agenda setting, within and across all EAC provinces, when issues of regime legitimacy are raised. Yet for the SADC, education is a statistically significant predictor of agenda setting within and across the five South African provinces that were examined in the survey, when issues of regime legitimacy are raised; but it is not significant within the five provinces of Zambia.

The news media did not influence citizens within and across provinces in the EAC on issues of the rule of law, but they did for SADC across all five provinces of Zambia and South Africa, although not within each province. One of the consistent public opinion findings in the analysis is that when education levels are higher across ESA provinces—regardless of the country—media influence tends to decrease.

Agenda building on matters of democratic rule in East African provinces is not the same across different education levels and gender. The same findings apply to South Africans and Zambians of different education levels and gender. EAC governments influenced public attitudes on matters of the rule of law in each province with increased influence across provinces when education is considered. However, this did not apply for social class. The increase in government influence on public attitudes towards the rule of law is even higher for the

Zambian and South African governments across provinces when social class and education are considered.

The influence of ESA governments on public attitudes concerning the rule of law at the individual level is not affected by gender differences, especially for Ethiopia, South Africa, Zambia, and Burundi (in that order) in terms of statistical significance. The EAC governments had no statistically significant influence on individuals within provinces and across provinces when issues of regime legitimacy are raised. The SADC governments also had no statistically significant influence on individuals within and across provinces, regarding issues of regime legitimacy. Even when gender differences were included in the hierarchical statistical calculations, there is no government influence on male or female attitudes toward the legitimacy of the regime.

In a nutshell, educated individuals in each province in the EAC are likely to reject the government stance on matters of the rule of law and regime legitimacy, but the majority of citizens who have less than a college education generally accepts that stance. SADC citizens are most likely to reject the government stance on matters of the rule of law and regime legitimacy, but more individuals in Zambia with less than a college education generally accept that stance than in South Africa. The following results are merely selected outcomes of public attitudes in ESA provinces.

Data collected on questions concerning regime legitimacy in EAC show diverse attitudes among respondents in each province of each country. In Uganda, for example, the majority of respondents from four provinces found the regime under President Yoweri Museveni to be illegitimate, while residents from the western province said it was legitimate. In Kenya, the majority from the southern and western provinces found the regime illegitimate, while those from the central and eastern provinces said the regime under President Mwai Kibaki was legitimate. Meanwhile, respondents from all five provinces in Tanzania supported their regime's legitimacy. In fact, 15 percent (n=465) of respondents from all provinces of Tanzania said the regime under President Jakaya Kikwete was legitimate.

To further explore the issue of regime legitimacy, respondents were also asked whether their president is a dictator. In Zambia, for instance, in the Copperbelt and Luapula provinces, about 72 percent of the respondents indicated that the president was above the law, and 63 percent reported that the president used excessive authority to dictate policies and pass laws. The numbers for the former were slightly lower in Kafue (44%), Livingstone (48%), and the southern provinces (48%). In these areas, respondents also provided similar responses to the question of whether the president used excessive authority to dictate policies and pass laws through the media.

When asked whether political coverage was impartial, more than three-quarters of respondents surveyed in Zambia responded in the affirmative. However, when respondents were asked which media type provides biased political news coverage, about 70 percent from all provinces identified state-owned news media as the culprit. In Rwanda, respondents from Butare (southern province) and Ruhengeri (northern) indicated that the president was a dictator. The data also show that three-quarters of respondents from Kibuye (western province) and Gitarama (west-central) in Rwanda said the president was authoritarian. In Kenya, most respondents from the northern, southern, and western provinces also saw Kibaki as a dictator, but none of the provinces in Tanzania saw Kikwete as a dictator.

As might be expected in countries that still hold on to archaic laws and authoritarian tendencies that are inimical to democratic rule, the majority of respondents across the EAC reported that there is less protection of human rights and justice than what is stipulated in their constitutions. On the question of whether the regimes violate some provisions of the constitution, 60 percent of the respondents from central, eastern, northern, and western provinces in Uganda agreed that the regime violates the constitution. In Ethiopia, in the northern province of Tigray, 92 percent of the respondents strongly disagreed that the Ethiopian regime violates the constitution. Note that the last four heads of state in Ethiopia have come from Tigray. Respondents were also asked whether all citizens have equal rights before the law. The mean aggregate of their responses shows that more respondents from Shewa and Wello provinces strongly disagreed that all citizens have equal rights before the law.

Agenda Setting Influence

Attention is restricted to three predictor variables at the individual or citizen level and the provincial level of the analysis, which tests the influence of the media on public attitudes towards democratic rule. The goal was to determine whether the provinces with more highly educated citizenry vary in their responses within and between provinces. Also of importance is whether the strength of association between the respondents' gender, social status, and levels of education predicts media influence on public attitudes towards the regime and the rule of law across provinces, and whether attitudes toward the rule of

Table 8.1. Agenda setting means and standard deviations for ESA

Variable Name	Individual Citizens (within each province)		All Citizens in a Province (across all provinces)	
	Mean	Std. Dev.	Mean	Std. Dev.
Regime Legitimacy	67.35	1.88	61.09	4.62
Political Patronage	67.29	11.20	73.93	4.96
Gender Identity	0.49	0.50	0.49	0.50
Education Levels	5.76	1.88	5.76	1.88
Social Status (class)	4.07	1.61	6.37	1.82
Rule of Law	42.86	8.02	64.15	4.68
Media Watchdog Role	4.64	0.94	4.47	2.26

Notes:
- Results simply indicate that the HLM read the agenda setting variables data correctly.
- Level 1 N = 3,339 individual citizens; Level 2 N = 40 provinces from eight countries.

law and regime legitimacy are strong predictors of media influence in some provinces and not in others when they interact with the citizens' levels of education.

Results show that there is variability in media influence within the forty provinces of the eight ESA countries. The estimated value of the variance, or the proportion of variance in media influence occurring between the forty ESA provinces, is .36. In statistical terms, it is known as the intraclass correlation (ICC). This simply means that 36 percent of the total variance in the public attitude scores on media influence is accounted for by between-province differences. The results in all of the models suggest that gender differences still have a significant effect on how the media influence public attitudes in all provinces of Ethiopia, Kenya, Tanzania, and Uganda. However, this is not true in all provinces of Burundi, Rwanda, South Africa, and Zambia. Unless regime legitimacy and social status are accounted for or interact in the model, the effect of gender differences does not vary significantly across provinces.

As for agenda setting, the probability values for these significant predictors in the model are as follows. The estimated media influence for attitude scores that estimate regime legitimacy, when accounting for gender differences, is significant at p = .001 for regime legitimacy and .013 for gender differences. As shown in Table 8.2, I cautiously interpret media influence on public attitudes towards the rule of law at a provincial level, since the influence predicted with aggregated mean-rule of law (between provinces) was not significant. What can be specifically estimated is that the news media in ESA have a significant influence on public attitudes regarding regime legitimacy from province to province. Individual ESA citizens who reported media influence within a province regarding regime legitimacy also collectively reported greater media influence across provinces.

Table 8.2. HLM models for intervening factors of media influence

Fixed Effects at **Level 1**			
Fixed Effect	**Coefficient**	**Std. Error**	**df**
β_{0j}, *Intcpt* γ_{00}	4.583	0.037	39
Social Status β_{01}, γ_{10}	4.701*	0.029	39
Gender β_{01}, γ_{10}	4.343*	0.021	39
Variance Components (with robust standard errors) at **Level 2**			
Random Effect	**Std. Dev.**	**Var. Comp.**	**df**
β_{0j},*Intcpt* γ_{00}	4.583	0.06*	39
Social Status β_{01}, γ_{10}	4.701	0.029	39
Gender β_{01}, γ_{10}	0.136	0.09*	39
Education β_{02}, γ_{20}	-0.023	0.19	39

Notes:
- HLM model: Means-as-Outcome Regression ($Y_{ij} = \gamma_{00} + \gamma_{01}W_j + u_{0j} + r_{ij}$).
- The asterisk (*) denotes a p< .001, for a two-tailed test.
- Level 1 estimates how much variance in the DV exists at the individual-level.
- Level 2 estimates variance at the EAC province-level (or ANOVA model).
- This analysis in Table 8.2 is for all eight ESA countries examined in this volume.
- These are primary survey data collected by the author in 2007 and 2008–2009.

Respondents were also asked to rate the performance of the news media during the democratization process, in addition to covering pertinent issues relating to the rule of law, human rights, and political accountability, among others. In the case of Uganda, as one example, almost 57 percent (n=481) of the respondents from the central and southern provinces indicated that the news media in general (both the state-owned and privately owned media) make elected officials accountable. However, in the eastern, western, and northern provinces, only 37 percent reported that the news media in general make elected officials accountable.

Table 8.3. HLM full model—Predictors of media influence in EAC

Fixed Effects at **Level 1**			
Fixed Effect	**Coefficient**	**Std. Error**	**df**
β_{0j}, Intcpt γ_{00}	4.106	0.157	14
Mean Rule, γ_{01}	0.034	0.036	13[a]
Regimes β_{01}, γ_{10}	0.012*	0.024	13[a]
Mean Reg β_{1}, γ_{11}	0.012	0.023	13[a]
Gender β_{02}, γ_{20}	0.121	0.059	14[a]

Variance Components (with robust standard errors) at **Level 2**				
Random Effect	**Std. Dev.**	**Var. Comp.**	**Chi-Sq.**	**df**
Intcpt-1, u_0	0.466	0.22	19.84	14[3]
Regimes, u_{01}	0.009	0.00	26.88	14[3]
Gender, u_{02}	0.120	0.02	19.13	14[3]
Intcpt-1, u_0	0.458	0.21	18.71	13[a]
Regimes, u_{01}	0.009*	0.00	27.20	13[a]
Gender, u_{02}	0.114	0.01	18.13	13[a]

Notes:

• Random-Coefficients Regression:

$$Y_{ij} = \gamma_{00} + \gamma_{10}(X_{ij} - \overline{X}_{.j}) + \mu_{0j} + \mu_{1j}(X_{ij} - \overline{X}_{.j}) + r_{ij}.$$

• The full mixed model, or the intercept- and slopes-as-outcome model, allows testing of the main effects and interactions within and between provinces.

• The asterisk (*) denotes a p< .001, for a two-tailed test.

- This analysis is only for Kenya, Tanzania, and Uganda.
- These are primary survey data collected by the author in 2007.

In southern, eastern, and northern Uganda, about 75 percent of the respondents indicated that political coverage is impartial; while over 80 percent from the central province consider political coverage to be impartial. However, when subjects were asked which media type provides biased political news coverage, more than 79 percent from all five Ugandan provinces indicated the state-owned news media. Furthermore, three-quarters of Ugandan respondents indicated that the privately owned news media cover politics and other national issues more responsibly. About 58 percent of the respondents across all provinces indicated that the state-owned media are not responsible.

In Kenya, the media's watchdog function on government received the highest approval from respondents across all regions in all three EAC partnerstates. On average, about 73 percent of the respondents from all five regions in Kenya indicated that the news media in general (both the state-owned and privately owned media) were a watchdog on government. However, respondents from the northern region of Kenya showed less agreement that the news media were a watchdog on government. In Kenya, a majority of the total number of respondents said that the news media, both private and state owned, were not trustworthy. In the central region, 56 percent did not trust the news media and a slim majority of respondents from the southern region did not trust the news media. However, more than 60 percent (n= 448) of all respondents from all Kenyan provinces found the news content truthful. Three-quarters of the respondents indicated that news content in the privately owned media was truthful. Respondents from the southern, eastern, and central regions of Kenya were skeptical about the truthfulness of news content in general.

Unlike Uganda, almost two-thirds of Tanzania's respondents from the central and southern regions indicated that the news media in general make elected officials accountable. In contrast, 52.8 percent of the respondents in the eastern region of Tanzania said the news media do *not* make elected officials accountable. In terms of exposing corruption and embezzlement of public funds, 71 percent of the respondents across all regions of Tanzania said the news media in general (privately owned and state-owned) perform that duty somewhat well, well, or very well. Furthermore, about 63 percent (n=465) indicated that the state-owned news media are not responsible when they cover national politics, and 77 percent across all regions indicated that the state-owned media do not equitably provide a forum for political debates. Figure 8.2 illustrates how often all respondents surveyed between 2007 and 2010 read, watched, or listened to news about Eastern Africa or Southern Africa in a typical week, and how many days in a typical week they followed news or current affairs about their country.

Agenda Building Influence

For the analysis on agenda building, the outcome here is a basic measure of government influence on public attitudes. It involves the summation of five interrelated items pertaining to governmental political persuasion or government authority. Attention is also restricted to two citizen-level variables that test the influence of the government on public attitudes, accounting for individual characteristics within and across provinces. Hierarchical linear modeling (HLM) results show that there is high variability in government influence within the EAC provinces and low variability in SADC provinces, particularly South Africa and Zambia. The mean and standard deviation for the intervening predictors are supplied in Table 8.3.

The analysis tested whether ESA provinces with more highly educated citizenry, or with citizens of higher social status, contribute to public opinion variations within and between provinces despite state authority and influence. Also of importance in this HLM analysis is whether the strength of association between the respondent's level of education, social status, or gender intervenes in their attitudes towards the regime and the rule of law across provinces. In other words, is being less educated or poor an important predictor of government influence over matters of the rule of law and regime legitimacy?

When the variance in the outcome is partitioned into its within- and between-province components, the proportion of variance in government influence between provinces was relatively higher than for media influence. The ICC in government influence occurring between the EAC provinces is .43 and the SADC proportion of variance for between provinces is .40. This means that more than 40 percent of the total variance in the public attitude scores on government influence was accounted for by province-to-province differences in ESA. This ICC indicates that throughout the ESA, finding influence based on regional alignment and sectarianism, or geopolitical effects, is more likely in government than it was in the media.

The next step was to model the between-province proportion of variance as a function of individual characteristics in provinces. The average variability for provinces about the mean, which is due to differences in the mean number of individuals' within-province scores on government influence (Y_{ij}), is .84.

Figure 8.2. Media exposure: News and current affairs in ESA

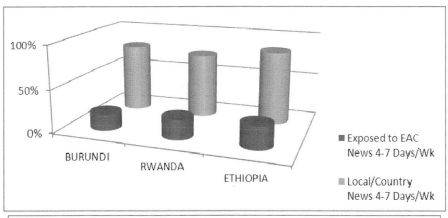

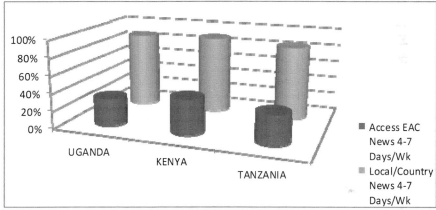

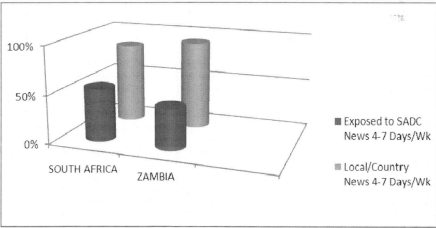

Table 8.4. Agenda building means and standard deviations in ESA

Variable Name	Individual Citizens (within each province)		All Citizens in a Province (across all provinces)	
	Mean	Std. Dev.	Mean	Std. Dev
Regime Legitimacy	69.38	9.13	4.18	1.41
Political Patronage	77.68	11.20	31.39	4.87
Gender Identity	0.49	0.50	0.49	0.50
Education Levels	5.76	1.88	5.76	1.88
Social Status (class)	4.07	1.61	6.37	1.82
Rule of Law	68.85	9.03	33.12	4.86
Media Watchdog Role	48.19	6.72	37.47	4.77

Notes:
- Results simply indicate that the HLM read the agenda building data correctly.
- Level 1 N = 3,339 individual citizens; Level 2 N = 40 provinces from eight countries.

The effect of both education level and social status was larger than gender differences as predictors of government influence on public attitudes toward regime legitimacy, rule of law, and overall democratic rule. In other words, the level of education and social status (economic class or political patronage) levels for individual citizens were statistically significant across ESA provinces at the P-value of .009, but not at the individual level. The conclusion is that there is no significant variation across individuals on the influence of government regarding attitudes towards the rule of law and regime legitimacy.

It explained only 21 percent of the variance at within-province levels. Gender was dropped as an intervening factor from further multilevel modeling because individual gender differences within provinces did not yield statistically significant government influence.

The rule of law had a significant association across provinces in Zambia and South Africa, but government influence on public attitudes towards regime legitimacy between the provinces of South Africa still had no significant association when social status was added to the equation.

Agenda setting is associated with differences in gender and education, while agenda building is associated with differences in social status and education, but not gender.

Table 8.5. HLM full model—Predictors of government influence in ESA

Fixed Effects at the Individual Level			
Fixed Effect	**Coefficient**	**Std. Error**	**df**
Social Status β_{01}, γ_{01}	0.487*	0.102	39
Education β_{01}, γ_{01}	-0.561	0.18	39
Gender β_{01}, γ_{10}	4.701	3.91	39
Rule of Law β_{01}, γ_{20}	0.033**	0.003	39
Regime Legit β_{01}, γ_{30}	0.069*	0.011	39
Variance Components (with robust standard errors) at Provinces			
Random Effect	**Std. Dev.**	**Var. Comp.**	**df**
Intcpt-1, U_0	2.31*	0.42	39
Rule of Law, U_{01}	0.054	0.00	39
Regime Legit, U_{02}	0.055	0.00	39
Democratic Rule, U_{03}	0.039*	0.01	39
Government Role, U_{04}	0.28	0.01	38

Notes:
- Full mixed model or the intercept- and slopes-as-outcome model allows testing the main effects and interactions within and between provinces.
- The asterisk (*) denotes a $P < .05$, (** $P < .001$). L-1, R = 0.86 Var. Component.
- This analysis is for all eight ESA countries examined in this volume.
- These are primary survey data collected by the author in 2007 and 2008–2009.

Overall, media performance on democratic rule in ESA is undercut by government influence on matters of the rule of law, but not regime legitimacy. The ICC and the full model outcomes reveal that EAC governments have a stronger influence on public attitudes towards democratic rule, and the propagation of their legitimacy, than the news media. On the other hand, SADC governments do not have as much influence as EAC governments, but it is still statistically significant.

Determinants of Issue Salience

Based on these findings, it appears that looking at the role of media only in shaping public opinion on issues of democratic rule may not be sufficient without considering government influence and the nature of geopolitical sectarianism. The results also show agenda building influence on matters concerning the rule of law and other indicators of democratic governance, even when accounting for individual characteristics such as levels of education and social status.

There are both positive and negative evaluations of media performance in Burundi, Ethiopia, Kenya, Rwanda, South Africa, Tanzania, Uganda, and Zambia. Most respondents in all eight ESA countries stated that coverage of politics is impartial. The results support the argument that media exposure to issues leads to attitude changes towards that issue and that when individuals are highly interested in national issues, they are more likely to be influenced by the media. The data also show that the news media exert a positive influence on public attitudes at the individual level, based on gender differences, with increased influence within provinces where citizens feel marginalized. Media influence on individual citizens increases significantly within the provinces when social status and gender differences are included and is markedly more significant where citizens decry authoritarianism and government mistrust (regime legitimacy). However, education is not a significant factor in media influence on citizens within the provinces.

Previous literature has showcased the role of media and democracy in ESA since the time when media have been in the forefront of political education, fostering public debate, and sensitizing society about the virtues of democracy.[22] So, it was unexpected that the media influence on individual citizens towards democratic rule would be based on the geopolitics within a province. One possible reason for such an outcome is that governments selectively insinuate geopolitical sentiments using regional radio stations and national television stations to seek public support and dissuade critics from launching successful campaigns against the regime. As previously articulated in Chapters One, Four, and Five, regional media are owned and controlled by individuals connected with the government or who purposefully seek state patronage for economic gain.

The type of media agenda created in each province has a facilitative role, as crusaders of democratic rule in their respective markets. In this case, the media had a significant influence on individuals within provinces when issues of regime legitimacy were raised. There is a dichotomy in ESA countries, however. The media in some marginalized and unstable provinces may report incidences of human rights abuse in their community, while the media in other provinces may support such abuses by reporting them as law enforcement, evenhandedness, security, and justice. In this case, both media agendas influence citizens in their provinces in significantly different ways. Arguably, the regional or community media are regarded as the voice of the nation and are used by state leaders to infuse their authority directly to the people. This is done in a way that influences listeners in rural or community areas to conceive of community media as a government mouthpiece. The national radio is most often used to sustain the political legitimacy of state leaders and to stabilize the broader polity.[23]

Results indicate that regarding issues of the rule of law, the news media do not influence citizens at the individual level within provinces in East Africa. The best explanation for this could be that in East Africa, the media are disempowered by archaic press laws and the lack of unconditional freedom of expression. Consequently, journalists and citizens are not free to express their opinions about the government through the media. As outlined in Chapters Four and Five, government bureaucrats across Eastern Africa do not fully safeguard and respect constitutional rules, the rights of citizens, and the news media. As a result, existing media laws throughout ESA are not seen as conducive for building the rule of law and advocating for good governance. For example, leaders use state-owned radio and TV stations to manipulate voters. They incite ethnic divisions, selectively labeling opponents as terrorists and opportunists, and in the process they dissuade critics of the regime from launching successful campaigns.

The significant influence of the media on public attitudes towards regime legitimacy was confirmed across all ESA provinces. As reported earlier, the relationship between the media and education was negative in some ESA countries, suggesting that when levels of education are higher across the provinces, media influence tends to decrease. The findings also suggest that there are gender differences moderating media influence (agenda setting) on the attitudes of citizens toward regime legitimacy, both at the individual level within a province and comparatively across all EAC provinces. This is also the case for social status. The news media in general have the greatest impact when they induce an audience to reject authoritarian rule. This is especially true in provinces where citizens do not trust government and where the majority of respondents agree to a statement that calls the president a dictator. Listening, reading, and watching news makes Eastern Africans in particular more likely to label their regime

Figure 8.3. Graphic summary of agenda building and agenda setting in ESA

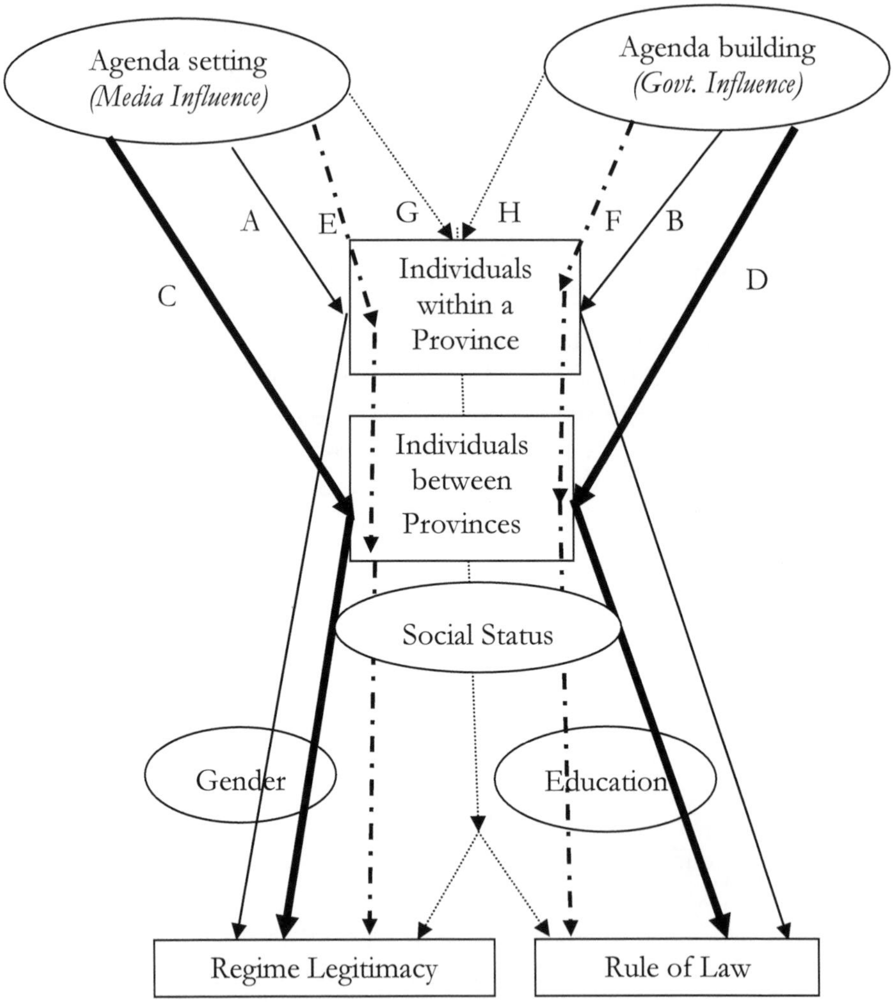

Notes:

- Abbreviations below refer to **AS** for media influence, **AB** for government influence.
- Arrow A (⟶): **AS** = regime legitimacy; increased by gender at the individual level.
- Arrow B (⟶): **AB** = rule of law; increased by education at the individual level.
- Arrow C (➡): **AS** = regime legitimacy; increased by gender at the regional level.
- Arrow D (➡): **AB** = rule of law; increased by education at the regional level.
- Arrow E (‑ •▶): **AS** = regime legitimacy; gender not a factor within/across provinces.
- Arrow F (‑ •▶): **AB** = rule of law; increased by education within/across provinces.
- Arrow G (·····▶): **AS** = rule of law; increased by social status within/across provinces.
- Arrow H (·····▶): **AB** = regime legitimacy; social status a factor across provinces.

illegitimate, although the effects of media influence are not particularly strong when education levels are higher.

The findings, as illustrated in Figure 8.3 as well as Table 8.4 and 8.5, add considerable weight to the hypotheses in previous chapters about the role of governments on issues of democratic rule in ESA. Governments do not exert positive influence on public attitudes at the individual level, based on gender differences. Very likely this is because the issues concerning the rule of law affect both women and men in the same way. Yet in contrast, education was a significant factor in the way governments influenced citizens within provinces. Most revealing for agenda building is that the influence on public attitudes towards democratic rule has a negative effect within each province when education levels are high.

Less educated individuals in each province were more likely to agree with the government stance on the rule of law and regime legitimacy, whether or not that province has a state-media presence. One possible reason for this relates to the current situation in which governments build an agenda of absolutism to maximize their political power by taking advantage of citizens who are less educated and lack an understanding of basic human and political rights. Provinces with a relatively high number of educated respondents are more attuned and politicized about the rule of law. Results support previous research which argues that EAC governments build legitimacy and maximize their absolutist tendencies from unsuspecting citizens by trumpeting socioeconomic successes, justice, and voting rights.[24]

It is important to recognize that some provinces across ESA are highly populated, industrialized, and economically developed, while others are densely populated with poor uneducated peasants. It is arguable that such a scenario creates some variations in government influence on many important issues of democratic rule, including regime legitimacy and the rule of law. The data in previous chapters support the conclusion that educated citizens know how to determine the legitimacy of a regime. They understand how to evaluate the manner in which state actors come to power—through free and fair elections—and that they should guarantee basic human and political rights with respect to the rule of law. It is conceivable that this also explains why education is *not* a strong predictor of government influence on public attitudes towards regime legitimacy within heavily populated, urbanized, and "civilized" provinces, yet it *is* an influential factor for the citizens' positive attitudes across provinces.

The alternate set of cross-level interactions involving the rule of law, social status, and education levels is what produces the positive attitudes for government influence across provinces.

One of the most striking aspects of these findings is that government actions on most matters of democratic rule were not tolerable to citizens within and across provinces, yet their leaders always found a way to win re-election by wide margins. State actors attempted to convince citizens that their regimes protect individuals against arbitrary governance, sectarianism, and each other. But the agenda of these state actors was ineffective in trying to influence citizen attitudes that their regimes exercise political accommodation for all geopolitical constituents. Ethnic cleansing in Burundi and Rwanda during the last four decades and the ethno-political genocide in 1994 come to mind here. In theory, when political leaders behave in a responsible manner by caring for economically marginalized groups regardless of their creed, ethnicity, or social status, and do not engage in geopolitical nepotism or favoritism, they sustain their political legitimacy and stabilize the broader polity.[25]

It appears that regimes in ESA are still struggling to build strong public attitudes that would show their government's mandate to protect their people from militaristic dictatorship and sectarian anarchy. Moreover, citizens have not come to terms with the efforts of current ESA governments to provide political and economic equality and justice for all, regardless of ethnic or gender identities, or to pacify their societies and provinces through established laws. In the next chapter I discuss the link between media coverage and economic development, a key component of successful democratization.

Chapter Nine

Media and the Political Economy of Development

Global awareness of Africa is driven by international media coverage, which often focuses on war, state collapse, famine, and disease. One of the main complaints from state actors and policy makers about Africa's international image is that the global media do not present the continent's promising economic indicators and progress to the rest of the world. Much of Africa has a favorable economic climate, indicators of consistent—albeit slow—growth, and sound economic and regulatory frameworks. The media can play a crucial role in disseminating such economic information, which can effectively guide international public opinion about Africa's potential.

The global media have already proven to be a powerful tool for mobilizing resources to Africa for humanitarian intervention and disaster management. A positive global response to Ethiopia's national drought and famine in the 1980s occurred, for example, after the international media showed images of a starving child feeding on her mother's corpse. National broadcasts and global media also covered the HIV/AIDS crisis in Botswana, Kenya, South Africa, and Uganda during the last two decades. These national emergencies were successfully brought under control partly because the world learned about them from media reports.

This chapter focuses on media performance in covering economic development, a necessary precursor to substantive democracy. Specifically, it discusses the link between media coverage and economic development, assesses the state of the economies in Eastern and Southern African (ESA) nations, suggests an approach to economic liberalization, and presents results from a study of economic coverage and key economic indicators in thirty Sub-Saharan African countries. The study examined content in South Africa's *Business Day* and economic data from the World Bank.

The study's results show that indicators of growth and good governance influenced *Business Day* coverage, while other salient indicators rarely appeared in print. Why is this important? Because press coverage of economic trends can help the image of ESA as its nations struggle to attract multilateral trade and international investment to expand job growth and help liberate people from poverty, creating a much-desired middle class. The middle class can then act to enforce good fiscal governance, in order to protect its newly acquired prosperity. Bigger markets and global investments can also strengthen the EAC and SADC regional economic communities and promote state accountability.

Why choose only the South African media here as a case study to examine how a major press covers development news on the continent? The answer is threefold. First, South Africa is Africa's largest economy and has the continent's biggest and most diverse media industry. Second, South Africa has enjoyed accelerated economic growth since 2000, slowed its population growth, and recorded an increase in household disposable income and living standards. These are all important indicators of good growth, which has enhanced South Africa's integration into the global economy. Third, the relatively stable political situation and increasing business and investor confidence have also resulted in a stable currency, higher direct foreign investment, and soaring portfolio investment into South African equities and debt instruments.[1] For these reasons, the South African press is better suited than others to champion comprehensive and consistent coverage of economic news on the African continent.

International press coverage of Africa's positive economic trends and good governance can contribute to its integration into the global economy as an attractive destination for multilateral trade and investment. The African press itself can do the same with new communication technologies, such as the Internet, modern cellular mobile phones, and other new media. Most African nations depend on direct foreign investment as well as multilateral donors to promote national economic growth and reduce poverty, improve health, and promote good governance.[2] In order to attract foreign investment and donor support, both the global and national mass media ought to equitably portray Africa's economic progress with respect to each country's democratic and economic reforms.

The Press and Economic News Coverage

An examination of press coverage of economic news suggests that the portrayal of the economic environment in third world regions by the international media is highly associated with ethnocentricity, and some of that coverage is not entirely accurate.[3] Studies indicate that coverage of economic news affects people's perceptions of their economies and the welfare of the featured societies. For instance, what the international media cover and choose to report about ESA nations may determine what the citizens of industrialized countries know about Eastern and Southern Africa. Africa is politically and socially perceived as having an extremely risky business environment and, as a result, tourism and the international flow of foreign capital are stalled by such views.[4] This negative perception of Africa is linked to the international media's coverage of socioeconomics and the human rights atmosphere.[5] In addition, ESA's slow trajectory from dictatorial and corrupt regimes to the present era of viable nation building also has had a negative effect.

While there is adequate news coverage of some African nations in the major local media and international news media, it is difficult to characterize that coverage as positive or thematically balanced. The emphasis is almost always on conflicts, wars, and other crises.[6] In the minds of those in ESA who depend on the mainstream media for information, the coverage of political instability and crises in some regional areas overshadows the good economic news about the pace of growth and good governance. The perennial and constant depiction of third world regions in international news as economically risky and politically unstable is detrimental for foreign investment opportunities, particularly in Sub-Saharan Africa, because it renders the continent an international investment risk. The images of poverty on international media, for example, reinforce misconceptions of that region's economic potential and contribute to its continued impoverishment. Demby argued:

> Stereotypes of subservient incompetence and rampant and unbridled corruption coupled with images of poverty and starvation all combine to reinforce the

subconscious perception that Africa is a place where business may only occur at great risk to the investor.[7]

Moreover, press coverage of the economy during bad economic times often distorts reality as journalists become more vigilant during coverage of an economic crisis.

When the press consistently covers the economy of a nation by focusing on one time events like a trade demonstration, a labor dispute and picket, inflation, and job losses, these spot news events may diminish any long-term positive growth and investment potential. For example, Fogarty found that the news media in the United States emphasizes the negative, reporting on trade deficits, unemployment, and business outsourcing.[8] He found that in deciding what is newsworthy, the American press do not consider all economic statistics equally and ignore key economic indicators. Fogarty's results suggest that the public's exposure to economic news coverage tends to highlight the negative, and fails to report and illustrate pure economic data. He concluded that economic reality and growth have little effect on the contemporary press coverage of these economic indicators.

The recent economic history of tropical Africa includes encouraging episodes regarding the prospects for long-term economic growth. Some ESA countries have seen remarkable economic growth without substantive liberal democracies. Democracy is neither a necessary condition for growth nor a generator of growth-creating reforms, according to Austin.[9] The Western press gave modest coverage to democratic transitions and positive economic reforms in various parts of tropical Africa throughout the 1990s.[10] International news coverage of democratic movements did not provide any context on Africa's economic growth or good governance. The lack of adequate information about Africa creates pessimism with respect to economic performance and its feasibility as an attractive investment zone.

The inaccurate portrayal of the economic situation in developing regions has a negative impact that reduces multilateral trade relations with developing nations. Whether negative media coverage of developing countries is deliberate or accidental, citizens in ESA cannot be expected to know how to deal with pervasive disinformation, especially information that provides a disturbing view of reality. The power of the Western media, with their agenda setting function on economic issues, strongly contributes to what people think about the welfare of developing nations.[11] None of the ESA countries are as substantively democratic as Canada or Australia, but their economic progress has been visible and steady in the 2000s. Of concern is how media coverage by the African business press and the international business press on economic issues like poverty reduction, controlling the rate of inflation, and per capita income affect developing nations in ESA and other Sub-Saharan African countries.

Economic Growth and Good Governance

The assumption presented here is that a country's economic policies and the ensuing press coverage of economic news can accelerate or cripple economic growth. Sound economic development is only possible once the engine of growth is supported by investment, capital accumulation, and industrialization.[12] One of the primary prerequisites for institutional growth and economic prosperity is a coherent and stable leadership, coupled with market-oriented economic policy and the rule of law.[13]

Research indicates that an increasing number of Sub-Saharan African nations demonstrate sound economic progress, signaling implementation of better economic policies and structural reforms.[14] But this significant progress is little known to the rest of the world and may be attributed to a lack of fair publicity on growth and good governance from the international press. Miguel argued that for the first time in a long while:

> There is genuine hope today that Africa is on the path to real economic and political progress and may finally catch up to the rest of the world economy. International trade is rising; better roads and new technologies like cell phones are improving millions of lives, and more countries than ever are turning to democracy. The economic boom and political opening I witnessed in Kenya shows what is possible.[15]

Research by the International Monetary Fund (IMF) in 2009 disclosed that Africa's GDP growth and per capita income reflect continued macro-stability based on prudent fiscal and monetary policy. These include cash-crop agriculture, minerals, and receipts from tourism, as well as improved political stability in thirty of the forty-six Sub-Saharan African countries. Seven of these countries are in ESA; Burundi is the only exception. The manufacturing sector still derails most of ESA's economic boom, except for South Africa. The other seven ESA countries rely heavily on natural resources, tourism, and some agricultural exports, which continue to expand and to drive ESA's economic growth.

Gross Domestic Product (GDP) and the inflation rate (IR) are key determinants of growth and good governance in fiscal policy. GDP and IR are the determinants of the GDP growth rate (GGR) for economies as prescribed by the Washington Consensus. The GGR economic indicator, which is one of the independent variables examined here, stipulates that the capitalist norms of private property, rule of law, and some degree of stability are necessary for GDP growth to occur. GDP growth rate reflects cash flow and is considered a more precise look at the rate of economic growth of the thirty African nations. This growth determinant is not distorted by the effects of extreme inflation or deflation since it is expressed in percentages and adjusted for inflation. Using such a market-oriented economic determinant, a nation can sustain household consumption and business investment.

The stable growth of an economy should generate new jobs consistent with the normal expansion of per capita GDP, in order to support consumer confidence and help sustain a moderate growth of domestic demand.[16] However, the IMF reported that some Sub-Saharan African nations continue to face major challenges in raising growth and reducing poverty, and competitively integrating into the global economy. When the incomes of the poor move up simultaneously with overall average incomes, it is an indication that growth is adequate.

Economic scholars like Ihrig and Moe examined the relationship between government policies, the labor force, and real GDP per capita. They assessed long-run growth regressions linking government policies, informal employment, and real GDP per employee. They found that changes in government taxation policies and tax enforcement significantly affected growth in the informal sector in thirty-two developed and developing countries.[17] Their goal was to quantify how changes in national tax policy affect the informal sector and how that affects the long-run growth rate of real GDP for each employee. The authors found that government policies caused an increase in the growth rate of real GDP per worker by 0.1 percent, which explains 6 percent of the growth rate.

The argument here is that the relationship between government policies and economic growth holds for both industrialized and developing countries, whether that nation is democratic or not. As for ESA, some economists view that argument with pessimism. They argued that the lack of autonomy for financial institutions coupled with autocracy undermines government policies and the overall political economy of growth. Thus the lack of civil liberties and autonomy of financial institutions makes it difficult to compare how government policies and economic growth hold for industrialized and ESA nations. Prosperity and democracy are measured by civil liberties, which require freedom of expression, rule of law, and protection of intellectual property rights. So, economic development cannot last if it does not move alongside pertinent fundamentals of democracy such as the ability to liberalize commerce and markets, and to maintain economic freedoms and private property. Barro's data from thirty-five African countries show that a few African countries still had below-target levels of democracy in the mid-1990s.[18] Prominent among them were Nigeria, Rwanda, Somalia, Sudan, and Swaziland. The strength of these cross-country studies, as pointed out by Barro, is that they provide the understanding required to assess government policies and other determinants of long-term economic growth.

In this era of global capitalism punctuated by stiff competition, third world nations in their quest for integration are facing universal corporate structures dominated by industrialized Western and some Asian countries. Economic growth and good governance are central to realizing this integration. The international reputation of a nation is dependent on its governance, and whether state actors promote anti-corruption policies, individualism, democracy, fair competition, and free trade.[19]

Africa's Economic Growth

Because close to 30 percent of the world's poor live in Sub-Saharan Africa, most African nations still have the slowest growth rates in the world. According to the World Bank's Africa Development Indicators (ADI), the average individual annual income in 2009 in Sub-Saharan Africa, including South Africa, was USD 461. This is the worst average individual income in the world. Yet in light of these challenges, most of ESA has made progress in crucial areas. The creation of a new African Union and the New Partnership for Africa's Development (NEPAD) has accelerated development on the subcontinent.[20] Sub-Saharan Africa's economy in general grew by 5.7 percent in 2006 and 5.8 percent in 2008. Domestic incomes in most of the subcontinent grew by a substantial 3.9 percent, and poverty slowly began to diminish.

According to Bio-Tchané, most of Sub-Saharan Africa adopted and implemented principles of good political economic and corporate governance.[21] The implementation of these principles contributed to the reduction of poverty levels in some African countries and accelerated human development by 3.2 percent from 2003 to 2006. African countries have benefited from high commodity prices and affordable Chinese imports; growing investment, especially in extractive industries; and development-aid packages for education and health.[22] The United Nations Development Program (UNDP) reported in 2006 and also in 2008 that there were considerable gains in the industrial and service sectors in most of Sub-Saharan Africa. Some agricultural sectors in ESA, such as Burundi and Ethiopia, exhibited a weaker performance between 2005 and 2008. Some African nations have applied the International Monetary Fund's (IMF) basic policy advice on privatization, deregulation, fiscal balance, and open trade in order to boost their international trade portfolio from agricultural products and attract direct foreign investment.

The World Bank's ADI determined that growth and good governance alone are not sufficient to reduce Africa's poverty levels substantially.[23] According to the World Bank report, Africa's share of world trade dropped from 3.5 percent to 1.5 percent between 1970 and the mid-1990s. Despite the progress noted here in some Sub-Saharan African countries, overall growth in ESA from 2000 to 2008 averaged about 3.9 percent instead of the 5 percent needed to significantly reduce poverty, and the 7 percent needed to achieve the

goal of halving poverty by 2015.[24] According to a UNDP report, the GDP and GGR in Sub-Saharan Africa were only 4.3 percent from 2003 to 2005, which was below the target rate of growth set by the Millennium Development Goals. This low growth is closely linked with the lack of multilateral international trade. More work needs to be done by the ESA governments to reform institutions and safeguard the autonomy of the private sector from state patronage and bureaucratic corruption.

Figure 9.1. Typical cash earning small-scale economic activities in ESA. Typical African markets. Many small traders in ESA's major cities and towns work as market vendors, merchandize hawkers, or operate small grocery and clothing boutiques. Photos by Yusuf Kalyango in Nairobi, Kenya, and Kampala, Uganda.

EAC Economies and Regional Integration

The existence of the EAC has contributed significantly to the strength of a common economic bloc through the East Africa Customs Union (EACU). One of the goals of the EACU is the creation of a common currency, which will be handled by the finance ministers of each member state, the East African Legislative Assembly, and the central bank governors. In their quest to help the EAC achieve monetary integration, the central banks are also faced with the challenge of promoting the convertibility of their currencies amid a low volume of cross-border trade and investment flows.

The 2004 regional summit revealed that in 2003, the EAC Common Market boasted a combined population of 95 million and a total GDP of more than USD 32 billion dollars. Economists argued that progress toward the harmonization of monetary and fiscal policy in the EAC was hampered by disparities in measuring and computing macroeconomic indicators such as inflation.[25] Governors of the central banks and the permanent secretaries of the ministries of finance examined indicators that would allow a more accurate comparison of economic development and fiscal discipline. Economic disparities make it difficult to compare and harmonize micro- and macroeconomic performance across partner states. The regional body must consider resolving the role of banking institutions, taxation policies, and financial sector reforms, and then focus on stabilizing the macroeconomic environment among the partner states. This must be embarked upon with a neo-liberal approach.

In order to convert the currencies of the partner states, economists have proposed that the EAC enhance wage and price flexibility, equitably strengthen the financial sectors of partner states, and harmonize monetary policy under a common monetary arrangement. All these factors have so far challenged the establishment of a single East African currency. Furthermore, economic disparities themselves impede the harmonization of micro- and macro-economic performance. For instance, by the end of 2007, Burundi was the poorest member state with a purchasing power of less than USD 500 per capita, while Rwanda's was USD 609.[26]Tanzania's was less than USD 780, compared to Kenya's USD 1,540 and Uganda's USD 1,820. Kenya has the largest economy in the region, although Uganda has experienced faster growth in the past twelve years. In 2007, Kenya's share of regional GDP declined from 33 percent to 30 percent, while Uganda's grew from 32 percent to 33 percent and Tanzania's declined from 27 percent to 26 percent. Rwanda's and Burundi's share remained at 15 percent.

Meanwhile, the broader economic environment remains backward and volatile. A ranking of business and cross-border trading in 2008 and early 2009 showed that Tanzania ranked 103rd out of 181 countries, Uganda placed 145th, Kenya was 148th, Rwanda ranked 168th, and Burundi ranked 170th.[27] The concern is that economic disparities in one state could trigger a move of labor forces toward the better economy of another and thus destabilize the region. The uncertainty of this economic integration is further increased by poor fiscal discipline, corruption, and embezzlement. Corruption in public office also stifles East Africa's struggle to eradicate poverty.[28]

According to Kalyango and Eckler, the more industrialized and economically viable a society is, the greater is the diversion of resources from investments and commercial markets to the masses through media advertisements. They added:

> Arguably, economic development is necessary in East Africa for a vibrant and independent media. Consequently, if the private media and civil society are successful in securing a fair share of revenues from competing business and commercial services, they could restrict dictatorships and demand resource accountability, so that

democratic institutions and a middle class are established and the regimes begin to act in the general societal interest.[29]

The data in Table 9.1 show variations in the scores of three countries. History accounts for some of the variability. Uganda emerged from a long period of civil conflict and numerous *coups d'état,* while Tanzania was a socialist state under Presidents Julius Nyerere and Ali Hassan Mwinyi. But during President Mwinyi's reign, Tanzania liberalized its economy and embraced capitalism. Kenya suffered a prolonged regime of monocracy and absolutism under Presidents Jomo Kenyatta and Daniel Toroitich arap Moi.

A 2007 World Bank study of the investment climate in 178 countries demonstrated that the broader economic environment in ESA remains backward and volatile. The rankings consider ten aspects as crucial for providing a transnational investment environment. These aspects dealt with the ease of starting a business, dealing with commercial licenses, employing workers, property registration, tax payment, getting credit, contracts enforcement, trading across borders, and investor protection.

Economic Liberalization and Democratization

It is important to note that barely twenty years ago, most of the subcontinent was under authoritarian military rule. So, authoritarian leadership did not significantly stall economic gains. However, the adoption of democratic principles by some Sub-Saharan African regimes did create an enabling environment for investment in infrastructure, new technology, and promotion of the private sector and small enterprises.[30] In the early 2000s, the GDP in fifteen countries grew at a consistent annual rate of over 6 percent for five consecutive years, supported by a substantial improvement in economic governance across Sub-Saharan Africa since the mid-1990s.[31]

Some African governments, with the support of the international community, have sustained good political, economic, and corporate governance and, thus, have reduced poverty. For instance, Rwanda has shown appreciable signs of economic recovery in the years since the 1994 genocide, after conducting two presidential and parliamentary general elections. Other countries on the subcontinent have also made tremendous turnarounds by implementing strong democratic measures, promoting political stability, and combating corruption by encouraging more transparent institutions. There could well be a connection between Sub-Saharan Africa's recent progress in both political accommodation and improved freedoms, and its steady economic growth. Most African countries today hold regular elections, and political leaders in Africa are significantly more likely to leave power voluntarily than to resort to military *coups d'état* or assassinations. However, decades of dictatorships, coupled with continued corrupt state bureaucrats and sustained authoritarian regimes, prolong economic stagnation and delay the creation of a middle class.

The issue of economic liberalization is part of a wider and more controversial debate over national prosperity and the way in which it can be achieved. The following discussion touches on the issues that comprise the economic liberalization debate.

There was an increase in economic liberalization in the late 1980s and 1990s. Economic liberalization can be defined as

> a reduction in the direct involvement of the state in economic activity (state enterprises); a reduction of state control of economic processes and activity (prices, production directives, etc.); giving leeway and encouragement to the private sector; and liberalizing foreign trade. The latter includes not only the reduction of trade barriers for imports, but also the halting of policies that favored import substitution over production for export.[32]

Market forces are more capable than the state in producing lasting economic growth, but there has also been a neo-liberal economic and political influence in the new paradigm.

Neo-liberalism is, according to Campbell, a "heterogeneous set of institutions consisting of various ideas, social and economic policies, and ways of organizing political and economic activity."[33] This includes formal institutions such as welfare-states, taxation, and business regulation programs. None of the ESA countries are welfare states, but they enforce heavy taxation and have a great influence on the private sector. The neo-liberal framework of economic liberalization that can lead to economic growth also calls for flexible labor markets, decentralized capital, and labor relations.[34] ESA labor relations, unlike those in South Africa, Tanzania, and Zambia, ought to have strong unions and collective bargaining.

The absence of barriers to international capital mobility is equally important for economic liberalization. Government economic policies in ESA ought to favor free market solutions to economic problems, rather than bargaining or indicative planning. Another element of economic liberalization that has

Table 9.1. Some socioeconomic indicators from the earliest tripartite EAC

INDICATORS	KENYA	TANZANIA	UGANDA
Literacy Rate	Male, 78.9 Female, 70.2	Male, 78.7 Female, 62.4	Male = 77.3 Female, 58.1
Life Expectancy at Birth *(in years)*	Male, 51 Female, 50	Male, 47 Female, 50	Male, 48 Female, 51
Population: Access to Water	Urban, 89 Rural, 46	Urban, 92 Rural, 62	Urban, 87 Rural, 53
Energy: Access to Electricity	Urban, 47.3 Rural, 4.3	Urban, 27.3 Rural, 1.1	Urban, 43.9 Rural, 2.4
Agriculture: Crop Produce *(in %)*	GDP, 23	GDP, 42	GDP, 29
EMPLOYMENT:			
• Self-Employed	Male, 49 Female, 38	Male, 53 Female, 38	Male, 69 Female, 57
• Wage & Salaried	Male, 33 Female, 18	Male, 29 Female, 12	Male, 27 Female, 16
• Agricultural Labor	Male, 59.8 Female, 50.3	Male, 80.2 Female, 84	Male, 60.1 Female, 77.3
• Youth Unemployment	Overall, 34	Overall, 40	Overall, 36

Notes:
- Data are drawn from the national Bureau of Statistics (or National Statistics System) of each country and from the national archives and population secretariat/bureau of each country in 2008.
- The scores are reported in percent (%), unless indicated otherwise.

consistently failed many ESA countries, and across Sub-Saharan Africa, is the ability to control inflation even at the expense of loaded employment in the civil service. Free market policies have not been enforced by the ministries of finance in most of the ESA countries.

Liberalization can be defined as follows: "Any policy action which reduces the restrictiveness of controls—either their complete removal, or the replacement of a more restrictive set of controls with a less restrictive one."[35] Economic liberalization should allow the input of new resources from foreign investment and domestic liquidity, and also allow private market initiatives that are unencumbered by state controls.[36] If ESA developing nations enacted such policies, they would help produce more wealth with long-term viability. The neo-liberal approach to economic progress allows countries to provide a basic socioeconomic infrastructure with media and judicial autonomy, all within a legal framework that safeguards private property and encourages the market to function unhindered.

As state accountability, freedom of the press, and governance with more credible and autonomous non-state institutions are introduced in ESA, perhaps the economic dividends of good growth and substantive democracy will be realized. Using this backdrop, an analysis of the relationship between economic news and economic indicators was performed. The study sought to answer the question: Do economic indicators really matter in press coverage of Africa's economic development?

The following analysis requires some knowledge of basic statistics. For readers who want to skip to analysis of the results, please go to the "*Business Day News Coverage of Africa*" section.

Assessing Economic News Coverage

The specific economic indicators analyzed were the growth of Gross Domestic Product (GDP-Growth), trends in the GDP growth rate (GGR), per capita GDP (PCG), and the inflation rate (IR). Political economic models were analyzed to explain any variations in economic news coverage. Two research questions were posed. What is the relationship between the GDP-Growth, GGR, PCG, IR and *Business Day*'s coverage of economic news? Which one of the four indicators of growth and good fiscal governance of the thirty countries in Sub-Saharan Africa influenced coverage in *Business Day*?

Economic survey data from the World Bank were compiled to determine the relationship between economic indicators of thirty Sub-Saharan African countries and economic news coverage by South Africa's *Business Day* newspaper. Data for the press coverage were generated from the LexisNexis Academic–*Business Day* index, representing the total number of news stories in which the newspaper focused coverage on an individual country. *Business Day* is one of South Africa's financial and economic news presses. It is a privately owned publication and one of the most widely read South African daily business newspapers. *Business Day* was chosen for this study based on its editorial interest and frequent inclusion of economic news, analysis, and business features beyond South Africa.

The focus was on business and economic stories, which *Business Day* published on each one of the thirty African nations examined between January 1, 2006, and December 31, 2008. Data from the newspaper were collected based on stories that featured the economic indicators examined (GDP-Growth, GGR, PCG, and IR), and all stories that covered social and economic development trends from each individual country. A total of 684 business or economic stories from all thirty countries published in *Business Day* during the study period were sampled.

Data for the economic indicators were generated from the World Bank Data Group compiled under the World Development Indicator (WDI), accessible to the public and updated every month. These databases are generated by World Bank economists for poverty assessments, research studies, and other economic and sector initiatives used in the preparation of each country's development assistance strategies. The WDI has compiled data for the last three decades and can be used by researchers and economists to trace and analyze trends in social and economic development for cross-country comparisons. These databases contain a series of data on economic indicators for all regions and nations in the world on a wide range of issues related to macroeconomics and growth, living standards of the rich and poor nations, and the finance of individual nations. The data used were collected by the World Bank research team. Table 9.2 shows a complete outline of the WDI data for each country.

Ordinary least squares (OLS) regression analysis was used to explain whether press coverage of economic news was related to the general trends of real economic data, as well as to determine which of the four economic indicators influenced press coverage.

First, descriptive statistics showed that *Business Day*'s economic news coverage of each of the thirty African countries was strongly correlated with the

Table 9.2. Africa's development indicator data, World Bank Data Group 2007/2008

Country	GDP	PCG	GGR	IR
Angola	23.17	21	11.7	43.8
Benin	3.338	12	5	2.8
Botswana	15.05	92	3.5	7
Burkina Faso	15.74	12	4.8	2.4
Burundi	4.001	6	3	8.5
Cameroon	30.17	19	4.9	1
Central African Republic	4.248	11	0.5	3.64
Dem. Rep. of Congo	42.74	7	7.5	14.01
Republic of Congo	2.324	8	3.7	1.8
Côte d'Ivoire	24.78	15	−1.0	1.4
Eritrea	4.154	9	2.5	10
Ethiopia	54.89	8	11.6	2.4
Gabon	7.966	59	1.9	1.5
Ghana	48.27	23	5.4	13
Guinea	19.5	21	1	18
Kenya	34.68	11	2.2	9
Lesotho	5.892	32	3.3	5.3
Liberia	2.903	9	21.8	15.01
Malawi	7.41	6	4	12
Mozambique	23.38	12	8.2	12.8
Namibia	14.76	73	4.8	4.2
Niger	9.716	9	3.5	3.03
Nigeria	125.7	10	6.2	16.5
Rwanda	10.43	13	0.9	7
Senegal	18.36	17	3.2	0.8
Sierra Leone	3.335	6	6	1.03
Tanzania	23.71	7	5.8	5.4
Uganda	39.39	15	5	3.5
Zambia	9.409	9	4.6	18.3
Zimbabwe	24.37	19	−8.2	133

Notes:

- GDP is the Gross Domestic Product calculated in billions of U.S. dollars.
- PCG is the Per Capita GDP calculated by the World Bank Data Group in hundreds.
- GGR is the GDP Growth Rate calculated by the World Bank Data Group in percentages.
- IR is the Rate of Inflation calculated by the World Bank Data Group in percentages.

GDP of each of those countries at R = .862. The correlations for the other independent variables (IVs) on *Business Day*'s economic news coverage were not significant.

The values from the OLS hierarchical model indicated that all four predictors, IR, GDP, GGR, and PCG, were strongly correlated with *Business Day*'s economic news coverage (R = .893). The relative impact of the thirty African countries' economic realities of growth and good governance was strong at R^2 = .798. In other words, 79 percentage of the variance in the *Business Day* coverage was explained from the four predictors of growth and good governance. The adjusted R^2 for this model was .765.

In the stepwise model, which is considered a good OLS linear model for such predictions, the results show GDP as the strongest predictor of news coverage, with an overall adjusted R^2 = .778 in this model. This shows that *Business Day* economic news coverage was significantly influenced by the GDP and IR of the thirty African countries.

Partial correlation helps to sort out or control the variance of other intervening factors, while studying the correlations of other variables. As shown in Table 9.3, overall, the results indicate that GDP and IR play a pivotal role in influencing the economic news that *Business Day* reports about the countries.

Business Day News Coverage of Africa

The purpose of this study was to determine whether press coverage of economic news in Sub-Saharan Africa was influenced by key economic indicators of growth and good governance. Economic issues such as poverty reduction, controlling the rate of inflation, and per capita income affect the subcontinent, and the central purpose was to determine if such issues predict the pattern of financial news coverage. Of particular interest was the relationship between the Gross Domestic Product (GDP), GDP growth rate (GGR), per capita GDP (PCG), inflation rate (IR) and *Business Day* coverage of economic news. Also examined was the extent to which the GGR, PCG, IR ,and GDP of thirty countries account for variance in *Business Day*'s economic news coverage. In brief, do Africa's economic indicators and steady economic growth really matter in the financial or business press coverage of economic news?

Table 9.3. Predictors of *Business Day* economic news coverage

Predictors	Coeff. & S.E.
Gross Domestic Product	.319 (.020) ***
Inflation Rate	.115* (.038)
GDP Growth Rate	.031 (.040)
Per Capita GDP	-.057 (.199)
N = 30	Adj. R^2 = .765

Notes:
- The asterisk (*) indicates a statistical significance at $p < .05$ and the asterisks *** denote significance at $p < .001$ alpha level.
- The figures in parentheses indicate Standard Errors.
- Dependent Variable (DV): *Business Day*'s coverage.

Regression analysis of the relationship between the real economic indicators and *Business Day* coverage found that GDP and IR of the thirty African countries strongly influenced economic news coverage. Thus, the data show that some key economic indicators of growth and good governance matter in *Business Day* coverage more than others. Results show that *Business Day* was more likely to cover political and economic issues pertaining to GDP and IR, than economic issues related to GGR and PCG. This supports the argument that the news media emphasize mostly provocative developments such as trade deficits, inflation, and high taxation, which are components of the GDP and IR variables.

Other fundamentals for growth and good governance such as the GGR and PCG, which are synonymous with poverty reduction and institutional development, were not reported as much in *Business Day*. The IMF reports that Africa's political economy reflects continued macro-stability based on prudent fiscal and monetary policy and improved political stability. However, this assumption is not supported by the coverage of the thirty countries by *Business Day*. The implication here is that if the major financial media have not featured the GDP growth rate and the sound macroeconomic policies on the continent, how can the international media be expected to do any better?

During the 1990s, the international press gave modest coverage to fiscal policy and economic governance and their roles in democratic transitions in Africa.[37] The findings here show that coverage of real economic indicators was also modest in *Business Day*, just as it was in the 1990s. Without considerable press coverage of the contribution of GGR and PCG to growth and good fiscal governance in Africa, the subcontinent might continue to be perceived as being extremely unsafe for foreign multilateral trade. Third world regions have benefited from the outsourcing of jobs from the United States to low-wage-paying countries, including even the volatile Afghanistan. Yet apparently, Sub-Saharan Africa, particularly ESA, has not been as successful at attracting such needed foreign investment in human capital.

In conclusion, modest press coverage of the fundamentals of growth and good governance may deny the continent a platform to attract foreign trade and investment. There is great concern that Africa will fail to meet the millennium development goals of halving poverty by 2015, a commitment agreed to by African leaders and the United Nations in 2011. Press coverage of Africa continues to at least partially paint a gloomy economic picture. To underscore what was argued earlier, the role of the international press in portraying Africa's growth and good governance has not prominently played out. The assessment of what specific issues were ignored by press coverage is beyond the scope of this book. Further investigation should look into these and other fundamental issues using a few countries, or a single case, across time.

It is important also to acknowledge that this is not an attempt to present and hype all thirty African countries as beacons of good governance in all aspects of political economic leadership. In fact, the UNDP and other institutions have documented that poverty still exists in almost half of the thirty African countries examined here and that a large number of citizens in those nations still live in absolute poverty. Small-scale political and ethnic conflicts are still raging in some provinces in half of these thirty African countries. In addition, according to the Human Poverty Index report of 2005, Sub-Saharan Africa has some of the most deprived and backward societies on the planet today. This analysis supports the notion that press coverage of the subcontinent still paints social and economic reality even worse than it is, ignoring some of Africa's positive political and economic growth and good governance.

Many of the past dictatorial regimes in ESA who wished to sustain their grip on power also tried to suppress economic liberalization because some of the dictators were convinced that economic liberalization pluralizes control and authority. Private enterprises must be provided with incentives and tangible state guarantees that there would be no influence and control from state agencies. Obviously, such policies in the ESA regimes would permit the private sector and other autonomous non-state institutions to accelerate national growth and foster development. An autonomous media would not cover stories that favor only governments in power because of fear of retaliation. Chapters Seven and Eight show that governments build their agenda through media because these media slant political and economic news coverage to appease the status quo. The South African media are not to a large extent biased and *Business Day* in particular cannot be regarded as a phony or unprofessional newspaper. *Business Day*'s scribes simply slant coverage towards their editorial policies. That is not biased journalism, because news slant is different than news bias. In the field of journalism and media studies, bias represents patterns of the intentional twisting of news using distorted facts that persist across time, message dimensions, and media outlets.

If the private sector, which includes the commercial privately owned media and a robust middle class, is to compete with political authority without slanting coverage for financial and political patronage, then economic liberalization and national economic development have to be considered as critical to that balance of power. Without such a regimen in each ESA country, accountable and responsible open governments would be unlikely. Regimes that do not enforce proper economic liberation have also crippled the autonomy of news media and press freedom. ESA regimes that do not guarantee the requirement of a substantive consolidated democracy, which includes the rule of law, regime legitimacy, conducive media policies, and economic liberalization, cannot also attract the international investments and the sustainable economic development that many ESA governments desire.

Here is the zero sum game that many of these regimes must come to terms with. The eight ESA governments are evidently in dire need of fast economic growth so that they can free their countries and economies from foreign aid and international loans, which have enslaved them almost more than their previous colonial masters. But to achieve economic development, these countries must be willing to support the private entrepreneurial initiatives of their citizens.

However, that would come at the price of encouraging their citizens to resist authoritarianism and to protest non-democratic policies.

Chapter Ten

Conclusion and Prospects

I embarked on this work about seven years ago (from 2003 to 2010) with the idea of exploring the complex and strenuous role that the African media have played over the last thirty years. I wanted to see how the media in Africa advocated for the rule of law, good governance, and other structures of democratization that inform and empower citizens, as well as help them make rational decisions about how they should be governed. My goal was to determine how the governments of Eastern and Southern Africa (ESA) pursue the basic structures of democratic rule during the second wave of democratization. ESA was a comfortable place for me to conduct scholarly research because I know the region quite well through my previous work as an international news correspondent. Throughout this period of social scientific inquiry, I learned that none of the ESA countries can fully democratize and the media cannot fully be autonomous without establishing a strong foundation in the basic elements of democracy. I hope that the preceding chapters show the efforts of that endeavor.

Preceding chapters explored how the news media in Burundi, Ethiopia, Kenya, Rwanda, Tanzania, South Africa, Uganda, and Zambia have shaped the political and socioeconomic agenda on issues of democratization. These countries vary in the way they safeguard and respect the rule of law based on constitutional governance. They also approach sectarianism differently; some openly induce ethno-politics while others prosecute opponents under the guise of preventing ethno-politics.

Attitudes towards Governance

Regardless of their levels of education, gender, or social status, Eastern and Southern Africans want their state institutions and their regimes to provide the necessary checks and balances of political power. The majority believes that democracy is a good thing but that even non-democratic governments are necessary. I conceptualized democratic rule in ESA based on principles of regime legitimacy and the rule of law, whereby a government accommodates free expression, allows political competition, respects human rights, and exercises transparency and accountability.

The majority of ESA citizens said that their regimes are somewhat, but not entirely, legitimate. To fully accept and embrace their governments and regimes, respondents stated that they support freedom of the press, and they want an independent judiciary and a functioning civil society where all citizens freely and effectively participate in their own governance.

Although citizens agreed that their regimes in ESA are somewhat legitimate, they also stated that they do not trust their governments. Government mistrust, especially in Eastern Africa, could be due to misuse of the judiciary by state leaders, as well as the misuse of presidential authority, which disrupts the political opposition and the privately owned independent media with unwarranted arrests. An American entertainment legend during the depression of the 1930s, Will Rogers once said that people can have plenty of confidence in their country, but the country might also be a little short of good men who deserve the people's confidence. His sentiment about governance in the United States in the 1920s and 1930s conveys public attitudes in ESA in this millennium.

In most of these countries except South Africa, citizens in some provinces are denied the right to freely protest. In focus groups conducted during 2008–2009, participants stated that they were frustrated with worsening economic situations, their lack of personal development, and poor public infrastructure. They lamented the lack of basic public services such as uninterrupted distribution of electricity, health care services, and quality education for their children and for their professional development. Public attitudes towards government in these areas were low across all countries, regardless of the availability of free universal education up to the university level.

The findings support the argument that African governments lose public trust and legitimacy when political leaders have not equitably provided economic opportunities to their citizens.[1] Unfortunately, as the ESA countries seek to build their economic infrastructure, they must first accomplish three things. First, they must enforce the rule of law that safeguards media freedoms, compulsory universal education, and judicial independence. Second, governments must restore peace and political order without state militarization by allowing political competition and a dynamic civil society. Third, they must reinforce economic liberalization with an accountable government and an incentivized private sector that can attract foreign investment. In his first trip to Africa as President of the United States of America, Barack Obama told Africans in Ghana that the economic growth and development of Africa depend on good governance. "That's the change that can unlock Africa's potential. And that is a responsibility that can only be met by Africans," President Obama told the Ghanaian Parliament in late 2009.

> Repression can take many forms, and too many nations, even those that have elections, are plagued by problems that condemn their people to poverty. No country is going to create wealth if its leaders exploit the economy to enrich themselves, or if police can be bought off by drug traffickers. No business wants to invest in a place where the government skims 20 percent off the top, or the head of the Port Authority is corrupt. No person wants to live in a society where the rule of law gives way to the rule of brutality and bribery. That is not democracy; it is tyranny, even if occasionally you sprinkle an election in there. And now is the time for that style of governance to end.[2]

The rule of law is another important issue for African democracy. Public attitudes toward the rule of law throughout ESA indicate that these regimes still exploit policies that clearly violate their constitutions. Popular support of equal rights for all citizens is high, and the majority of Eastern Africans in particular stated that citizens do not have equal rights before the law. A clear majority somewhat disagreed that the judiciary was independent from the regimes in ESA. Reports of government repression, torture, and detention without trial of civilians in Burundi, Ethiopia, Kenya, and Uganda during the previous and current regimes[3] may explain these public attitudes. Throughout ESA, the sentiments of respondents are best interpreted as an outcry regarding the terms and conditions surrounding the presidential appointment of compromised judges whose political views and interests align with those of the president. These findings are a strong signal that citizens assign their concerns to the undue and improper political pressure that their governments have exerted on the judiciary and used to convict the opposition on politically motivated charges.[4]

The people of northern, central, and eastern Uganda said President Museveni was a dictator. This is not a surprising finding because of the ongoing war in the north and the extrajudicial killings, which many people in that region say were perpetuated by Museveni's government and the military. The same regions also labeled the regime as authoritarian. Perhaps these results can be understood in the context of what occurred in the late 1980s to 1990s when the Ugandan army under Museveni's regime ethnically marginalized the Acholis and Langis in the north during the rebellion. In more than twenty years of Museveni's reign, the northern, eastern, central, and northeastern regions have been deprived of basic social services in education, health, and economics. A similar geopolitical sectarianism or favoritism can be assigned to other countries such as Ethiopia, Kenya, and Tanzania. Citizens from provinces that have produced the president and the majority of the ruling elites tended to give a positive nod to governance and regime legitimacy. Citizens from provinces of the presidents' ethnicity have greater positive attitudes towards the rule of law and the performance of state-owned media than do citizens from other provinces where the presidents do not enjoy ethnic support. This is true across all ESA countries.

I have come to mixed conclusions on the matter of public attitudes towards authoritarianism and presidential dictatorship in some ESA countries. For instance, Kenyans could not draw a clear distinction between those who considered the president a dictator and those who did not. Notably, Kenyans from the central and eastern regions said they do not consider the president a dictator, but they do not trust the government. Clearly, government bureaucrats in Kenya perform poorly, but the citizens in these two regions did not attribute the country's failures to the head of state. Most Tanzanians did not trust their government but the majority still believed the regime is legitimate. This means that Tanzanians did not associate governmental trust with regime legitimacy, even as the Chama Cha Mapinduzi (CCM) continues to dominate politics, stifle the opposition, and control all state institutions. Tanzanians also were torn between those who consider the regime authoritarian and those who do not. So were Burundians. It is likely that those who do not trust the government had the ruling parties in mind.

Take Tanzania as an example. For three decades, CCM has sustained its authoritative influence on the governing state institutions and encouraged political patronage to achieve legitimacy. Previous chapters presented specific instances when CCM bureaucrats committed extrajudicial killings and corruption in the 1990s, but were set free by state prosecutors. CCM also controlled provincial power and sustained the regime's grip on state power for over thirty years through "nation building." I place "nation building" in quotes because the CCM was quite successful at creating a multi-ethnic ruling elite and embraced inclusiveness in regional politics, characterized by the appointment of cabinet portfolios (national executive ministerial positions) and institutional sector representation to all major ethnic groups.

In order to consolidate political ties, state leaders in ESA reward their elite supporters from the same geopolitical ethnic regions to the detriment of other citizens.[5] This kind of nepotism, coupled with discrimination, has fractured the spirit of nationalism in many ESA states and in other African nations. Governments favor people from their own ethnic lineage and totally forget about serving all citizens without preferential treatment. This reminds me of a famous quotation about racial discrimination that I saw on a television documentary from U.S. civil rights leader the Reverend Martin Luther King Jr.: "We may have all come on different ships, but we are in the same boat now." Geopolitical sectarianism in ESA may explain some of the significant variations between provinces in public attitudes concerning regime legitimacy.

Attitudes towards Media

The public opinion data and the hierarchical linear modeling (HLM) analysis show that the media in ESA enhance public attitudes on issues of regime legitimacy, with increased effect when other individual characteristics are examined within and between provinces. That influence is a function of the media's agenda setting effect on public attitudes toward important issues. Chapters Four through Seven show that the state-owned media do not fully constrain the exercise of authoritarian power, nor do they object to unethical state action that controls and manipulates editorial independence.

The majority of EAC respondents from all regions indicated that the news media do not hold elected officials accountable, whereas respondents from SADC were evenly divided on the same issue. In Tanzania, a slim majority indicated that the media make elected officials accountable. In addition, most Tanzanians and South Africans trusted the news media, while Kenyans were evenly divided from a regional standpoint. A slim majority of Ugandans and Rwandese indicated that the news media are not trustworthy. This uncomplimentary pub-

lic opinion of media performance by ESA citizens reflects the prevailing political volatility and working conditions of journalists in ESA under authoritarianism and totalitarianism, which are enumerated in Chapter Seven.

The uncomplimentary opinions about media performance in both the EAC
and SADC countries can be attributed to the states' attempts to control and
suppress the independent press. Chapter Five discusses how regimes enact unfavorable media regulatory statutes and use law enforcement to intimidate journalists.[5] The state-owned media also deny opposition politicians a platform to
air their views.[6] The press becomes a purveyor of state propaganda, where the
state either owns the national media, or where private media owners enjoy state
patronage for tax relief benefits and other economic arrangements.

The survey and focus group data reveal that the majority of citizens in ESA
(except for Ethiopia and Rwanda) rated private media as more responsible than
state-owned and community media. The privately owned media had a more
responsible role to play in the realization of democratic rule, a collective ac-
knowledgement that was articulated in focus group discussions throughout
ESA. However, the extent of private media influence was not the same in provinces and in some countries, as established from the HLM analysis. On the
whole, focus group participants attributed these regional variations to two major reasons: The first is identity politics and the politics of sectarianism (otherwise known as "divide and rule politics"); and the second is the archaic laws
that are set up to limit press freedom. These press laws derail privately owned
independent media and community media in their advocacy for state accountability.

The majority of East Africans indicated that the news media expose corruption or embezzlement of public funds. In focus groups, citizens stated that the
news media have been truthful yet timid about exposing the abuses of dictatorial governance. The media are not impartial about the government and those
who oppose it. However, it is pretty clear from the focus group discourse that
truth in journalism has several interpretations, especially in the countries examined here. For instance, citizens may feel that the news media, when they
chronicle the activities of state actors, are a watchdog on government even
when they promote state propaganda. The media might also be viewed as truthful when they accurately report government business that reflects good checks
and balances. But an even more important truth may be when media investigate
and accurately expose wrongdoing and state excesses in the public interest and
well-being of society. However, some of the focus group participants, particu-

larly from the EAC, argued that even the privately owned media never report corruption in top government offices that are closely connected to the presidency and only investigate and expose junior politicians and mid-level civil servants. Thus, citizens rated the media as truthful in their coverage of news but partially prejudicial because of coverage that tends to favor state actors and friends of media proprietors and the government.

To resolve this quagmire, I propose that militarized states, or authoritarian governments, paradoxically receive more positive coverage of their tyrannical actions than their more liberal and democratic counterparts. Democratic governments get their proposed policies into government white papers or bills in the legislature, where they are openly debated and critically scrutinized by lawmakers and activists. Then, of course, the privately owned independent media descend upon the scene and aggressively publicize the controversy. I give credit where it is due, however. Some countries such as South Africa, Tanzania, and Zambia are moving quickly toward achieving sustainable, free, and fair electoral democracy, but some provinces throughout ESA are still faced with a myriad of impediments. These problems include geopolitical sectarianism, political distrust, regional economic inequality, disregard of the rule of law, and manipulation of the state media. The question of how the news media set the public agenda to facilitate political debate is imperative. Citizens rated the independent, privately owned media as more crucial than the state-owned media in mobilizing and politically energizing them to de-legitimize autocracy.

After examining the focus group findings, I agree that the independent media are more crucial to mobilizing and politically energizing citizens to de-legitimize autocracy than are the state-owned media. But that has not been the case in ESA, due to the fear of retribution from some of the dictatorial governments. For instance, the privately owned media, such as Kenya's *Daily Nation* and Uganda's *Daily Monitor*, exerted pressure on President Daniel Moi and President Yoweri Museveni in the 1990s to allow multiparty democracy, even when experiencing extreme hostility from those governments. It is my contention that state leaders try to tear down the adversarial role of the press when coverage is aimed at state institutions because such coverage gives citizens the information they need to make the right decisions in a democratic society. U.S. president Barack Obama told African lawmakers and civil society that:

> You have the power to hold your leaders accountable, and to build institutions that serve the people. You can serve in your communities, and harness your energy and education to create new wealth and build new connections to the world. You can con-

quer disease, and end conflicts, and make change from the bottom up. You can do that. Yes you can![7]

Although I use the U.S. president to contextualize my broader points, I fully recognize that the United States does not have a perfect model of democracy. In fact, it is far from being perfect. The 2000 U.S. presidential election, involving Republican governor George W. Bush and Democratic vice president Al Gore, is testament to its imperfection. That election was decided by the United States Supreme Court, which had a predominantly conservative (Republican) bench, and produced the conservative George W. Bush as the winner. The Florida vote recounts, and widespread allegations of ballot malpractices, were testimony to the problems with national elections not just in the United States but in many countries around the world.

Clearly, no system of democracy is perfect. However, some democratic systems are lesser evils than others. A renowned nineteenth-century publisher and political genius, Sir Ernest Benn, famously referred to the Western style of democracy as the art of looking for trouble and diagnosing it incorrectly with the wrong remedy. Whenever I follow U.S. politics, Ameringer's famous quotation about democracy comes to mind: "Politics is the gentle art of getting votes from the poor and campaign funds from the rich, by promising to protect each from the other."[8] A colleague (in academe) and friend who teaches international relations and comparative politics at the University of Southern California (USC), James Patrick, sent out an e-mail that contained this widely cited quotation from an unknown author about the U.S. system of democracy: "We no longer live in a society but live in an economy, where right and wrong is determined not by fairness, but by profitability; and where the law no longer dictates corporate behavior, but corporate behavior dictates the law."

In Eastern and Southern Africa, even basic procedural democracy can culminate in the worst of evil. Take, for example, the 2010 presidential elections in Rwanda. Three months before the elections, two newspapers were suspended, an international human rights expatriate was deported, two opposition political parties were banned from political contestation, and a total of five journalists were arrested. One of the deadly outcomes of Rwanda's 2010 election cycle was the assassination of journalist Jean-Leonard Rugambage at the gate of his home. Rugambage had earlier reported that the Rwandan government was allegedly involved in the botched assassination attempt in South Africa of the country's exiled former lieutenant general Kayumba Nyamwasa.

African Journalists and Media Performance

Do the media influence public attitudes (agenda setting) on the issue of regime legitimacy and matters of the rule of law? Does the government influence public attitudes (agenda building) towards democratic rule more than the news media? A succinct answer to both questions is yes and no. Some of my findings support earlier arguments that the coming of multiparty politics and the new wave of democratization, from the early 1990s to 2007, have not changed the way the news media perform. Governments still impact public opinion on several key elements of substantive liberal democracy; for example, how the public views the basic functions of government in safeguarding the rule of law. Governments succeed in maintaining public support because the majority of citizens are less educated and are not aware of the disintegration of civil order and the collapse of the rule of law.

The major challenge facing the future of the EAC and the SADC is that governments still have control of the state media and independent press. Many African journalists are also disempowered by their countries' weak economies and underdevelopment, which explain their poor remuneration and lack of professional training. Understandably, low-educated citizens and lack of well-trained and well-equipped local journalists create an electorate who are influenced by government and who are most likely to legitimize the regime. Astonishingly, almost three-quarters of citizens with less than a college diploma, and who endure authoritarian governments, agreed that their regimes are legitimate. The intentions of some selfish totalitarian politicians are to keep citizens uninformed and less educated about citizenship and their basic inalienable rights. Martin Luther King Jr. cynically declared that nothing in the entire world is more dangerous than sincere ignorance and conscientious stupidity.

Consequently, we see that many ESA governments have a stronger impact than the news media on public attitudes towards democratic rule. It is my belief that the impediments on media performance—to freely advocate and educate citizens about the gross violation of the rule of law in these countries and the fragility of political contestation—will continue to derail robust growth and tangible economic development. However, Africa is not totally at a loss, and the African media and some international media have done a commendable job of holding state leaders and their regimes accountable for their actions. Many journalists have languished in jail and hundreds of others have sacrificed their lives in the past two decades to prove that the pen can be mightier than the sword. Some of these selfless independent journalists remind me of an old wise

Figure 10.1. A majority of ESA journalists cover planned events like this one. I termed these types of stories "Microphone Journalism." Photo taken by Yusuf Kaly-ango in December 2010.

saying that "righteous social agents may be temporarily defeated by evil empires, but their will and resilience are always stronger and everlasting than those temporarily triumphant evil empires."

In most cases, local African journalists suffer the brutality of their governments. The weaker among them simply pursue brown envelope journalism, where stories are paid for by newsmakers who want to spin the agenda in their favor. These journalists avoid any confrontational investigative work in favor of public relations stories.

I cannot conclude this volume without paying my utmost respect to the many journalists and editors who have endured tyranny to expose corrupt governments and extrajudicial militarized states in Africa. Many of these professionals are African international journalists who work for the Western media but who dedicate their work to promoting change for good government, economic development, and democratization in Africa. Some of these extraordinary journalists include Joel Kibazo in London, U.K., Oius Njawe from Cameroon (rest in peace), Darwit Isaac from Eritrea (languishing in Eritrean military prison), Andrew Mwenda in Uganda, Charles Onnyango Obbo in

Kenya, Fahem Boukadous from Tunisia (languishing in Tunis prison), Wa Africa from South Africa, and many others. Regardless of the ruthless attacks on top investigative journalists, they keep fighting the good fight. The Ugandan Acholi people say, "The growing millet does not fear the sun." It is a euphemism that describes the mission of these courageous journalists. In fact, many African journalists would tell you that their pens and microphones are mightier than the army's bayonets.

I could fill another book with accolades for a handful of prominent African journalists who have made a mark for positive change. I will highlight one particular journalist who has excelled and lit the torch of professionalism for Africa's democratic renewal at the international level. His name is Dr. Shaka M. Ssali. He is passionately and simply called *Ndugu* (which means friend) Shaka. He has worked with the Voice of America in Washington, D.C., for almost twenty years. What makes him special among the exclusive club of Africa's top independent journalists?

Ssali has been a role model to society and for many African journalists who listen to both VOA radio and television. In retrospect, Ssali is living proof for aspiring African journalists who personify ambition, hope, hard work, dedication, and the commitment and the resilience to seek knowledge. He was enlisted in the Ugandan army as a cadet officer under President Idi Amin when he was only sixteen years old. He rose to the rank of lieutenant, but his ambition was to seek knowledge about world affairs. In the mid-1970s, he developed an interest in reading both local and international news magazines such as *Drum* and *Africa*. That is when his desire to become a journalist began. He left Amin's brutal dictatorial regime and sought political asylum in the United States in 1976. He pursued higher education at the State University of New York (SUNY) in Albany, where he began writing opinion columns in student magazines about African dictatorship. After college at SUNY, he worked briefly with *Newsday* newspaper in New York City. He quit and went back to school at the University of California in Los Angeles (UCLA). His hope was to work with a well-established international news organization such as *Time* magazine or the *BBC World Service*. In 1988, his hard work in school earned him a Ph.D. in cross-cultural relations at UCLA. Ssali has previously worked as deputy director of *Radio Unamir* in Rwanda, a regional editor for the New York State Public Broadcasting Co., in New York City, and a radio program editor for *Sautiza Africa* in Troy, New York.

Figure 10.2. Journalist Shaka Ssali covers Africa for the global audience. Dr. Shaka M. Ssali, managing editor and host of *Straight Talk Africa* on Voice of America. Photo taken in Washington, D.C., by Sally Ann Cruickshank, doctoral student at Ohio University.

He became managing editor of Eastern Africa at VOA, and a film and television producer for the editor of the Voice of America's *English-to-Africa* service. He is an analyst on VOA's *Africa Journal* program and serves as host and senior editor of *Straight Talk Africa*, a weekly live call-in international radio talk show. He has interviewed hundreds of political leaders, including more than twenty current and former African presidents. *Straight Talk Africa* has a loyal following across Africa and Europe, and it has been the number one current affairs television show in six ESA countries for six consecutive years. Some ordinary citizens have actually called in live on *Straight Talk Africa* and talked directly with their heads of state. Such media empowerment of citizens to participate in political discourse with state leaders is unprecedented on the African continent.

Ssali's work represents the epitome of global media's power to impact national decision making and the strategic international relations of African governments with the West through journalism and mass communication. Although his work in particular has not been empirically tested in African media research, several focus groups, discourse reveal that Shaka Ssali is one of a se- lect few "African" journalists with the ability to influence the policy agenda of some African nations, especially when he consistently reports on an issue as a priority. For instance, when pressed for further clarification, focus group par- ticipants in Rwanda, Tanzania, Uganda, and Zambia stated that Ssali's VOA reports and shows have prompted state reaction or intervention on corruption scandals, triggered government action to provide medical assistance, and forced politicians to change their authoritarian agenda. As I said earlier, further empiri- cal analysis of these qualitative findings is needed to ascertain their validity or robustness.

I should point out that such journalistic influence at the national level can predictably occur when the national policy agenda expressed by the government is either inconsistent or undecided. Then Ssali's work can impact a wavering national agenda. Equally important is the idea that for such effects on the na- tional policy agenda to occur, VOA's *Straight Talk Africa* or the aura of Shaka Ssali's influential reporting would have to provide consistently, strong passion- ate, and pointed critiques, with heavy coverage, sustained over several days. The question remains whether the influence of prominent African journalists like Ssali is made through direct media effects and exposure of state actors, thereby challenging them to act. Or is that influence an indirect effect, affected by other factors such as the international donor agencies applying pressure or national outrage from the public?

During an informal discussion with Ssali in 2010 at the VOA studios in Washington, D.C., he said that some political leaders across Africa now do whatever is possible to avoid appearing on his show. Unlike some renowned African journalists such as Darwit Isaac, Andrew Mwenda, Fahem Boukadous, and Wa Africa, whose great investigative work has landed them in trouble with their governments, Ssali and a handful of other international African journalists have kept hope alive for journalism in Africa. Ssali's journalistic accomplish- ments are an anecdotal but apparent example of the impact that the media and journalists can have on democratization and good governance in Africa.

Future of Mass Communication in ESA

African mass communication is on the move with developments in new media technology. Communications and delivery of content concerning politics and democracy, especially during election campaigns, have significantly changed how the media work in ESA. The reality now is that the institutionalized media's monopoly of mass communication is no longer tenable. Equally important is that institutionalized government's monopoly and control of media content are no longer tenable. The flow of messages has ceased to be horizontal and one-dimensional. The opportunities for ESA citizens to construct and share information through the Internet, social media outlets such as Facebook, and text messaging have posed new challenges to authoritarian governments and dictatorial leaders. Mobilizing citizens for political participation has become multidimensional and easily implemented[9] outside of the three traditional mediums of radio, television, and newspapers.

By the end of 2009, the use of cellular and mobile phones and the Internet had quadrupled in three years throughout ESA. My colleague Uche Onyebadi and I determined in our 2010 research that the penetration of new media technology, especially cellular phones, has quadrupled opportunities for the expression and exchange of political information among citizens of the East African region. According to the *World Factbook*, cell phone use was 490,000 users in Burundi; 2.2 million in Ethiopia; 16.6 million and 9.3 million, respectively, in Kenya and Uganda; and 14.7 million in Tanzania. South Africa has about 45 million cell phone users while Zambia had about 4.9 million cell phones in use. Internet access in Uganda was 2 million in 2007 and 400,000 in Tanzania in the same year. Kenya's figure for 2008 was 3 million. These data show a modest explosion in the availability and use of new media communication channels for mass mobilization and political discourse. Building political agendas or strategic communication in ESA is no longer confined to traditional mass communication that channels through state actors straight through media for consumption by the public. It is now a public dialogue between the elite, who use savvy social media and mobile and Internet technology, and the potential consumers of the multitudes of media channels.[10] Thus the one-to-many or candidate-to-electorate model of political communication is increasingly making way for the more interactive many-to-many system brought about by new communication technologies.[11]

While it is relatively easy for governments throughout ESA to muzzle traditional media outlets and independent investigative journalists, the introduction of new media outlets such as the Internet poses a threat to their control of the national agenda. In Kenya, for example, in the wake of the 2007 presidential elections, the government used extrajudicial means to ban or suspend live news broadcasts about the government and national politics, amidst allegations of election fraud by the incumbent president, Mwai Kibaki. Upon the suspension of the traditional media, citizens remobilized via mobile phone text messaging and the Kenyan blogosphere. The eruption of violence and the subsequent deaths, as well as the impact of new media actions, are documented in Chapters One through Five.

In 2011, the world witnessed the model of this revolutionary mass mobilization with the new communication technologies in North Africa and in some Middle Eastern countries. Citizens of Tunisia, Egypt, Libya, and Bahrain learned about the choice between democratization and autocracy from the new online media. It appears that as the new information technology avails "new" content to third world masses about the alternative types of governance, authoritarian regimes will not have many choices but to transform how they govern in order to participate in their country's futures. These new social media proxies enhance political participation to all citizens across the spectrum who reject totalitarianism and authoritarianism, and for the opposition who wish to uphold equality and force the regimes to play by democratic rule.

Those examples in North Africa and elsewhere show the power, influence, and prospects of mass communication in the third world and particularly in ESA for the next generation of media professionals and consumers. Onyebadi and I concluded in our research that new media platforms are quickly filling the void in a political environment where African governments have traditionally intervened to suppress information gathering and dissemination by the established media. Interestingly, an important segment of the population that did not have access to information through traditional media found such exposure via some of these new technologies. Table 10.1 illustrates this point.

What Next?

I hope that this work has enriched our understanding of public attitudes towards the African media, democratization, and other indicators of democratic rule in Eastern and Southern Africa. I previously argued that the watchdog role of the press in a substantive liberal democracy implies a duty to promote transparency, the rule of law, and good governance. The press should alert citizens about the misuse of power through sectarianism, authoritarianism, militarization of states, dictatorships, state patronage, and corruption. Many of the citizens surveyed and interviewed in focus groups somewhat agreed that the media fulfill some of these roles, which is a necessary condition for effective checks on democratic governance.

Table 10.1. New Media trends and the national political discourse in East Africa

	Kenya	Tanzania	Uganda
Trust political information in newspapers	5.97	4.08	4.93***
Trust political information on radio	4.74	5.19	5.87*
Trust political information on television	4.60	4.33	3.98*
Trust political information on Internet	6.13	6.28	6.40
Emergency phone texting messages necessary	6.88	6.91	6.93
Government should regulate information texting	1.13	1.31	1.07
Have texted a message to inform or alert others	6.89	6.91	6.76
Have phoned/texted talk-radio about politics	6.33	6.16	6.59
Have called/texted TV talk shows about politics	6.11	5.83	6.39*
Written letters to newspaper editors about politics	1.29	1.21	2.29 *
Used or would use the Internet to discuss politics	6.83	6.34	6.49
Internet/phone texting is good for democracy	7.0	5.01	6.31***
The government wire taps my mobile phone	5.78	3.39	5.21*
Government often suppresses politics discourse	6.01	5.11	6.22*

Notes:
- For mean differences between provinces: * = p < .05; *** = p < .001. Sample σ^2 explained = .64 across East Africa. Two-tailed tests of significance with robust SEs.
- The scores are based on a scale of 1 to 7 (1 = strongly disagree and 7 = strongly agree).
- These are primary survey data collected in the first wave in 2007 by the author.

The nuances of this watchdog role, as seen by the survey respondents from the media ownership perspective (privately owned or state-owned media), were not adequately assessed here. But they certainly warrant further research.

Democratization is an especially likely time for political elites to turn to ethnic sectarianism using geopolitical rhetoric. Control and influence over media are the main ways that elites are able to manipulate and persuade the people.[12] Such elites aim to make ethnicity the only politically relevant identity— especially if any other identities might threaten them. State actors in ESA also construct propaganda as a national agenda that is primarily defined by the best interests of the provinces or constituents that they claim to represent. People in these provinces may then be persuaded to take actions that would otherwise be completely against their best interests.

Some independent journalists have played their role despite a series of barriers and decrees imposed by governments to limit media influence. I found that the media are still relevant and central to providing electoral masses with a forum for public debate, notwithstanding the constraints of government influence and control of the press. However, these positive developments can still be destroyed by authoritarian reversals related to political influence and meddling that hinder free expression, free speech, and political participation. A fully unfettered press can emerge if it can be supported with adequate training of journalists, a continued commitment to universal formal education for all citizens, and respect for the rule of law.

Despite the constraints outlined here, there is a good indication that a fairly critical independent media, with the support of the civil society, have played a central role in mobilizing the masses to recognize bad regimes and expose authoritarianism in ESA and also in other parts of Africa. Despite the persistent draconian measures against media in Africa, independent journalists continue to push for regime legitimacy in order to change the political landscape of presidential monocracy and absolutism. This assessment of the ongoing challenges of democratization indicates that agenda building is central to the political control of messages and attitudes towards the rule of law and has helped some leaders like Meles Zenawi of Ethiopia, Yoweri Museveni of Uganda, Paul Kagame of Rwanda, and Mwai Kibaki of Kenya to sustain their imperial grip on state power. It is still unknown whether the current problems with governance are temporary conditions on the way to greater freedom and peace throughout ESA.

Although my work generally paints a gloomy picture on the question of governance and examines some positive developments of media performance and democratic rule in ESA, the next phase of research should consider how new media technologies and media use may change the political landscape. It is still unknown whether current problems with the performance of the news media, and in democratic rule, are temporary conditions but within reach to a permanent fixture for greater prosperity for all the people of ESA.

May the people of Eastern and Southern Africa achieve and prevail in whatever they wish for: peace, prosperity, opportunity, substantive democracy, and in particular, unfettered responsible media and the rule of law.

Appendix

Conducting Research in Africa

As a Western scholar, conducting research in Eastern and Southern Africa (ESA) is a major challenge with a lot of frustrations, delays, and setbacks. Examining the link between media and Africa's state governance on specific issues of democratization is a daunting task in countries where the governments and regimes are still semi-authoritarian. Also, there is a scarcity of national trend data on democracy. I will address theses challenges in more detail in the last section of this appendix.

For this project, I conducted cross-sectional surveys of citizens in Burundi, Ethiopia, Kenya, Rwanda, South Africa, Tanzania, Uganda, and Zambia in ESA from June 2 to July 27, 2007, and December 4, 2008, to January 14, 2009. The goal was to survey 500 citizens of voting age from each country. A "citizen" was defined as an individual over 18 years of age who resides in one of the ESA countries. A total of 3,339 questionnaires were returned out of the 4,000 surveys that were randomly handed out in eight countries. A total of 216 respondents from Burundi, 467 from Ethiopia, 448 from Kenya, 403 from Rwanda, 465 from Tanzania, 409 from South Africa, 482 from Uganda, and 449 respondents from Zambia completed the surveys. Public opinion and attitudes were sought on issues ranging from media use, exposure, ownership, and performance to the rule of law, governance, the presidency, presidentialism, conflicts, sectarianism, and many other variables.

I collected cross-sectional survey data that are hierarchical in nature so that I could have citizens nested within their provinces. For the hierarchical linear modeling (HLM) analysis, the data were not all weighted or centered on provinces. These citizens were nested in only five provinces in each country because of how the data were clustered in stages. Citizens were randomly selected using a stratified random sampling and, where required, a multistage cluster sampling technique.

Survey Overview

I used a stratified multistage cluster random sampling for these surveys. The purpose of a stratified multistage cluster random sampling is to get comparison groups of equal size and demographics from each country, despite some variations in the population parameters. To avoid unreliability in the data due to unequal probabilities of selection, respondents were stratified on a "citizen" variable instead of on ethnicity or regional variables. For instance, the national census population estimates of the year 2000 in Uganda, as well as in Kenya and Zambia, indicated extreme variance in population. This unevenness is due to the geography of provinces or the multitudes of ethnic groups in ESA countries. The stratified random sampling ensured that the sample of 500 citizens from each ESA country was proportionately categorized for comparative purposes.

Since the ESA countries are heterogeneous, an equitable sample of respondents that represents the opinions, attitudes, and demographics of citizens in each ESA country was taken. For instance, there are more than twenty different ethnic tribes and dozens of languages in each ESA country. In these diverse societies, a stratified random sampling achieved a better representation with a reasonable sample size than would a simple random sampling.

The following stratification was followed in order to give every citizen an equal chance of participating:

- 50 unemployed workers were randomly selected from available records from the departments or bureaus of labor.
- 50 students were randomly selected from major universities or other tertiary two-year diploma institutions of ESA countries. For example, in Uganda respondents were selected from a random sample of students from Mbarara University, Makerere University, the International University in Kampala, Islamic University in Mbale, and Nkumba University. Similarly in

Kenya, the respondents were randomly selected from Kenyatta University, Nairobi University, Egerton University, Moi University, and the United States International University (USIU) in Nairobi. In Tanzania, for example, respondents were drawn from a random sample at the University of Dar es Salaam, The Open University, St. Augustine University, Mount Meru University, and Sokoine University of Agriculture. Similar academic institutions were used across all eight ESA nations.

- 50 civil servants were randomly selected from available lists of names and mobile phone contacts provided by the ministries or departments of public service.
- 50 members of the business community were randomly selected from available membership lists of the national chambers of commerce and industries.
- 50 housewives were selected from the central provinces or the capital seat within each ESA country because the majority of female spouses do not work. They are referred to as housewives.
- 150 citizens representing farmers and peasants from other districts and counties of each ESA country were also selected. The subsample for the farmers and peasants was larger because these particular groups make up more than 60 percent of the population.
- 50 professionals, such as teachers, nurses, and lawyers, were randomly selected from a list provided by the ministries of education.
- 50 entertainers, including artists and sports personnel, were also randomly selected from a list provided by the departments of youth, culture, and sports.

Out of each pool of respondents, I attempted to sample gender equally at 50 percent, but age was not considered a critical weighting factor during the data collection stage. Within each list of population record, citizen records were drawn until a stratified distribution was generated for each category in each ESA country.

In situations where there were no official records of residents, such as the Ugandan and Kenyan farmers in some remote counties, a multistage cluster sampling method was used. The first stage was to randomly select a cluster of small villages from a list provided by district officers. From that list of small village towns that are located within the district, a second cluster of homes was then randomly selected. Finally, a respondent was randomly picked in a household. With both the stratified sampling and the multistage cluster sampling technique, an approximate representation of adult citizens of the population was assured.

ESA societies are permeated with political mistrust and concerns over government spies and infiltrators, and there were several challenges to overcome in order to get a fair representation of the national population. I recruited a total of sixty-seven field research assistants from all eight ESA countries to administer these surveys. ESA citizens in particular are usually less than willing to participate in academic projects like this one due to personal security reasons, especially if questions concern national leaders and regime legitimacy. For instance, during data collection some of the participants demanded more assurance of anonymity and required to know how their responses would bring a loaf of bread and medicine to their households. Survey respondents were not given incentives to fill out the questionnaire. See a list of field survey coordinators from each country by visiting the author's website, www.kalyango.com.

Field survey coordinators from each ESA country were recruited from post-graduate schools at colleges and universities. A few field survey coordinators, who collected data from persons located in provinces and areas outside urban centers, were recommended by researchers who work with organizations, such as the African Medical and Research Foundation (AMREF), the Bureaus of Statistics, and the African Population and Health Research Center (APHRC). Some organizations, like the Zambia Association for Research and Development (ZARD) and the Centre for Basic Research (CBR) in Uganda, provided assistants. All field survey coordinators had to be fluent in both English and at least one local language. They had to demonstrate communication skills that would elicit voluntary cooperation from respondents.

Instrumentation and Measurement

The field coordinators gave the survey instrument to respondents in hard copy (paper format). In Kenya and Tanzania, most respondents preferred to fill out an English version of the survey, although translated versions in Kiswahili and other major languages in East Africa were at hand. A translated copy in Kiswahili was not used at all in Burundi, Rwanda, and Uganda. Two primary reasons compelled me to conduct an in-person survey instead of using other data collection methods. First, more than 80 percent of the population throughout ESA has no access to either a conventional land telephone line or a cellular phone. Therefore, a valid telephone survey was impossible. Second, an estimated 60 percent of residences or citizens in ESA do not have access to a physical-address infrastructure where a self-administered mail survey could be sent. Those two common data collection methods for surveys can cause validity problems and social class biases in third world regions like the East African Community (EAC) or the Southern African Development Community (SADC).

Although the survey instrument was piloted on ESA citizens residing in both the United States and in some of the ESA countries before it was approved, there were a few occasions when the field survey coordinators had to spend about ten minutes explaining the purpose of the exercise to some individual respondents. The survey instrument was piloted on a total of twenty-nine individuals from four of the countries examined here and on another nine individuals who went to Ohio University in Athens, Ohio, and to the University of Missouri in Columbia, Missouri. In spite of the detailed instructions and explanation, about 43 out of 3,339 questionnaires were filled out incorrectly, as some participants marked more than one option on the seven-point scale of a few questions. In a few cases whenever possible, field survey coordinators handed respondents another questionnaire as soon as they spotted this.

It certainly helped to know about the literacy levels, cultural norms, and ethno-political tensions of each province prior to the fieldwork. Field survey coordinators were matched with a province of their ethnicity or residence. In this way, their presence created trust and brought comfort to respondents in order to minimize sensitivity, inaccuracy, and biased responses. I knew from my experience and political knowledge of the provinces that if I had not matched field survey coordinators to a "friendly" stratum, the response rate would have been lower and the feedback would have been biased or inaccurate. The data would have been distorted by respondents in order to cautiously please the "alien" field survey coordinators. Matching field survey coordinators to particular strata considering gender, ethnic language, religion, and appropriate caste minimized the respondents' perceived fears of a political trap from their governments that would have impacted the validity of the data.

To manage the survey, the assistants and I separately visited the locations or residences of each selected respondent. The assistants also managed the survey in most upcountry areas where respondents were randomly selected. I doubled as a supervisor of the self-administered exercise. Respondents who had no time to fill out the questionnaire were given three days to complete it. Research assistants picked up questionnaires from those respondents on the fourth day.

Whenever questionnaires were not yet completed, respondents were asked to complete and mail them to a hotel where I was staying or to the addresses of my principal survey coordinators.

All the countries had one survey instrument that contained a set of identical questions applicable to the ESA, thus making countries comparable. The first items were concerned with media exposure, measuring behavioral patterns (media use) of respondents on a particular medium during a one-week period, and about a specific country. Some items utilized perceptual measurements of news coverage to assess how citizens in ESA rate news coverage on salient issues related to governance and the rule of law. The third batch of items utilized attitude measurements on media performance, democratic rule, and regime legitimacy. They measured the citizens' degree of strong agreement or strong disagreement on matters of trust, interest, influence, thoughts, and effectiveness.

The field survey coordinators asked each respondent to select only one choice that best rated or indicated their opinion about the following issues: the performance of the media, the coverage of news, the privately owned and state-owned media, the regime and the rule of law, and their ideas or beliefs about democratic rule. Respondents also provided their opinions on statements regarding the role of state institutions and their experiences with public services. In a scale that measured "attitudes toward the regime and other state institutions in each ESA country," respondents were asked to check the response that best corresponded with their opinion, using point values assigned for items as follows: strongly disagree = 1, neutral = 4, and strongly agree = 7. All items were coded such that a more positive attitude toward the regime received the higher response value.

The survey had ten items that measured how citizens rated news media performance under the prevailing laws and political dispensation. The items were scored using the following seven point scale: very poorly = 1, somewhat poorly = 3, neutral = 4, somewhat well = 5, and very well = 7.[1] A maximum score of 7 indicated a position that would imply approval of something well done, and that when performance was generally unacceptable based on their personal judgments or expectations, it was indicated with a minimum score of 1.[2] For the twenty items measuring attitudes towards the news and the media, respondents were asked to select only point value assigned as follows: strongly disagree = 1, neutral = 4, and strongly agree = 7. All items were coded such that a more positive attitude towards the news and media received the higher response value.

To prepare data for the HLM analysis, all items were coded such that a more positive (accepting) attitude towards the outcome variable received the higher response value. The scale was scored by summing the point values of the responses and dividing by the total number of responses. Lower mean scores, which ranged from 1 to 4, indicated a strong agreement or higher level of approval for media performance. Higher mean scores indicated a better rating for media performance in the coverage of the citizens' issue concerns.[3] However, the scores do not provide answers to the agenda setting and agenda building influence on the media. Those scores were set up in the Statistical Package for the Social Sciences (SPSS) and downloaded in HLM6 for an advanced estimation of media influence (agenda setting) and government influence (agenda building) on public attitudes, at both the individual level and nested within the geopolitical (regional) context.

Nested Analysis Using HLM

In a study of this nature, comparisons between the regime types of the partner states must be interpreted cautiously because there is no control over the choice of who resides in what province or their ethnicity. The survey data consist of citizens of voting age who are nested within the provinces of ESA. To better analyze the data structures that are nested within each ESA country requires going beyond the conventional multivariate techniques, which treat a country or even the community as one unit of analysis. Such simple regression techniques ignore the variation between-citizens within each province of a country and at the same time treat the ESA countries as unique units of analysis by ignoring a between-geopolitical regional component. I employed a statistical technique called hierarchical linear modeling (HLM). HLM properly reflects the structure of the ESA dataset with citizens grouped by provinces in the partner states. HLM is a class of techniques that has a nested structure.[4]

Multilevel, hierarchical, nested, and *clustered* are terms used interchangeably in social science research, but they all essentially mean and do the same thing in the general linear models (GLM).[5] All those terms refer to a type of statistical procedure that belongs to the family of GLM, which are used to analyze data baring some inherent group membership or cluster.[6] A typical example given most often by researchers is a dataset that consists of students within schools, or patients within hospitals. Since the present study uses comparative data, the hierarchical nature permits testing of cross-level interactions between the contexts in which the news media perform under the current political culture, as well as the individual characteristics.[7]

This method estimates how differentiation in attitudes towards the regime, democratic rule, and individual characteristics vary across forty provinces that shape geopolitical alignment in the ESA provinces. The dataset includes citizen characteristics because of the existing assumption that they are open to the influence of regional politics. Regional composition can bias estimates, if they are included in statistical adjustments for citizen background. I refer here to (a) the ethnicity or political identity of citizens, (b) the gender imbalance in political discourse, and (c) and the prevalence of low income and educationally disadvantaged citizens. By *statistical significance*, I simply refer to the reported outcome being due to some systematic analysis of a relationship, or influence, or difference between the groups, and that the influence was not due to chance.

Nested Analysis Research Design

This study used the HLM6 program software and SPSS, which handle the multilevel modeling data structure. The HLM application consisted of two sets of linear regression equations that incorporate predictor variables at each level. The output of the level 1 regression estimated how much of the variation in attitudes towards media exposure between citizens, and within provinces, can be accounted for by differences in individual characteristics. This lower (first) level decomposed the total variance into between-individuals on a media exposure outcome. In using the nested framework, the idea was to depart from a conventional Ordinary least squares (OLS) regression approach to a two-level model. Using multilevel modeling (or HLM) allowed individual-level predictors of news media exposure to be separated from differences in the context and characteristics of citizens based on their geopolitical identity.

It meant that differences stemming either from individual attitudes towards the news media or from attitudes towards the regime could be altered by the random effects arising from social economic status and democratic rule across all provinces. Furthermore, considering that the news media is both privately owned and state owned, an additional measure of media type was useful. In reference to both types of media, respondents were asked attitude questions concerning their trust and their interest in these media, as well as the accountability and independence of the media. These measures constructed an index that afforded an indicator of media type usage. Likewise, for basic demographic comparisons, dummy indicators of gender and education levels were analyzed and included as predictors in the multilevel estimation models. Their relevant interactions were also explored. To achieve this, the assessment was whether the various predictors tested in the first-level individual model demonstrated significance when nested in a two-level (ESA provinces) hierarchical model. HLM helped to retain variable information that could have been easily lost with a simple multivariate technique. Although most regression studies would stop at reporting findings at the OLS equation ($Y_i = \beta_0 + \beta_1 X_1 + r_i$), the scores on public attitudes towards the regime or democratic rule may be affected by randomization, even after adjusting for other characteristics such as gender, education, and socioeconomic status.

The level 1 HLM questions in the first and second model for the agenda setting (or media) influence were as follows:

- What is the variability in media performance within the ESA provinces?
- What is the proportion of variance in media performance between the ESA provinces (this is also referred to as the intraclass correlation, or ICC)?
- What is the reliability of each province's sample mean, as an estimate of its true population mean?
- How much do individual ESA citizens vary within and between the forty provinces in their attitudes towards media performance?
- Do provinces with a large population of highly educated citizenry vary in their evaluation of media performance within and between provinces?
- Is the strength of association between gender characteristics and regime legitimacy, controlling for the rule of law, similar across provinces? Or is being educated a more important predictor of regime legitimacy in some provinces than others?

This statistical approach was important because I tested the news media influence on individuals within each ESA country and also estimated whether the predicted agenda setting influence significantly varied or diminished between provinces as a function of other geopolitical characteristics. Drawing from Raudenbush and Bryk's example,[8] I estimated whether a significant amount of random variation existed in any related individual-level predictor coefficients associated with the initial model estimation. This type of assessment involves cross-level interactions at the second level, and the random variation in the second-level coefficient is predictable as a function of province-level variables.[9] What this means statistically at level 2 is that there might be a violation of the independent assumptions, particularly the biased estimates of standard errors of means and regression weights, related to the influence of the media on public attitudes (Type II error). Based on Dickinson and Basu's methodology,[10] multi-level modeling (or HLM) produces a decomposition of the total variance established in level 1 into a between-citizen, within-province, and a between-province component.

In this study, the nested approach at level 2 tested how much variation in the province-means, or adjusted province-means, can be accounted for by differences in media exposure and media type. The relationship between attitude scores on media exposure (the outcome variable) and democratic rule as the independent predictor can differ from one province to another given the nature of geopolitics and regime type. Consequently, each province's set of regression coefficients is predicted by one or more regional characteristics (media accessibility, media type, attitudes towards the regime, and demographics such as gender, the social economic status). For this study, the primary nesting centered on how inclusion of multiple predictor variables at the citizen level affected the estimated average difference in province-means between privately owned media and state-owned media in each province. Four output models in level 2 estimated how much of the variation in province-means can be accounted for by differences in mean-regime type and province characteristics such as education and social economic status. The following were some of the questions tested in the multilevel models:

- How much of the explained variance within each ESA province is reduced by adding gender as a predictor of media performance?
- How much variance can be accounted for by adding individual education levels to the model?
- What is the average effect or the rate of change (regression slope) within the provinces? How much of the explained variance within each ESA province is reduced by adding citizen attitudes towards regime legitimacy as a predictor of media performance?
- How much variance can be accounted for by adding gender to the model?
- What is the impact of variation in gender-based effects or the rate of change (regression slope) on attitudes towards the legitimacy of the regime within the provinces?

Level 2 yields each province's set of regression coefficients, which are predicted by one or more province characteristics such as geopolitical identity, mean-regime type, and education composition. These averages are weighted at different levels in an HLM analysis in two specific components: a component applied to citizens within a province and a component applied to sets of provinces. The full HLM model tested the following questions for the agenda setting influence:

- Does mean–rule of law and mean–regime legitimacy account for variability across ESA provinces (predict the intercept)?
- Are there cross-level interactions within the ESA provinces in terms of citizen attitudes towards regime legitimacy and the rule of law on media performance (predict the slope)?
- Finally, how much variation in the intercepts and the slopes is explained by using mean-rule and mean-regime as predictors of citizen attitudes towards media performance?

The overriding utility of the nested two-level analysis in this research is the ability to pull out the variance into components that explain the effects of different levels of analysis. It adjusts for correlated error terms by not underestimating standard errors and not assuming that errors within components are independent.[11] HLM partitioned the errors between individual attitude scores and across all the ESA provinces in the dataset, and also estimated cross-level effects in individual attitudes. Any possible increment in standard errors and the likelihood of Type I error were avoided or reduced within the sample size variations across units.

One of the purposes of this advanced statistical analysis was to provide preliminary information about how much variation lies within and between the ESA provinces. It determines the reliability of each ESA province's sample mean as an estimate of the true population mean: $Y_{ij} = \beta_{0j} + r_{ij}$. Model 1 also allows each ESA province to have unique intercepts (mean media influence), slopes (effects of citizen characteristics on media influence), and error terms. In level 1 of the first model, the outcome variable Y_{ij}, which is media influence, is first tested as a one-way analysis of variance (ANOVA) with random effects to get a preliminary understanding of whether media influence in each province (the intercept as mean β_{0j}) is highly correlated. The model at level 1 accounts for the unique increment to that intercept associated with a particular province, r_{ij}.

In this case, the r_{ij} are the error terms (residuals) that estimate how ESA citizens vary around a particular ESA province mean.

In addition, level 2 in model 1 estimates whether provinces vary around the overall grand mean from a one-way ANOVA with random effects. When we predict the media influence in ESA, the level 2 model, $\beta_{0j} = \gamma_{00} + u_{0j}$, is fully unconditional and it helps to estimate the reliability of each province's sample mean as an estimate of its true population mean (between-province variability). Accordingly, the combined level 1 and 2 one-way ANOVA with random effects model estimates one fixed effect and two random effects: $Y_{ij} = \gamma_{00} + u_{0j} + r_{ij}$. The three primary concerns here are:

- What is the variability in media influence within the ESA provinces?
- What is the proportion of variance in media influence between the ESA provinces (this is also referred to as the intraclass correlation, or ICC)?
- What is the reliability of the ESA province's sample mean as an estimate of its true population mean?

The estimated value of the variance or the proportion of variance in media influence occurring between the forty ESA provinces is .36. The ICC variation between the ESA provinces makes a statistically significant contribution to the analysis, and is necessary for HLM analysis, despite the reality that about 64 percent of the variance in the outcome of these data is at the citizen level.[12] Typically, an ICC coefficient of 36 percent indicates that a multilevel or hierarchical model would provide considerable benefits over a standard fixed effects model for the analysis of these data. However, some research disciplines in the social sciences, such as sociology and psychology, prefer an ICC that is higher than 30 percent to provide substantial benefits for the HLM analysis. My rationale for continuing with the HLM despite a less than 30 percent ICC is based on the rationale used by several scholars, such as Dickinson and Basu, who argue that, "Obviously, the degree to which individuals within a practice are more similar than individuals in different practices depends on the outcome of interest, as well as other factors, and will vary from one study and situation to another."[13] To use HLM, significant variance in the parameters must exist before researchers attempt to account for systematic variation within each ESA province.

At level 2 of model 1, which measures the variance components with random effects, the value of the likelihood function at iteration was statistically robust, as shown in Chapter Eight. This likelihood function is important for the veracity of the model. The variance component ($\tau00$), as shown in the tables in Chapter Eight, is the variability within the individual ESA provinces. The average variability for individual provinces about the mean is .87. This tells us that 87 percent of the variability is due to differences in media influence (Y_{ij}) in each province, decomposed on the total variability of that number into the between-provinces (level 2) component.

For model 2, this phase of the analysis considered how the media influenced citizen attitudes across provinces, and beyond individual differences, accounting for a citizen's level of education, social status, and gender. First of all, the logic of the random coefficient model is to allow both the intercept and the slope to be specified as random variables that show individual regressions for each province in ESA. It accounts for variability in both the mean attitudes from media influence based on gender and education levels (as intercepts). Second, it accounts for the effects of gender and education levels across the provinces (as slopes). The questions that inspire this consideration are listed below.

The *fixed effects* results in Chapter Eight and elsewhere show the significance of intervening variables as a strong factor in estimating the association of individual characteristics with media influence within-provinces ($\gamma01Wj$). This simply means that the grand mean is different from a random number (0). At level 2, $\tau00 =.87$ is the variability (87% of the variance) within the individual ESA provinces around the mean. When intervening variables for individual characteristics are included in the model, there is a slight average variance increase of 6 percent in the Chi-Square (χ^2), which also increases by 2.15, yielding a 99 percent confidence interval.

The *ß02* in the tables in Chapter Eight shows that the relationship between media influence and the intervening factors is actually either negative or positive, suggesting that when levels of education are higher across the provinces, media influence tends to decrease. In cases where the P dimensional space at the education slope is greater than α .05, I have to remove it from the next phase of the HLM model. One-way ANOVA with random effects in the tables in Chapter Eight contrasts with model 2, which estimates the means-as-outcome regression. The P dimensional space at the gender slope diminishes significantly when regime legitimacy is added into the model. I therefore retain regime legitimacy for the next full model as a strong predictor of media influence across provinces.

Level 1 Model: $Y_{ij} = \beta 0j + \beta 01*$(Regimes) $+ \beta 02*$(Gender) $+ r_{ij}$

Level 2 Model: $\beta 0j = \gamma 00 + \gamma 01*$(Mean Rule)$j + \gamma 02*$(Mean Regime)$j + \mu 0j$

$\beta 1j = \gamma 10 + \gamma 11*$(Mean Rule)$j + \gamma 12*$(Mean Regime)$j + \mu 1j$

Three questions also motivated the HLM analysis:

- Does mean–rule of law and mean–regime legitimacy account for variability across ESA provinces (predict the intercept)?
- Are there cross-level interactions of regime legitimacy, rule of law, and individual characteristics within the ESA provinces to predict the slope?
- Finally, how much variation in the intercepts and the slopes is explained by using mean–rule and mean–regime legitimacy as predictors of media influence?

Results of the intercept-as-outcome models for the multilevel equation $(Y_{ij} = \gamma_{00} + \gamma_{01}W_j + u_{0j} + r_{ij})$ show that regime legitimacy is not a significant predictor of government influence within the provinces. The slopes at the individual level 1 of government influence (outcome variable) were as follows: (Government influence $\beta 0j$) $= \gamma 00 + \gamma 01*$(Education) $+ \gamma 02*$(Rule of Law) $+ \gamma 03*$(Regime Legitimacy) $+ r_{ij.}$

There were also some challenges in collecting cross-sectional data without such hierarchically nested structures. Although the ESA data were sufficiently collected in respect to the proper HLM multistage random sampling survey design, some of the characteristics were not appropriately weighted for HLM within provinces, notably the respondents' age and social economic status. I went forward with an ICC less than .51 because it is only .30 ICC that is required in mass communication research. The most conventional cutoff point is also debatable because in some social science subdisciplines, it can weaken data requirements.

On the issue of media influence in ESA, province characteristics such as geopolitical sectarianism and media ownership may enable or impair the occurrence of agenda setting and present a third category of contingent conditions of the model. The scope of this book, however, did not allow an exploration of this possible weakness. Media type, whether state-owned or privately owned media, and autocratic media impediments in ESA do not automatically help the perceived attitudes towards an issue like the rule of law among the public. However, it can be a controllable latent variable that was not addressed. Issue and media correlations in this study show that the media in ESA are important in telling people what to think about democracy and authoritarian rule, but this specific traditional "media agenda" was not content analyzed in the national and regional media of the ESA. Nonetheless, the individual characteristics and regional contexts that are traditionally required by the HLM method have shown that the agenda setting effects and agenda building aspects shape both communication processes and have significant impact on public attitudes.

Future research on ESA should consider the interaction effects between media ownership and media performance in the coverage of political crises related to presidential elections. For instance, does political absolutism, which militates against democratic governance in many parts of Africa, restrain state-owned media in ESA from promoting democracy? Do the privately owned media in ESA, which succumb to the interests of proprietors and the marketplace, restrain their journalists from informing citizens about democratic governance? How can the news media challenge the past leadership record of an authoritarian regime while, at the same time, tout a weak opposition's political manifesto without crossing the line of becoming partisan? Do journalists simply defend dominant partisan interests based on ownership bias, or do they provide political information about national affairs that offer other political alternatives? The relationship between economic conditions, poverty, and regime legitimacy should also be examined.

Comparative Nested Case Analysis

In Chapter Seven, I used the comparative nested case analysis of how Nigerians and Ugandans exercise their democratic rights and participate in politics as a result of media exposure. This is done by combining the results of the statistical tests of four hypotheses from a large-scale survey with an inductive exploration of the deeper meanings of these results.

H1: Heavy media exposure in Nigeria and Uganda will lead citizens to express stronger attitudes towards democracy.

H2: Heavy media exposure in Nigeria and Uganda will lead citizens to show greater levels of political participation.

H3: Stronger attitudes towards democracy in Nigeria and Uganda will lead citizens to greater levels of political participation.

H4: Greater media control by proprietors and government in Nigeria and Uganda will lead citizens to express negative attitudes towards democracy.

This is achieved by nesting some of the salient abstract statistical findings into an in-depth comparative case analysis of the two regimes. The nesting used here draws from Lieberman, who suggested that one of the goals of such analysis is ultimately to make inferences about the unit of analysis that is shared *between-* and *within*-case variation. Nested analysis bridges the gap between the highly abstract statistical conclusion and the detailed reality.[14]

This design also works well in comparative studies to provide insights about rival statistical explanations and bridges the gap between the highly abstract statistical conclusion and the detailed reality.[15] For instance, if the hypothesis concerning the impact of media exposure on attitudes towards democracy in Nigeria is statistically insignificant, while the same hypothesis in Uganda is statistically significant, a within-case exploration is appropriate to compare and illuminate the significance of those variations in each case. A single-unit case analysis is best explored for comparative purposes to illuminate variations exhibited with another measured case that is pulled from the large N units.[16] In other words, when a single-unit case is drawn from the larger unit, it makes the nesting plausible and likely to be comparable to the other cases within that larger unit.

For the subsection in Chapter Seven, data were drawn from the 2004 Afrobarometer surveys conducted in Nigeria and Uganda, which measured public opinion on democracy, governance, and the use of the news media, *inter alia*. In 2004, the Afrobarometer conducted a randomly selected sample of 2,400 respondents each in Nigeria and Uganda, using clustered, stratified, and area probability samples. The survey instrument asks a set of similar questions that provide for a comparable analysis of the countries. The Afrobarometer conducts each interview with a randomly selected individual from a randomly selected household. Some questions are grouped in subparts with a distinctive variable name such as attitudes, participation, and cognitive awareness, among others. Only the data related to media exposure, attitudes towards democracy, and political participation were analyzed. Data indicating the following multiple-scale responses "refused to answer," "not applicable," and "other" were excluded from the sample. Also categories with missing data were excluded. A total of 1,643 cases were used in that subsection.

Focus Group Overview

Focus groups were conducted for qualitative assessment of audience discourse. I embarked on a triangulation of methods in this project (surveys, focus groups, content analysis) by setting up three different focus groups in each ESA country. Focus groups in Kenya, Tanzania, and Uganda were conducted in 2008; in Burundi, Ethiopia, and Rwanda in 2009; and in South Africa and Zambia in 2010. The age of the participants was between 18 and 55.

Each focus group was planned to have fourteen participants. All three focus groups in each country were set up in major towns. In each focus group, a moderator was hired to assist with the interview process. A total of six moderators were recruited to assist with the three focus groups in each of the countries. In some African cultures, in order for women (or men) to make useful discussions and comparisons, separate groups of men and women have to be considered. In order to make participants feel at ease, the participants in each group belonged to the shared milieu. It is a technique that helps participants to feel more comfortable and to share their thoughts in a discourse.

The focus groups in each country were composed of a male-only group, a female-only group, and one mixed-gender group. The way these focus groups can provide desirable data from such political cultures is through segmentation.[17] The segmented approach provides a platform for an effective dialogue (homogeneity) that not only allows for more free-flowing conversations among participants within groups but also facilitates an effective discourse.

The participants responded to an oral consent statement giving moderators the right to record them on audio tapes and giving me the right to use the collected data in any form for my research presentations, my articles, and in this book. The moderators also assured participants that their personal information would remain anonymous. As you can tell from the chapters, the participants' discourse was summarized according to the following criteria that we agreed upon: range, abstract and anonymous specificity, no direct quotes that identify country specifics, and no depth or identifying personal contexts.

Challenges of Conducting Research in Africa

To conduct academic research in any part of Africa can be a tall order. Many African scholars face challenges that include a lengthy process to secure research permits from African governments. They also endure suspicion when citizens are asked to participate in studies. There is also red tape and bureaucracy at some institutions where scholars collect data. The challenges faced by scholars perhaps explain why little empirical (or primary) research has been done in Africa. I will use Dr. Musa Olaka's example to illustrate some of the challenges. Dr. Olaka is a lecturer and information science coordinator at the Holocaust and Genocide Studies Center, at the University of South Florida. He collected data in Kenya in 2009 for his dissertation at the University of Missouri, but he faced many challenges similar to what I experienced in some of the ESA countries.

Securing a research permit in Kenya began as a challenge because it took half a day to locate the Kenya National Council for Science and Technology (KNCST). This is the agency charged with issuing research permits. KNCST has changed the location of its offices many times around Nairobi. A researcher has to physically visit the KNCST offices to obtain a research permit. If all the required papers are in order, it takes between two to three weeks to process the permit. Some of these requirements require two *stamped* and *signed* copies of one's research proposal by the researcher's institution of employment. Unfortunately, many documents from universities in the United States do not bear stamps or seals.

Affiliation with an ESA university is a requirement, and my friend Olaka also faced the same challenge. He recalls that one of the sections of the research permit application form requires a signature and stamp from the head of the Kenyan institution the researcher is affiliated with, as testimony that the applicant is truly affiliated with that institution. Being affiliated with an institution in Kenya was the most challenging obstacle to Olaka's research. Even the university where Olaka completed his undergraduate and master's degree studies did not understand this requirement or what it meant. The research permit application form required that the vice chancellor of a university in Kenya (university president) approve that the researcher was affiliated with the institution. Unfortunately, it is almost impossible to have a face-to-face dialogue with senior university administrators in Kenya and elsewhere in ESA.

Olaka met with several officers and presented his predicament. KNCST was willing to process the research permit without meeting all the conditions set in the research permit application form. It took three weeks from the time he completed the application for the research permit to the time he got it. That was just one university out of a dozen with whom Olaka had to negotiate.

Meanwhile, he realized that waiting for approval of a government-issued research permit before seeking approval from individual universities would cost him more time than expected. To make matters worse, the University of Missouri had set a strict deadline for the completion of the dissertation. Olaka targeted libraries in Kenyan universities where senior librarians were his former classmates. In most of Africa, such personal connections normally work very well. In my situation, I used my connections as a well-known former journalist in East Africa and beyond to get approvals and collect data in a timely manner.

This is how Olaka correctly summarizes the hurdles of academic research in Africa:

> Knowing procedures beforehand is critical to the success in collecting data. However, having a strong network of friends will in most cases reduce hurdles that one would have experienced. Anybody undertaking research ought not to ever think that by virtue of the government giving him a research permit, he will be able to collect data. The level of bureaucracy in many Kenyan institutions seems to cause many researchers frustration. It is very unfortunate that there is too much centralization of management in most of the academic institutions in Kenya, meaning data collection took longer than the researcher had anticipated. Potential researchers ought to be wary of doing studies in one institution lest they have their request to collect data in that institution denied. However, doing research in multiple institutions also brings about increased hurdles to overcome and thus it takes longer to collect data. What was amazing is how secretaries of administrators play a critical role in either enabling your documents to be processed faster, or simply acting as obstacles.

Another major problem with research in Africa is that many junior employees, particularly secretaries at private organizations and public institutions, wield immense power. They tend to determine who can meet their superior or what documents can be processed and presented to the superior's desk for approval. Research permits can sometimes take as long as six months to be approved in some ESA countries. And that may be just one of many offices where a signature must be sought before you get the final seal of approval.

Notes

Chapter 1

1   Including Burundi, Ethiopia, Tanzania, and Zambia
2   Bratton et al. (2005); Kalyango (2008)
3   Interview was conducted for CNN's *Inside Africa* in 2001.
4   Rubongoya (2007)
5   Bourgault (1995)
6   Sekalala (1968)
7   Barnett (1999)
8   Horwitz (2001); Kalyango (2009)
9   Jennings (2001)
10   Lemarchand et al. (1996)
11   Frère (2007)
12   Philippart (2000)
13   Frère (2007)
14   Frère (2007)
15   Henze (2000)
16   Henze (2000)
17   Allen and Seaton (1999)
18   Jacquin-Berdal and Plaut (2005)
19   Fessehatzion (2003); Allen and Seaton (1999)
20   Abbink (1994)
21   Allen and Seaton (1999)
22   IFJ (2007)
23   Amogne (2005)
24   Gebremedhin (2006)
25   Amogne (2005)
26   Amogne (2005)
27   Munene (2001)
28   Faringer (1991)
29   Abuoga and Mutere (1988)
30   Munene (2001)
31   Munene (2001)
32   Ibelema and Bosch (2004)
33   Mbeke (2008)
34   Uvin (1998)
35   Uvin (1998)

36   Hachten (2004)
37   Karnell (2002); Olorunnisola (1995)
38   Chalk (1999); Karnell (2002)
39   Snyder and Ballentine (1996)
40   Frohardt and Temin (2003); Mamdani (1996)
41   Kalyango (2008)
42   Rotberg and Weiss (1996); Sonwalkar (2004)
43   Karnell (2002)
44   Reyntjens (2004)
45   Reyntjens (2004)
46   Berger (2000)
47   Berger (2000); Emdon (1998)
48   Bond (2000)
49   Louw (1993)
50   Louw (1991, 1993)
51   Barnett (1999); Domatob and Hall (1983)
52   Teer-Tomaselli and Tomaselli (2001)
53   Emdon (1998)
54   Tettey (2006)
55   Kamuhanda (1990)
56   Kambenga (2005)
57   Ansell and Veriava (2000)
58   Shivji (1995)
59   Kambenga (2005)
60   Ochs (1987)
61   Kambenga (2005)
62   Tripp (2000)
63   Rubongoya (2007); Kannyo (2004)
64   Museveni and Kanyogonya (2000)
65   Rubongoya (2007)
66   Oloka-Onyango (2004)
67   Okuku (2002)
68   Ocitti (2006)
69   NIJU (2000)
70   Mwesige (2004)
71   Moore (1992)
72   Posner (2005)
73   Moore (1992)
74   Moore (1992); Pitts (2000)
75   Mudhai et al. (2009)
76   Mudhai et al. (2009)
77   Matibini (2006)
78   Matibini (2006)
79   Anderson (1991), 5.
80   Connor (1994); Geertz (1994)
81   Posner (2004)
82   Brown (2000)
83   Snyder (2000); Gagnon (1995); Kissopoulos (2004)
84   Horowitz (1985)

Chapter 2

1   Alcoff (2006)
2   Berman (1998); Cornell (2000)
3   Fearon and Laitin (2003)
4   Nyang'oro (2004)
5   Young (1998)
6   Fearon and Laitin (2003)
7   Connolly (2002)
8   Mamdani (1997)
9   Gyimah-Boadi and Asante (2006)
10 Weber (1968), 389.
11 Connor (1994); Cornell and Hartmann (1998)
12 Brown (2000), 21.
13 Ndarubagiye (1996)
14 Uvin (1999)
15 Uvin (1999)
16 Uvin (1999)
17 Uvin (1999); Ndarubagiye (1996)
18 Uvin (1999)
19 Uvin (1999)
20 Ndarubagiye (1996)
21 Ndarubagiye (1996)
22 BBC (2008)
23 Uvin (1999)
24 Habtu (2004)
25 Joireman (1997)
26 Habtu (2004)
27 Joireman (1997)
28 Habtu (2004)
29 Aalen (2006)
30 Joireman (1997)
31 Habtu (2004)
32 Tronvoll (2008)
33 Tronvoll (2008)
34 Aalen (2006); Joireman (1997); Tronvoll (2008)
35 Abbink (2006)
36 Central Bureau of Statistics (2002)
37 Steeves (2006)
38 Brown (2004)
39 Ruteere (2006); Ihonvbere (1994)
40 Orvis (2006)
41 Hughes (2005); Brown (2004)
42 Ruteere (2006)
43 Murunga and Shadrack (2006); Holmquist (2005)
44 Steeves (2006)
45 Kanyinga et al. (1994)
46 Mukandala (2000)
47 Mukandala (2000)
48 Uvin (1999)
49 Adelman (2000)
50 Adelman (2000); Semujanga (2003)

51 UNHCR (2000)
52 Longman (2009)
53 Reyntjens (2004)
54 Forster et al. (2000)
55 Frankel (1960); Worden (2000)
56 Worden (2000)
57 Forster et al. (2000)
58 Worden (2000)
59 Worden (2000)
60 Worden (2000)
61 Worden (2000)
62 Worden (2000)
63 Dixon and Durrheim (2010)
64 Finchilescu and Tredoux (2010)
65 Finchilescu and Tredoux (2010)
66 Campbell (1999)
67 Campbell (1999); Miguel (2004)
68 Mpangala and Lwehabura (2005)
69 Miguel (2004)
70 Mushi (2001)
71 Hyden (1999)
72 Nyang'oro (2004)
73 Mpangala and Lwehabura (2005)
74 Mpangala (2004)
75 Ahluwalia and Zegeye (2001)
76 Mamdani (1996); Tripp (2000)
77 Ahluwalia and Zegeye (2001)
78 Kabwegyere (1974)
79 Kasfir (1976)
80 Hansen (1977)
81 Kasfir (1976)
82 Kasfir (1976)
83 Museveni (1997)
84 Speech by President Yoweri Museveni (July 26, 2005)
85 Hayward and Dumbuya (1983)
86 Mugisha (2004)
87 Mwenda (2007); Rubongoya (2007)
88 Rubongoya (2007)

Chapter 3

1   Hyden et al. (2002)
2   Elkins (2000); Rose et al. (1998)
3   Kalyango and Eckler (2010)
4   Dahl (1989); Held (2006)
5   Held (2006)
6   Dahl (1989); Lindberg (2006); Rubongoya (2007)
7   Diamond (1999)
8   Dahl (1989)
9   Horowitz (2003)
10 Hatchard et al. (2004)
11 Lanegran (2001); Lodge (1999); Mattes (2004)

12 Dahl (2006)
13 Lindberg (2006)
14 Huntington (1991); Hagopian and Mainwaring (2005)
15 Przeworski (2003)
16 Bratton et al. (2005); Kalyango (2010); Lindberg (2006)

Chapter 4

1   Schmitz (2006)
2   Hayek (1972), 73.
3   Hatchard et al. (2009); Shivji (1995)
4   Hatchard et al. (2009)
5   Takirambudde and Fletcher (2006)
6   Hatchard et al. (2009); Takirambudde and Fletcher (2006)
7   O'Donnell (2004), 29.
8   Fallon (1997)
9   Mahoney (1999); Deutsch (1977)
10 Deutsch (1977)
11 Morlino (2005); O'Donnell (2004)
12 Stromseth et al. (2006)
13 Oloka-Onyango (2004, 1995)
14 Okoye (2004); Juma (2004)
15 Grosswiler (1997); Jennings (2000); Schmitz (2006)
16 Brown (2003)
17 Kassahun (2003); Vestal (1999)
18 Merera (2003); Vestal (1999)
19 Vestal (1999)
20 Brown (2003)
21 Steeves (2006)
22 Manirakiza (2005)
23 Ahluwalia and Zegeye (2001)
24 Kaiser (2000a)
25 Kaiser (2000b)
26 Baker (2004)
27 Baker (2004)
28 Kamanyi (2006), 15.
29 Juma (2004); Mbunda (2004); Momba (2004)
30 Bratton and Mattes (2001)
31 Rubongoya (2007)
32 Hatchard, Ndulo and Slinn (2009)
33 van de Walle (2002)
34 Schatzberg (2001)
35 Schatzberg (2001)
36 Hatchard, Ndulo and Slinn (2009)
37 Ndulo (2003)
38 Hayward and Dumbuya (1983)
39 Bratton and Mattes (2001); Zafliro (1988)
40 Mwesige (2009); Kalyango (2009, 2010)
41 Mwenda (2007); Oloka-Onyango (2004)
42 Aldrich (1995); Morrison (2004)
43 Morrison and Hong (2006); Kuenzi and Lambright (2007)
44 Morrison and Hong (2006)

45 Lindberg and Morrison (2005)
46 Kuenzi and Lambright (2007, 2005); Morrison et al. (2006)
47 Jackson and Rosberg (1984)
48 Mugisha (2004)
49 Mamdani (1996)
50 Horowitz (2000)
51 Rubongoya (2007)
52 van de Walle (2002)
53 Ndulo (2009), 10.

Chapter 5

1   Lippman (1922)
2   Azurmendi (2008)
3   Braman (2004)
4   Melzer (2008)
5   Gebremedhin (2006)
6   Mute (2000)
7   Media Institute (2004)
8   Juma (2004); Okoye (2004)
9   Karlekar and Cook (2008)
10 Makali (2003)
11 Frère (2007)
12 Frohardt and Temin (2003)
13 Karnell (2002)
14 Reyntjens (2004)
15 Freedom House (2008)
16 Franklin and Love (1998)
17 Duncan (2009)
18 Mochaba et al. (2003)
19 Republic of South Africa (2001)
20 Louw (2005)
21 Ramaprasad (2003)
22 Konde (1984)
23 Kilimwiko and Mapunda (1998); Ramaprasad (2003)
24 Eribo and Jong-Ebot (1997)
25 Martin (1974)
26 Sturmer (1998); Kilimwiko (2006)
27 Ramaprasad (2003)
28 Sturmer (1998); Grosswiler (1997)
29 Kalyango and Eckler (2010)
30 Balikowa (2002)
31 Mwenda (2007)
32 Rubongoya (2007); Mwenda (2007)
33 *The Monitor* (March 15, 2010)
34 Moore (1992)
35 Moore (1992), 22.
36 Matibini (2006)
37 Makungu (2004), 5.
38 Moore (1992)
39 Mudhai et al. (2009)
40 Matibini (2006)

41 Banda (2006)
42 Matibini (2006)

Chapter 6

1 Kalyango (2009)
2 Hyden et al. (2002); Madamombe (2005)
3 Kalyango (2009); Madamombe (2005); Wanyeki (2002)
4 Kalyango (2009); Mwesige (2009)
5 Barker (2001); Nassanga (2009)
6 Some responses like this information came from personal and in-depth interviews; however, all of the named sources in this chapter are communication/media, or development, or political science scholars.
7 Kasoma (1990)
8 Opoku-Mensah (2000); Nassanga (2009), 45.
9 Nassanga (2009); Rogers (1983)
10 Kasoma (1990)
11 Soubbotina (2004)
12 Ansah (1988)
13 Kivikuru (2006); Nassanga (2009); O'Connor (1990)
14 Manyozo (2009),7.
15 Opoku-Mensah (2000)
16 Kivikuru (2006), 9.
17 Nassanga (2009), 52.
18 Wanyeki (2000), 31.
19 Jallov (2009)
20 Wanyeki (2000)
21 Jallov (2009)
22 Wanyeki (2000)
23 Manyozo (2009), 9.
24 Kivikuru (2006), 13.
25 Jallov (2005)
26 Kilimwiko (2006)
27 Ramaprasad (2003)
28 Kilimwiko (2006)
29 Wanyande (1996); Matende (2005)
30 Moggi and Tessier (2001)
31 Omosa and McCormick (2004)
32 Moggi and Tessier (2001)
33 Kemigisha (1998); Ocitti (2006)
34 Ocitti (2006)
35 IREX (2008)
36 IREX (2008)
37 IREX (2008)
38 IREX (2008)
39 Manyozo (2009)
40 Kivukuru (2006)
41 Manyozo (2009)
42 Manyozo (2009), 14.
43 Wanyeki (2000)
44 Barker (2001)
45 Barker (2001)

46 Barker (2001), 20.
47 Barker (2001), 19.
48 Kivikuru (2006)
49 Opoku-Mensah (2000), 165.
50 Kivikuru (2006), 27.
51 Kivikuru (2006)
52 Daloz and Verrier-Frechette (2000)

Chapter 7

1   Bahmueller (1995), 384.
2   Schapiro (1972), 39.
3   Roberston (2004), 136.
4   Robertson (2004), 137.
5   Schwarzmantel (1994), 48.
6   Spector (2007)
7   Linz (1964), 255.
8   Spector (2007)
9   Barry (1989)
10 Unless the statement is presented or attributed as a personal or in-depth interview (in which case the source was nonacademic), the rest of the named sources in this chapter are either communication/media, or law/legal, or political science scholars. Refer to chapter notes and bibliography for details.
11 Roberston (2005), 145.
12 Magalhães (1995)
13 Brooker (2000)
14 Brooker (2000); Burch (1964); Linz (1975); Spector (2007)
15 Brooker (2000)
16 Burch (1964)
17 Linz (1975), 63.
18 Brooker (2000)
19 Brooker (2000)
20 Brooker (2000)
21 Bratton et al. (2005)
22 Young (1976)
23 Lewis (1999)
24 Clark (2007); Suberu (2007); Young (1976)
25 Lewis (1999)
26 Smith (2005)
27 Alapiki (2005)
28 Sklar (2006); Clark (2007)
29 Sklar (2006)
30 Museveni and Kanyogonya (2000)
31 Ndulo (2003); Ofcansky (1996)
32 Kaweesa and Gorman (2003); Ofcansky (1996)
33 Afako (2006)
34 Afako (2006)
35 Therkildsen (2002)
36 Bratton and Lambright (2001)
37 Kalyango (2009); Ocitti (2006)
38 Kalyango and Eckler (2010)
39 Rubongoya (2007)

40 Ibrahim (2006)
41 Schedler (2010), 36.
42 Tripp (2004), 5.
43 Levitsky and Way (2002)
44 Schedler (2010), 37.
45 Schedler (2010)
46 Pareto (1935)
47 Magalhães (1995)
48 Robertson (2007), 223.
49 Stepan (1990)
50 Stepan (1990), 44.
51 Dahl (1971), 15.
52 Luckham (1998)
53 Pye (1962); Klare (1972)
54 Coleman and Brice (1962), 359.
55 Luckham (1997)
56 Horwitz et al. (1984), 67.
57 Luckham (1998), 2.
58 Welch (1970)
59 Onwumechili (1998)
60 Wiking (1983)
61 Luckham (1998)
62 Feffer (2008)
63 Uche (1989)
64 Ojo (2003)
65 Ette (2000)
66 Smith (2005)
67 Kalyango and Eckler (2010); Mwesige (2009)

Chapter 8

1 Nyang'oro (2004); Mamdani (1997)
2 Wanta (1997)
3 Lasorsa (1997); Wanta (1997)
4 Wanta et al. (2004)
5 Unless the statement is presented or attributed as a personal or in-depth interview (in which case the source was nonacademic), the rest of the named sources in this chapter are either communication/media, or law/legal, or political science scholars. Refer to chapter notes and bibliography for details.
6 McCombs and Shaw (1972)
7 Craft and Wanta (2005)
8 Peter (2003)
9 Shaw and McCombs (1977)
10 Wanta (1997)
11 Hyden et al. (2002)
12 Eribo and Tanjong (1998)
13 Scheufele (2000), 303.
14 Lang and Lang (1981)
15 McCombs and Ghanem (2003), 68.
16 Berkowitz (1987); Johnson et al. (1994)
17 Weaver and Elliot (1985)
18 Behr and Iyengar (1985)

[19] Berkowitz (1987)
[20] Tanner (2004)
[21] Weiler (1997)
[22] Kannyo (2004); Ocitti (2006)
[23] Schatzberg (2001); Ruteere (2006); Wanyande (1996)
[24] Weiler (1997); Rubongoya (2007)
[25] Schatzberg (2001)

Chapter 9

[1]   Milne and Taylor (2006)
[2]   Helleiner (2000)
[3]   Bhagavan and Bari (2001); Demby (2000); Fogarty (2005)
[4]   Collier and Pattillo (2000)
[5]   Addis (2003)
[6]   Adjibolosoo (2005)
[7]   Demby (2000), 152.
[8]   Fogarty (2005)
[9]   Austin (2000)
[10] Austin (2000)
[11] Wanta (1997); Wood (1985)
[12] Barro (1991); Barro and Salai-Martin (1995)
[13] North (1989)
[14] Basu et al. (2000)
[15] Miguel (2009), 45.
[16] Mussa (2005); Addison (2003)
[17] Ihrig and Moe (2000)
[18] Barro (1998)
[19] Dollar and Kraay (2000)
[20] Page (2005)
[21] Bio-Tchané (2006)
[22] Miguel and Ajakaiye (2009)
[23] Page (2005)
[24] Brian (2005); Miguel (2009)
[25] Goldstein and Ndung'u (2003)
[26] Lawson (2008)
[27] World Bank (2008)
[28] Transparency International (2007)
[29] Kalyango and Eckler (2010), 359.
[30] Brian (2005)
[31] Page (2005)
[32] Nonneman (1996), 4.
[33] Campbell and Pedersen (2001), 5.
[34] Campbell and Pedersen (2001)
[35] Krueger (1986), 16.
[36] Nonneman (1996)
[37] Dollar and Kraay (2000)

Chapter 10

[1]   Bratton et al. (2005); van de Walle (2002)
[2]   Obama (2009)

3   Brown (2003); Baker (2004)
4   Oloka-Onyango (1995); Mugisha (2004); Osaghae (2005)
5   Dicklitch and Lwanga (2003); Kilimwiko (2006); Kambenga (2005)
6   Kilimwiko (2006); Ocitti (2006); Omosa and McCormick (2004)
7   Obama (2009)
8   Ameringer (2005)
9   Anduzia (2009); Montero (2009)
10 Jackson and Lilleker (2009)
11 Karan et al. (2009)
12 Snyder (2000)

Appendix

1   Huesman et al. (1992)
2   Huesman et al. (1992)
3   Slaby (1984); Dickinson and Basu (2005)
4   Kang and Kwak (2003); Raudenbush and Bryk (2002)
5   Raudenbush and Bryk (2002)
6   Bryk and Raudenbush (1988)
7   Paek et al. (2005)
8   Raudenbush and Bryk (2002)
9   Kang and Kwak (2003)
10 Dickinson and Basu (2005)
11 Bryk and Raudenbush (1988)
12 Raudenbush and Bryk (2002); Berger and Milem (2000)
13 Dickinson and Basu (2005), 54.
14 Lieberman (2005)
15 Lieberman (2003)
16 Gerring (2004)
17 Thorne and Henley (1975)

Bibliography

Aalen, Lovise. 2006. "Ethnic Federalism and Self-Determination for Nationalities in a Semi-Authoritarian State: The Case of Ethiopia." *International Journal on Minority and Group Rights* 13(2/3): 243–261.

Abbink, Jan. 1994. "Refractions of Revolution in Ethiopian 'Surmic' Societies: An Analysis of Cultural Response." In *New Trends in Ethiopian Studies*, ed. Harold G. Marcus. Lawrenceville, NJ: Red Sea Press, 734–755.

Abbink, Jon. 2006. "Ethnicity and Conflict Generation In Ethiopia: Some Problems and Prospects of Ethno-Regional Federalism." *Journal of Contemporary African Studies* 24(3): 389–413.

Abuoga, John, and Absalom Mutere. 1988. *The History of the Press in Kenya*. Nairobi: African Council for Communication Education.

Addis, Adeno. 2003. "Economic Sanctions and the Problem of Evil." *Human Rights Quarterly* 25(3): 573–623.

Addison, Tony. 2003. "Africa's Recovery from Conflict: Making Peace Work for the Poor." *Policy Brief 6*, UNU-WIDER, Helsinki, Finland.

Adelman, Howard. 2000. "Rwanda Revisited: In Search of Lessons." *Journal of Genocide Research* 2(3): 431–444.

Adjibolosoo, Senyo. 2005. "Economic Underdevelopment in Africa: The Validity of the Corruption Argument." *Review of Human Factor Studies* 11(1): 90–112.

Afako, Barney. 2006. "Uncharted Waters: The Movement Approaches Transition in Uganda." Report Prepared for the Department for International Development (DFID)—Uganda Chapter, Makerere University, Kampala.

Ahluwalia, Pal, and Abebe Zegeye. 2001. "Multiparty Democracy in Tanzania." *African Security Review* 10(3), Article 4. Retrieved March 10, 2006, from http://www.iss.co.za/pubs/asr/10No3/AhluwaliaAndZegeye.html.

Ajakaiye, Olu. 2009. Forum: "Is It Africa's Turn?" *Boston Review.* Boston, MA: MIT Press.

Alapiki, Henry. 2005. "State Creation in Nigeria: Failed Approaches to National Integration and Local Autonomy." *African Studies Review* 48(3): 49–65.

Alcoff, Linda. 2006. *Identity Politics Reconsidered.* New York, NY: Palgrave MacMillan.

Aldrich, John. 1995. *Why Parties? The Origin and Transformation of Political Parties in America.* American Politics and Political Economy Series. Chicago: University of Chicago Press.

Allen, Tim, and Jean Seaton. 1999. *The Media of Conflict: War Reporting and Representation of Ethnic Violence.* London and New York: Zed Books.

Ameringer, Oscar. 2005. *Life and Deeds of Uncle Sam: A Satirical Look at U.S. History.* Charles Kerr Publishing Co.

Amogne, Getahun. 2005. "Public Access to Government Information in Ethiopia: An Assessment of Public Information Practice in Selected Government Institutions." Master's thesis in journalism. Addis Ababa University.

Anderson, Benedict. 1991. *Imagined Communities: Reflections on the Origin and Spread of Nationalism.* London: Verso.

Anduzia, Eva. 2009. "The Internet, Election Campaigns and Citizens: State of Affairs." *Quadernsdel CAC* 33: 5–12.

Ansah, Paul A. W. 1988. "In Search for a Role for the African Media in the Democratization Process." *African Media Review* 2(2): 1–16.

Ansell, Gwen, and Ahmed Veriava. 2000. *Human Rights Handbook for Southern African Communicators.* Johannesburg, South Africa: Institute for the Advancement of Journalism.

Austin, Gareth. 2000. "Markets, Democracy and African Growth: Liberalism and Afro-Pessimism Reconsidered." *The Round Table* 357: 543–555.

Azurmendi, Ana. 2008. "Communication Law and Policy: Europe." In *The International Encyclopedia of Communication*, ed. Wolfgang Donsbach. West Sussex, UK: Blackwell Publishing.

Bahmueller, Charles F. 1995. "Comparative Government." In *Survey of Social Science: Government and Politics Series (Vol. 2)*, ed. F. Magil. Pasadena, CA: Salem Press.

Baker, Bruce. 2004. "Popular Justice and Policing from Bush War to Democracy: Uganda 1981-2004." *International Journal of the Sociology of Law* 32 (4): 333–348.

Balikowa, David O. 2002, April. "MPs Dug Grave for Journalists." *The Daily Monitor.* Retrieved August 2006 from LexisNexis Academic.

Banda, Fackson. 2006. *Zambia: Research Findings and Conclusions.* American Media Development Initiative. London: BBC World Service Trust.

Barker, John M. 2001. "Is No Policy a Policy Goal?" In *Media, Democracy and Renewal in Southern Africa,* ed. Keyan Tomaselli and Hopeton Dunn. Colorado Springs, CO: International Academic Publishers.

Barnett, Clive. 1999. "The Limits of Media Democratization in South Africa: Politics, Privatization and Regulation." *Media, Culture and Society* 21(5): 649–671.

Barro, Robert J. 1991. "Economic growth in a cross section of countries." *Quarterly Journal of Economics* 106(2): 407–443.

Barro, Robert J. 1998. *Determinants of Economic Growth: A Cross-country Empirical Study.* Cambridge, MA: MIT Press.

Barro, Robert J. and Xavier Sala-i-Martin. 1995. *Economic growth.* New York, NY: McGraw-Hill.

Barry, Norman. 1989. An Introduction to Modern Political Theory. New York: St. Martin's Press.

Basu, Anupam, Evangelos A. Calamitsis, and Daneshwar Ghura. 2000. "Promoting Growth in Sub-Saharan Africa: Learning What Works." International Monetary Fund. *Economic Issues* 23.

Behr, Roy, and Shanto Iyengar. 1985. "Television News, Real-world Cues, and Changes in the Public Agenda." *Public Opinion Quarterly* 49: 38–57.

Berger, Guy. 2000. "Publishing for the People: The Alternative Press, 1980–1999." In *The Politics of Publishing in South Africa,* ed. N. Evans and M. Seeber. London and Scottsville: Holger Ehling and University of Natal Press.

Berger, Joseph, and Jeffrey Milem. 2000. "Organizational Behavior in Higher Education and Student Outcomes." In *Higher Education: Handbook of Theory and Research,* ed. John C. Smart. New York: Agathon.

Berkowitz, Dan. 1987. "TV News Sources and News Channels: A Study in Agenda-Building." *Journalism Quarterly* 64: 508–513.

Berman, Bruce. 1998. "Politics of Uncivil Nationalism: Ethnicity, Patronage and the African State." *African Affairs* No. 97.

Bhagavan, Manu, and Faisal Bari. 2001. "(Mis)Representing Economy: Western Media Production and the Impoverishment of South Asia." *Comparative Studies of South Asia, Africa and the Middle East* 21(2): 99–109.

Bio-Tchané, Abdoulaye. 2006. *Current Challenges for Sub-Saharan Africa.* International Monetary Fund, Africa Department.

Bloom, David E., and Jeffrey D. Sachs. 1998. "Geography, Demography, and Economic Growth in Africa." *Brookings Papers on Economic Activity* 1998(2): 207–295.

Bond, Patrick. 2000. *Elite Transition: From Apartheid to Neoliberalism in South Africa.* London and Pietermaritzburg: Pluto and University of Natal Press.

Bourgault, Louise. 1995. *Mass Media in Sub-Saharan Africa.* Bloomington, IN: Indiana University Press.

Braman, Sandra. 2004. "Where Has Media Policy Gone? Defining the Field in the Twenty-First Century." *Communication Law and Policy* 9(2): 153–82.

Bratton, Michael and Gina Lambright. 2001. "Uganda's Referendum 2000: The Silent Boycott." *African Affairs* 100: 429–452.

Bratton, Michael, and Robert Mattes., 2001. "Support for Democracy in Africa: Intrinsic or Instrumental?" *British Journal of Political Science* 31, 447–474.

Bratton, Michael, Robert Mattes, and Emmanuel Gyimah-Boadi. 2005. *Public Opinion, Democracy and Market Reform in Africa.* Cambridge: Cambridge University Press.

Brian, L. 2005. African Development Report: Human Capital Development. *African Development Bank.* New York: Oxford University Press.

Brooker, Paul. 2000. *Non-Democratic Regimes: Theory, Government and Politics: Theory, Government & Politics.* New York: St. Martin's Press.

Brown, David. 2000. *Contemporary Nationalism: Civic, Ethnocultural and Multicultural Politics.* London: Routledge.

Brown, Stephen. 2003. "Quiet Diplomacy and Recurring Ethnic Clashes in Kenya." In *From Promise to Practice: U.N. Capacities for the Prevention of Violent Conflict*, ed. C. L. Sriram and K. Wermester. Boulder, CO: Lynne Rienner.

Brown, Stephen. 2004. "Theorizing Kenya's Protracted Transition to Democracy." *Journal of Contemporary African Studies* 22(3): 325–342.

Bryk, Anthony, and Stephen Raudenbush. 1988. "Toward a More Appropriate Conceptualization of Research on School Effects: A Three-Level Hierarchical Linear Model." *American Journal of Education* 97(1): 65–108.

Burch, Betty (ed.). 1964. Preface. *Dictatorship and Totalitarianism: Selected Readings.* Princeton, NJ: D. Van Nostrand Company, Inc.

Campbell, John. 1999. "Nationalism, Ethnicity and Religion: Fundamental Conflicts and the Politics of Identity in Tanzania." *Nations and Nationalism* 5(1): 105–125.

Campbell, John L., and Ove K. Pedersen. 2001. *The Rise of Neoliberalism and Institutional Analysis*. Princeton, NJ: Princeton University Press.

Chakravartty, Paula, and Katharine Sarikakis. 2006. *Media Policy and Globalization*. New York, NY: Palgrave Macmillian.

Chalk, Frank. 1999. "Hate Radio in Rwanda." In *The Path of a Genocide: The Rwanda Crisis from Uganda to Zaire,* ed. Howard Adelman and Astri Suhrke. New Brunswick, NJ: Transaction.

Clark, John F. 2007. "The Decline of the African Military Coup." *Journal of Democracy* 18(3): 141–155.

Coleman, James S. and Belmont Brice, Jr. 1962."The role of the military in SubSaharan Africa." In *The Role of the Military in Underdeveloped Countries,* ed. J.J. Johnson. Princeton: Princeton University Press. 359–407.

Collier, David, and Steven Levitsky. 1997. "Democracy with Adjectives: Conceptual Innovation in Comparative Research." *World Politics* 49(3): 430–451.

Collier, David, and Robert Adcock. 1999. "Democracy and Dichotomies: A Pragmatic Approach to Choices about Concepts." *Annual Review of Political Science* 2, 537–565.

Collier, Paul, and Catherine Pattillo (eds). 2000. *Investment and Risk in Africa*. Basingstoke: Macmillan and New York: St Martin's Press.

Connolly, William. 2002. *Identity and Difference: Democratic Negotiations of Political Paradox*. Minneapolis: University of Minnesota Press.

Connor, Walker. 1994. *Ethnonationalism: The Quest for Understanding*. Princeton: Princeton University Press.

Cornell, Drucilla. 2000. *Just Cause: Freedom, Identity, and Rights*. Lanham, MD: Rowman and Littlefield.

Cornell, Stephen, and Douglas Hartmann. 1998. *Ethnicity and Race: Making Identities in a Changing World*. Thousand Oaks, CA: Pine Forge Press.

Craft, Stephanie and Wayne Wanta. 2005. "U. S. Public Concerns in the Aftermath of 9-11: A Test of Second-Level Agenda-Setting." *International Journal of Public Opinion Research* 16(4): 456–462.

Dahl, Robert A. 1971. *Polyarchy: Participation and Opposition*. New Haven: Yale University Press.

Dahl, Robert A. 1989. *Democracy and Its Critics*. New Haven and London: Yale University Press.

Dahl, Robert A. 2006. *On Political Equality.* New Haven and London: Yale University Press.

Daloz, Jean Pascal, and Katherine Verrier-Frechette. 2000. "Is Radio Pluralism an Instrument of Political Change?: Insights from Zambia." In *African Broadcast Cultures: Radio in Transition,* ed. Richard Fardon and Graham Furniss. Cape Town: James Currey Publishers, 180–187.

Demby, Joe. 2000. "Risk and Portfolio Investment into Africa: A Practitioner's Approach." In *Reducing the Risk of Investment in Africa,* ed. Paul Collier and Catherine Pattillo. Basingstoke: Macmillan.

Deutsch, Eberhard P. 1977. *An International Rule of Law.* Charlottesville, VA: University Press of Virginia.

Diamond, Larry. 1999. *Developing Democracy: Toward Consolidation.* Baltimore: Johns Hopkins University Press.

Dickinson, Miriam, and Anirban Basu. 2005. "Multilevel Modeling and Practice-Based Research." *Annals of Family Medicine* 3(3): 52–61.

Dicklitch, Susan, and Doreen Lwanga. 2003. "The Politics of Being Non-political: Human Rights Organizations and the Creation of a Positive Human Rights Culture in Uganda." *Human Rights Quarterly* 25(2): 482–509.

Dixon, John, and Kevin Durrheim. 2010. "Racial Contact and Change in South Africa." *Journal of Social Issues* 66(2): 273–288.

Dollar, David, and Aart Kraay. 2000. "Growth is good for the poor." Policy Research Working Paper 2587. *Development Research Group.* Washington, D.C: World Bank.

Domatob, Jerry K., and Stephen William Hall. 1983. "Development Journalism in BlackAfrica." *Gazette* (31)1: 9–33.

Duncan, Jane. 2009. "The Uses and Abuses of Political Economy: The ANC's Media Policy." *Transformation: Critical Perspectives on Southern Africa* 70: 1–30.

Eko, Lyombe. 2008. "Internet Law and Regulation." In *The International Encyclopedia of Communication,* ed. Wolfgang Donsbach. West Sussex, UK: Wiley-Blackwell Publishing.

Elkins, Zachary. 2000. "Gradations of Democracy? Empirical Tests of Alternative Conceptualizations." *American Journal of Political Science* 44(2): 287–294.

Emdon, Clive. 1998. "Ownership and Control of the South African Media." In *Media and Democracy in South Africa,* ed. J. Duncan and M. Seleoane. Pretoria: Human Sciences Research Council and Freedom of Expression Institute.

Eribo, Festus, and William Jong-Ebot (eds). 1997. *Press Freedom and Communication in Africa.* Trenton, NJ: Africa World Press.

Eribo, Festus, and Enoh Tanjong. 1998. "Reporting under Civilian and Military Rulers in Africa: Journalists' Perceptions of Press Freedom and Media Exposure in Cameroon and Nigeria." *Ecquid Novi* 19(2): 39-55.

Ette, Mercy. 2000. "Agent of Change or Stability? The Nigerian Press Undermines Democracy." *The Harvard International Journal of Press/Politics* 5(3): 67–86.

Fallon, Richard H. 1997. "The Rule of Law as a Concept in International Discourse."*Columbia Law Review* 97(1).

Faringer, Gunilla. 1991. *Press Freedom in Africa*. New York: Praeger Publishers.

Fearon, James D., and David Laitin. 2003. "Ethnicity, Insurgency and Civil War." *American Political Science Review* 97(1): 75–90.

Feffer, John. 2008, February. "Militarizing Africa (Again)." *Foreign Policy in Focus*. Retrieved August 22, 2010, from http://www.fpif.org/articles/militarizing_africa_again.

Feintuck, Mike, and Mike Varney. 2007. *Media Regulation, Public Interest and the Law*. Edinburgh: Edinburgh University Press.

Fessehatzion, Tekie. 2003. *Shattered Illusion, Broken Promise: Essays on the Eritrea-Ethiopia Conflict (1998-2000)*. Lawrenceville, NJ: Red Sea Press.

Finchilescu, Gillian, and Colin Tredoux. 2010. "The Changing Landscape of Intergroup Relations in South Africa." *Journal of Social Issues* 66(2): 223–236.

Fogarty, Brian J. 2005. "Determining Economic News Coverage." *International Journal of Public Opinion Research* 17(2):149–172.

Forster, Peter G., Michael Hitchcock, and Francis F. Lyimo. 2000. *Race and Ethnicity in East Africa*. New York: St. Martin's Press.

Frankel, Sally Herbert. 1960. *The Tyranny of Economic Paternalism in Africa: A Study of Frontier Mentality*. Johannesburg: Anglo-American Corporation of South Africa.

Franklin, Anita, and Roy Love. 1998. "Whose News? Control of the Media in Africa." *Review of African Political Economy* 78(25): 545–590.

Frère, Marie-Soleil. 2007. *The Media and Conflicts in Central Africa*. Imprint Boulder, CO: Lynne Rienner Publishers.

Frohardt, Mark, and Jonathan Temin. 2003. *Use and Abuse of Media in Vulnerable Societies* (special report 110). United States Institute of Peace, Washington, D.C., USA. Retrieved from March 2, 2009, at www.usip.org/pubs/specialreports/sr110.html.

Gagnon Jr., V.P. 1995. "Ethnic Nationalism and International Conflict: The Case of Serbia." In *Global Dangers: Changing Dimensions of International Security*, eds. Sean M. Lynne Jones and Steven E. Miller. Cambridge: MIT Press. 331–368.

Gebremedhin, Simon. 2006. "Media Coverage of the 2005 Ethiopian Elections." Unpublished paper presented at a workshop on Media and Good Governance. Addis Ababa: School of Journalism and Communication, Addis Ababa University and UNESCO.

Gebru, Amanuel (2006). "Job Satisfaction of Journalists in the Ethiopian Federal State Media." Unpublished Master's thesis. Addis Ababa University.

Geertz, Clifford. 2004. "What is a State If it is Not a Sovereign? Reflections on Politics in Complicated Places," *Current Anthropology,* 45(5): 577–93.

Gerring, John. 2004. "What Is a Case Study and What Is It Good for?" *American Political Science Review* 98(2): 341–354.

Goldstein, Andrea, and Njuguna Ndung'u. 2003. "Regional Integration Experience in the Eastern African Region." *OECD Development Centre Working Papers.*

Grosswiler, Paul. 1997. "Changing Perceptions of Press Freedom in Tanzania." In *Press Freedom and Communication in Africa,* ed. Festus Eribo and William Jong-Ebot. Trenton, NJ: Africa World Press.

Gyimah-Boadi, Emmanuel and Richard Asante. 2006. "Ethnic Structure, Inequality and Public Sector Governance in Ghana." In *Ethnic Inequalities and Public Sector Governance,* ed. Yusuf Bangura. Basingstoke: Palgrave Macmillan.

Habtu, Alem. 2004. "Ethnic Pluralism as an Organizing Principle of the Ethiopian Federation." *Dialectical Anthropology.* 28: 91–123.

Hachten, William. 2004. "Reporting Africa's Problems." In *Development and Communication in Africa,* ed. Charles Okigbo and Festus Eribo. Latham, MD: Rowman & Littlefield. 79–87.

Hagopian, Francis, and Scott P. Mainwaring. 2005. *The Third Wave of Democratization in Latin America: Advances and Setbacks.* Cambridge: Cambridge University Press.

Hansen, Holger B. 1977. *Ethnicity and Military Rule in Uganda: A Study of Ethnicity as a Political Factor in Uganda.* Uppsala: The Scandinavian Institute of African Studies.

Harguindéguy, Jean-Baptiste. 2007. "Government." In *Encyclopedia of Governance,* ed. M. Bevir. California: Sage Publications.

Hatchard, John, Muna Ndulo, and Peter Slinn. 2004. *Comparative Constitutionalism and Good Governance in the Commonwealth: An Eastern and Southern African Perspective.* Cambridge: Cambridge University Press.

Hatchard, John, Muna Ndulo, and Peter Slinn. 2009. *Comparative Constitutionalism and Good Governance in the Commonwealth: An Eastern and Southern African Perspective.* Cambridge University Press.

Hayek, Friedrich. 1972. *The Road to Serfdom.* Chicago: University of Chicago Press.

Hayward, Fred, and Ahmed Dumbuya. 1983. "Political Legitimacy, Political Symbols, and National Leadership in West Africa." *The Journal of Modern African Studies* 21(4): 645–671.

Held, David. 2006. *Models of Democracy*. 3rd Ed. Stanford, CA: Stanford University Press.

Helleiner, Gerry. 2000. "External Conditionality, Local Ownership and Development." In *Transforming Development: Foreign Aid for a Changing World*, ed. Jim Freedman. Toronto: University of Toronto Press.

Henze, Paul B. 2000. *Layers of Time: A History of Ethiopia*. New York: Palgrave, MacMillan.

Holmquist, Frank. 2005. "Kenya's Anti-politics." *Current History* 104: 209–215.

Horowitz, Donald. 1985. *Ethnic Groups in Conflict*. Berkeley, CA: University of California Press.

Horowitz, Donald L. 2000. *Ethnic Groups in Conflict*. Berkeley, CA: University of California Press.

Horowitz, Donald L. 2003. "The Contest of Ideas." *The Democracy Handbook*, ed. R. Dahl, I. Shapiro, and J. Cheibub. Cambridge, MA: MIT Press.

Horwitz, Iriving Louis, Augustus Richard Norton, and Claude E. Welch Jr. 1984. "Review Symposium: Beyond Empire and Revolution: Militarization and Consolidation in the Third World." *Studies in Comparative International Development* 19(2): 59–77.

Horwitz, Robert B. 2001. *Communication and Democratic Reform in South Africa*. Cambridge: Cambridge University Press.

Huesmann, Rowell, Leonard D. Eron, Leonard Berkowitz and Steven S. Chaffee. 1992. "The Effects of Television Violence on Aggression: A Reply to a Skeptic." In *Psychology and Social Policy*, ed. Peter Suedfeld and Philip E. Tetlock. 191–200. New York, NY: Hemisphere.

Huesmann, Rowell, Nancy Guerra, Laurie Miller and Arnaldo Zelli. 1992. "The Role of Social Norms in the Development of Aggression." In *Socialization and Aggression*, ed. Adam Fraczek and Horst Zumkley. 139–152. New York, NY: Springer.

Hughes, Lotte. 2005. "Malice in Maasailand: The Historical Roots of Current Political Struggles." *African Affairs* 104(415): 207–224.

Huntington, Samuel. 1991. *The Third Wave: Democratization in the Late Twentieth Century*. Norman, OK, and London: University of Oklahoma Press.

Hyden, Goran. 1999. "Top-Down Democratization in Tanzania." *Journal of Democracy* 10(4): 142–15.

Hyden, Goran, Michael Leslie, and Folu Ogundimu. 2002. *Media and Democracy in Africa*. New Brunswick, NJ: Transaction Publishers.

Ibelema, Minabere, and Tanja Bosch. 2004. "Sub-SaharanAfrica." In *Global Journalism: Topical Issues and Media Systems,* ed. Arnold S. de Beer and John C. Merrill. New York: Allyn and Bacon.

Ibrahim, Jibrin. 2006. "Legislation and the Electoral Process: The Third Term Agenda and the Future of Nigerian Democracy." Centre for Democracy and Development (CDD). Presented at a CDD Conference in London, U.K.

Ihonvbere, Julius. 1994. "The 'Irrelevant' State: Ethnicity and the Quest for Nationhood in Africa." *Ethnic and Racial Studies* 1(1): 42–60.

Ihrig, Jane and Karine S. Moe. 2000. "The Influence of Government Policies on Informal Labor: Implications for Long-Run Growth." *De Economist* 148(3): 331–343.

Ihrig, Jane, and Karine Moe. 2004. "Lurking in the Shadows: The Informal Sector and Government Policy." *Journal of Development Economics* 73(2): 541–57.

Jackson, Nigel, and Darren Lilleker. 2009. "Building an Architecture of Participation? Political Parties and Web.2.0 In Britain." *Journal of Information Technology & Politics* 6: 232–250.

Jackson, Robert, and Carl Rosberg. 1984. "Popular Legitimacy in African Multi-Ethnic States." *The Journal of Modern African Studies* 22(2): 177–198.

Jacobs, R. Lawrence, and Robert Shapiro. 1995. "The American Public's Pragmatic Liberalism Meets Its Philosophical Conservativism." *Journal of Health Politics, Policy and Law* 24(5): 1021–1031.

Jacquin-Berdal, Dominique, and Martin Plaut. 2005. *Unfinished Business: Ethiopia and Eritrea at War.* Lawrenceville, NJ: Red Sea Press.

Jallov, Birgitte. 2005. "Assessing Community Change: Development of a 'Bare Foot' Impact Assessment Methodology." *Radio Journal.* 3(1): 21–34.

Jallov, Birgitte. 2007. "Impact assessment of East African Community Media Project, 2000–2006." *Swedish International Development Cooperation Agency.* 1–51.

Jallov, Birgitte. 2009. "Stories of community radio in East Africa: Powerful Change." *Mazi* 18. Communication for Social Change Consortium. Retrieved 5 July 2010 from http://www.communicationforsocialchange.org/mazi.php?id=18.

Jennings, Christian. 2001. *Across the Red River: Rwanda, Burundi, and the Heart of Darkness.* London: Indigo.

Johnson, Thomas, Wayne Wanta, Timothy Boudreau, Janet Blank-Libra, Killian Schaffer, and Sally Turner. 1994. "Influence Dealers: A Path Analysis Model of Agenda Building during Richard Nixon's War on Drugs." *Journalism & Mass Communication Quarterly* 73(1): 181–194.

Joireman, Sandra Fullerton. 1997. "Opposition Politics and Ethnicity in Ethiopia: We Will All Go Down Together." *The Journal of Modern African Studies* 35(30): 387–407.

Juma, Monica K. 2004. "The Compromised Brokers: NGOs and Displaced Populations in East Africa," In *Human Rights, the Rule of Law, and Development in Africa,* ed. Paul Zeleza, Philip McConnaughay, and Teyambe Zeleza. Philadelphia, PA: University of Pennsylvania Press.

Kabwegyere, Tarsis. 1974. *The Politics of State Formation: The Nature and Effects of Colonialism in Uganda.* Nairobi, Kenya: East Africa Literature Bureau.

Kaiser, Paul. 2000a. "Elections and Conflict Management in Africa." *Journal of Asian and African Studies* 34(4).

Kaiser, Paul. 2000b. "Postmodern Insurgencies: Political Violence, Identity Formation and Peacemaking in Comparative Perspective." *The Journal of Modern African Studies* 38(3): 511–549.

Kalyango Jr., Yusuf. 2009. "Political News Use and Democratic Support: A Study of Uganda's Radio Impact." *Journal of Radio and Audio Media* 16(2): 200–215.

Kalyango Jr., Yusuf. 2010. "Media Accountability and Political Interest in East Africa." *Ecquid Novi: African Journalism Studies* 31(1): 1–23.

Kalyango Jr., Yusuf, and Petya Eckler. 2010. "Media Performance, Agenda Building, and Democratization in East Africa." *Communication Yearbook* 34: 355–389.

Kamanyi, Judy. 2006. "The East African Political Federation: Progress, Challenges and Prospects for Constitutional Development." *The 10th Annual Sir Udo Udoma Symposium,* KCK Study Series, 9.

Kambenga, Godfrey. 2005. "Tanzania: Media Sustainability Index 2006–2007." *International Research & Exchange Institute,* 2007.

Kamuhanda, Jean Baptiste. 1990. *East Africa Perspectives.*Nairobi, Kenya: East Africa Publishing House.

Kang, Naewon, and Nojin Kwak. 2003. "A Multilevel Approach to Civic Participation." *Communication Research* 30(1): 80–106.

Kannyo, Edward. 2004. "Change in Uganda: A New Opening?" *Journal of Democracy* 15(2): 125–139.

Kannyogonya, Elizabeth, and Yoweri Museveni. 2000. *What Is Africa's Problem?* Minneapolis, MN: The University of Minnesota Press.

Kanyinga, Karuti, Andrew Kiondo, Per Tidemand, and Peter Gibbon. 1994. *The New Local Level Politics in East Africa: Studies on Uganda, Tanzania, and Kenya.* Nordic African Institute, Questia Publications.

Karan, Kavita, Jacques Gimeno, and Edson Tandoc Jr. 2009. "The Internet and Mobile Technologies in Election Campaigns: The Gabriella Women's Party during the 2007 Philippine Elections." *Journal of Information Technology & Politics* 6: 326–339.

Karlekar, Karin D., and Sarah G. Cook. 2008. *Freedom of the Press: A Global Survey of Media Independence*. Plymouth, UK: Rowman & Littlefield Publishers.

Karnell, Aaron Phillip. 2002. "Counteracting Hate Radio in Africa's Great Lakes Region: Responses and Lessons." *Journal of International Communications* 8(1): 111–137.

Kasaija, Phillip A. 2004. "Regional Integration: A Political Federation of the East African Countries?" *African Journal of International Affairs* 7(2): 21–34.

Kasfir, Nelson. 1976. *The Shrinking Political Arena: Participation and Ethnicity in African Politics*. Berkeley: University of California Press.

Kasoma, Francis P. 1990. "Media Ownership: Key to Participatory Development Communication." *Media Asia* 17(2): 79–82.

Kassahun, Berhanu 2003. "Party Politics and Political Culture in Ethiopia." In *African Political Parties: Evolution, Institutionalization and Governance*, ed. Mohammed Salih. Lodon: Pluto Press.

Katz, Yaron. 2005. *Media Policy for the 21st Century in the United States and Western Europe*. The Hampton Press Communication Series. Cresskill, NJ: Hampton Press.

Kaweesa, Stephen, and Sheryl Gorman. 2003. *Through Persecution to Freedom: Uganda a Land of Tragedy and Hope*. Bloomington, IN: Authorhouse.

Kemigisha, Rosemary M. 1998. *A Handbook on the State of the Media in Uganda*. Kampala and Nairobi: Eastern Africa Media Institute & Freidrich Ebert Stiftung.

Kilimwiko, Lawrence. 2006. A *Report on Journalism in Tanzania*. Media Institute of Southern Africa, Dar es Salaam: MISA Publication.

Kilimwiko, Lawrence, and Joseph Mapunda, eds. 1998. *A Handbook on the State of Media in Tanzania*. Nairobi, Kenya: Friedrich Ebert Stiftung, Association of Journalists and MediaWorkers, and Eastern Africa Media Institute.

Kissopoulos, Lisa. 2004. "Democratization and Nationalist Conflict: Culture and Elite Manipulation in Serbia, 1988–1999." Presented at the Annual Meeting of the Midwestern Political Science Association, Chicago.

Kivikuru, Ullamaija. 2006. "Top-down or Bottom-up? Radio in the Service of Democracy: Experiences from South Africa and Namibia." *The International Communication Gazette* 68: 5–31.

Klare, Michael T. 1972. *War Without End: American Planning for the Next Vietnams*. New York: Vintage Books.

Konde, Hadji. 1984. Press *Freedom in Tanzania*. Arusha, Tanzania: Eastern Africa Publications.

Krueger, Anne O. 1986. *A New Approach to Sovereign Debt Restructuring*. Washington, DC: International Monetary Fund Publication Services.

Kuenzi, Michelle, and Gina Lambright. 2007. "Voter Turnout in Africa's Multiparty Regimes." *Comparative Political Studies* 40(6): 665–690.

Lanegran, Kimberly. 2001. "South Africa's 1999 Election: Consolidating a Dominant Party System." *Africa Today* 48(2): 81–102.

Lang, Gladys, and Kurt Lang. 1981. "Watergate: An Exploration of the Agenda-Building Process." In *Agenda Setting: Readings on Media, Public Opinion, and Policymaking,* ed. David L. Protess and Maxwell McCombs. Mahwah, NJ: Lawrence Erlbaum Associates.

Lasorsa, Dominic. 1997. "Media Agenda Setting and Press Performance: A Social System Approach for Building Theory." In *Communication and Democracy: Exploring the Intellectual Frontiers in Agenda Setting Theory,* ed. Maxwell McCombs, Donald Shaw, and David Weaver. Mahwah, NJ: Lawrence Erlbaum Associates.

Lawson, Fessou. 2008. "2007 Country Performance Assessment." *African Development Bank Group* 32: 1–14.

Lemarchand, René, Reni Lemarchand, and Lee Hamilton. 1996. *Burundi: Ethnic Conflict and Genocide.* Cambridge: Cambridge University Press.

Lewis, Peter M. 1999. "Nigeria: An End to the Permanent Transition?" *Journal of Democracy* 10(1): 141–156.

Lieberman, Evan. 2003. "Nested Analysis in Cross-National Research." *APSA Comparative Politics Section* 14(1): 17–20.

Lieberman, Evan. 2005. "Nested Analysis as a Mixed-Method Strategy for Comparative Research." *American Political Science Review* 99(3): 435–52.

Lindberg, Staffan. 2006. *Democracy and Elections in Africa.* Baltimore, MD: Johns Hopkins University Press.

Lindberg, I. Staffan, and Minion K. C. Morrison. 2005. "Exploring Voter Alignments in Africa: Core and Swing Voters in Ghana." *Journal of Modern African Studies* 43(4): 565–586.

Linz, Juan J. 1964. "An Authoritarian Regime: The Case of Spain." In *Cleavages, Ideologies and Party Systems,* ed. Erik Allard and Yrjo Littunen. Helsinki: Westermarck Society.

Linz, Juan J. 1975 (reprinted 2000). *Totalitarian and Authoritarian Regimes.* London: Lynne Rienner Publishers.

Lippman, Walter. 1922. *Public Opinion.* New York: Harcourt Brace Co.
Lodge, Tom. 1999. *Consolidating Democracy: South Africa's Second Popular Election.* Electoral Institute of South Africa, Johannesburg: Witwatersrand University Press.

Longman, Timothy. 2009. "An Assessment of Rwanda's *Gacaca* Courts." *Peace Review* 21(3): 304–312.

Louw, Eric. 1991. "Impact of the 1990 Reforms on the 'Alternative Media.'" In *The Alternative Press in South Africa*, ed.Keyan Tomaselli and Eric Louw. Bellville: Anthropos.

Louw, Eric. 1993. *South African Media Policy: Debates of the 1990s*. Bellville: Anthropos.

Louw, Jacques. 2005. "Journalism and the Law." In *Changing the Fourth Estate: Essays on South African Journalism*, ed. A. Hadland. Cape Town, SA: HSRC.

Luckham, Robin. 1998. "The Military, Militarization and Democratisation in Africa: A Survey of Literature and Issues." In *The Military and Militarism in Africa*, ed. Eboe Hutchful and Abdoulaye Bathily. Senegal: CODESRIA. 1–45.

Madamombe, Itai. 2005. "Community Radio: A Voice for the Poor: Better Local Communications Can Boost Development, Democracy." *African Renewal: United Nations Department of Public Information* 19: 4–5.

Magalhães III, Eduardo. 1995. "Dictatorships." In *Survey of Social Science: Government and Politics Series* (Vol. 2), ed. F. Magil. Pasadena, CA: Salem Press.

Mahoney, Paul G. 1999. "The Common Law and Economic Growth: Hayek Might Be Right." *Transition* 10(6): 28–37.

Majstorovic, Steven. 1997. "Ancient Hatreds or Elite Manipulation?" *World Affairs* 159(4): 170–183.

Makali, David. 2003. *Media Law and Practice: The Kenyan Jurisprudence*. Nairobi, Kenya: Phoenix Publishers Ltd.

Makungu, Kenny M. 2004. *The State of the Media in Zambia: From the Colonial Era to December 2003*. Lusaka, Zambia: Media Institute of Southern Africa.

Mamdani, Mahmood. 1996. *Citizen and Subject: Contemporary Africa and the Legacy of Late Colonialism*. Princeton, NJ: Princeton University Press.

Manirakiza, M. (2005). Nation-Building in Burundi: History and Its Impact on the Future. *Conflict Trends* Issue 2: 27–36. ACCORD, South Africa.

Manyozo, Linje. 2009. "Mobilizing Rural and Community Radio in Africa." *Ecquid Novi: African Journalism Studies*. 30(1): 1–23.

Martin, Robert. 1974. *Personal Freedom and the Law in Tanzania*. Nairobi, Kenya: Oxford University Press.

Matende, David. 2005. "The State of the News Media in Kenya." Presented at the Annual Meeting of the Kenya Union of Journalists in Nairobi, Kenya.

Matibini, Patrick. 2006. *The Struggle for Media Law Reforms in Zambia*. Johannesburg, South Africa: Media Institute of South Africa..

Mattes, Robert. 2004. "Trends in Political Party Support in South Africa." *AfroBarometer Briefing Paper* 6: 16.

Mazrui, Ali A. 1971. "Islam and the English Language in East & West Africa." In *Language Use & Social Change*, ed. W. W. Whiteley. London, UK: Oxford University Press for the International African Institute. 179–197.

Mbeke, Peter O. 2008. "The Media, Legal, Regulatory and Policy Environment in Kenya." BBC World Service Trust Policy Briefing No. 1. Retrieved March 16, 2009, from http://downloads.bbc.co.uk/worldservice/trust/pdf/kenya_media_legal_framework.pdf.

Mbunda, Luitfried. 2004. "Securing Human Rights through the Rule of Law in Tanzania." In *Human Rights, the Rule of Law, and Development in Africa*, ed. Paul Zeleza, Philip McConnaughay, and Teyambe Zeleza. Philadelphia, PA: University of Pennsylvania Press.

McCombs, Maxwell E. 1992. "Explorers and Surveyors: Expanding Strategies for Agenda Setting Research." *Journalism Quarterly* 69: 813–824.

McCombs, Maxwell, and Donald Shaw. 1972. "The Agenda-Setting Function of Mass Media." In *Agenda Setting: Readings on Media, Public Opinion, and Policymaking*, ed. David L. Protess and Maxwell McCombs. Mahwah, NJ: Lawrence Erlbaum Associates.

McCombs, Maxwell, and Salma Ghanem. 2003. "The Convergence of Agenda Setting and Framing." In *Framing Public Life: Perspectives on Media and Our Understanding of the Social World*, ed. Stephen Reese, Oscar G. Gandy, and August E. Grant. Mahwah, NJ: Lawrence Erlbaum Associates.

Melzer, Uta. 2008. "Africa: Where Information Is a Luxury Good." *World Press Freedom Review*, International Press Institute.

Merera, Gudina. 2003. "Ethiopia: Competing Ethnic Nationalisms and the Quest for Democracy, 1960–2000." PhD dissertation. Institute of Social Studies. The Hague, Netherlands.

Miguel, Edward. 2004. "Tribe or Nation? Nation Building and Public Goods in Kenya versus Tanzania." *World Politics* 56(3): 327–362.

Miguel, Edward. 2009. "Is It Africa's Turn?" *Boston Review*. Boston, MA: MIT Press.

Milne, Claire, and Anne Taylor. 2006. "South Africa AMDI Research Report." *Africa Media Development Initiative*. BBC World Trust Service Publication.

Mochaba, Khaliso, Carla Raffinetti, Sheetal Vallabh, and Justine White. 2003. *SADC Media Law: A Handbook for Media Practitioners* (Vol. 1). Johannesburg: Konrad Adenauer Foundation.

Moggi, Paola and Roger Tessier. 2001. "Media Status Report: Kenya." *Research and Technology Exchange Group*. Paris, France.

Momba, Jotham C. 2004. "Civil Society and the Struggle for Human Rights and Democracy in Zambia." In *Human Rights, the Rule of Law, and Development in Africa,* ed. Paul Zeleza, Philip McConnaughay, and Teyambe Zeleza. Philadelphia, PA: University of Pennsylvania Press.

Montero, Maria. D. 2009. "Political E-mobilisation and Participation in the Election Campaigns of Ségolène Royal (2007) and Barack Obama (2008)." *Quadernsdel CAC* 33: 27–34.

Moore, Robert. 1992. *The Political Reality of Freedom of the Press in Zambia.* Lanham, MD: University Press of America.

Morlino, Leonardo. 2005. "Anchors and Democratic Change." *Comparative Political Studies* 38(7): 743–770.

Morrison, Minion K. C. 2004. "Political Parties in Ghana through Four Republics: A Path to Democratic Consolidation." *Comparative Politics* 36(4): 421–442.

Morrison, Minion K. C., and Jae Woo Hong. 2006. "Ghana's Political Parties: How Ethno/Regional Variations Sustain the National Two-Party System." *Journal of Modern African Studies* 44(4): 1–25.

Mozaffar, Shaheen, and James R. Scarritt. 2005. "The Puzzle of African Party Systems." *Party Politics* 11(4): 399–421.

Mpangala, Gaudens. 2004. "Origins of Political Conflicts and Peace Building in the Great Lakes Region." Institute of Development Studies University Publication.

Mpangala, Gaudens, and Jonathan Lwehabura. 2005. "Zanzibar: Conflict Resolution and Human Security in the 2005 Elections." Institute for Security Studies.

Mudhai, Okoth, Wisdom Tettey, and Fackson Banda. 2009. *African Media and the Digital Public Sphere.* New York, NY: Palgrave Macmillan.

Mugisha, Anne. 2004. "Museveni's Machinations." *Journal of Democracy* 15(2): 140–144.

Mukandala, Rwekaza. 2000 March 25–26. "Political Cooperation: Perspectives on Regional Integration and Cooperation in East Africa." *Proceedings of the 1st Ministerial Seminar on East African Cooperation.* Arusha, Tanzania, 87–106.

Munene, Macharia. 2001. *The Politics of Transition in Kenya, 1995–1998.* Nairobi, Kenya: Friend of the Book Foundation.

Murunga, Godwin and Nasong'o Shadrack. 2006. "Bent on Self-Destruction: The Kibaki Regime in Kenya." *Journal of Contemporary African Studies* 24(1): 1–28.

Museveni, Yoweri. 1997. *Sowing the Mustard Seed.* London, UK: MacMillan Education Ltd.

Museveni, Yoweri, and Elizabeth Kanyogonya. 2000. *What Is Africa's Problem?* Minneapolis/St. Paul, MN: University of Minnesota Press.

Mushi, Samuel. 2001. *Development Democratisation in Tanzania: A Study of Rural Grassroots Politics.* Kampala: Fountain Publishers.

Mussa, Michel. 2005. *Global Economic Prospects: On Track for Strong Growth in 2004 but Worries about 2005.* Paper presented at 6th semiannual meeting on Global Economic Prospects, Institute for International Economics, Washington, D.C.

Mute, Lawrence M. 2000. "Media Policy in Kenya." In.*Media, Culture and Performance in Kenya* East Africa Media Institute (EAMI). Nairobi: EAMI Publications.

Mwenda, Andrew. 2007. "Personalizing Power in Uganda." *Journal of Democracy* 18(3): 23–37.

Mwesige, Peter. 2004. "Disseminators, Advocates, and Watchdogs: A Profile of Ugandan Journalists in the New Millennium." *Journalism* 5(1): 69–96.

Mwesige, Peter. G. 2009. "The Democratic Functions and Dysfunctions of Political Talk Radio: The Case of Uganda." *Journal of African Media Studies* 1(2): 221–245.

Nassanga, Goretti Linda. 2009. "An Assessment of the Changing Community Media Paramenters in East Africa." *Ecquid Novi: African Journalism Studies* 30(1): 42–57.

Ndarubagiye, Léonce. 1996. *Burundi: The Origins of the Hutu-Tutsi Conflict.* Nairobi: Léonce Ndarubagiye.

Ndulo, Muna. 2003. "The Democratization Process and Structural Adjustment in Africa." *Indiana Journal of Global Legal Studies* 10(1): 315–368.

Ndulo, Muna. 2010. "Rule of Law, Judicial Reform and the Reconstruction of Post-conflict and Failing States." In *Failed States and Failing States: The Experience of Africa,* ed. Muna Ndulo and Margaret Grieco. Cambridge: Cambridge Scholars Publishing.

Nonneman, Gerd. 1996. *Political and Economic Liberalization: Dynamics and Linkages in Comparative Perspective.* Boulder, CO: Lynne Rienner Publications.

North, Douglass C. 1989. "Institutions and Economic Growth: An Historical Introduction." *World Development* 17: 319–341.

Nyang'oro, Julius. 2004. "Ethnicity, Inequality and Public Sector Governance in Tanzania." In *Ethnicity, Inequality and Public Sector Governance,* ed. Yusuf Bangura. New York, NY: Palgrave Macmillan Ltd.

Obama, Barrack. 2009. "Presidential Address to People of Ghana at the National Parliament of the Republic of Ghana." *The White House Presidential Statements* 3–4.

Oberschall, Anthony. 2000. "The Manipulation of Ethnicity: From Ethnic Cooperation to War and Violence in Yugoslavia." *Ethnic and Racial Studies.* 23(6): 982–1001.

Ochs, Martin. 1987. *The African Press.* Cairo: American University in Cairo Press.

Ocitti, Jim. 2006. *Press Politics and Public Policy in Uganda: The Role of Journalism in Democratization.* London: Edwin Mellen Press.

O'Connor, Alan. 1990. "Radio Is Fundamental to Democracy." *Media Development* 37(4): 3–4.

O'Donnell, Guillermo. 2004. "The Rule of Law." *Journal of Democracy* 15(4): 32–47.

O'Donnell, Guillermo, and Philippe Schmitter. 1986. *Transitions from Authoritarian Rule: Tentative Conclusions about Uncertain Democracies.* Baltimore: Johns Hopkins UniversityPress.

Ofcansky, Thomas. 1996. *Uganda: Tarnished Pearl of Africa.* London, UK: Westview Press.

Ojo, Emmanuel. 2003. "The Mass Media and the Challenged of Sustainable Democratic Values in Nigeria: Possibilities and Limitation." *Media, Culture and Society* 25: 821–840.

Okoye, Ada. 2004. "The Rule of Law and Sociopolitical Dynamics in Africa." In *Human Rights, the Rule of Law, and Development in Africa,* ed. Paul Zeleza, Philip McConnaughay, and Teyambe Zeleza. Philadelphia, PA: University of Pennsylvania Press.

Okuku, Juma. 2002. *Ethnicity, State Power and the Democratisation Process in Uganda.* Uppsala, Sweden: Nordic African Institute.

Oloka-Onyango, Joseph. 1995. "Constitutional Transition in Museveni's Uganda: New Horizons or Another False Start?" *Journal of African Law* 39(2): 156–172.

Oloka-Onyango, Joseph. 2004. "Constitutional Change and Political Transition in Contemporary Uganda: A Socio-legal Analysis." Change Analysis in Uganda: Supporting Implementation of the PEAP. Study presented at the Department for International Development, Uganda, Confernce.

Olorunnisola, Anthony. 1995. "When Tribal Wars Are Mass Mediated: Re-evaluating the Policy of 'Non Interference.'" *Gazette* 56: 123–138.

Omosa, Mary, and Dorothy McCormick. 2004. "Universal Access to Communication Services in Rural Kenya: A Baseline Survey." Final Report to the International Development Research Centre. Nairobi, Kenya.

Onwumechili, Chuka. 1998. *African Democratization and Military Coups.* Westport, CT: Praeger Publishers.

Opoku-Mensah, Aida. 2000. "The Future of Community Radio in Africa: The Case of Southern Africa." In *African Broadcast Cultures: Radio in Transition,* ed. Richard Fardon and Graham Furniss. Cape Town: James Currey Publishers.

Opubor, Alfred E. 2000. "If Community Media Is the Answer, What Is the Question?" *Promoting Community Media in Africa* 11–24.

Orvis, Stephen. 2006. "Conclusion: Bringing Institutions Back into the Study of Kenya and Africa." *Africa Today* 53(2): 95–110.

Osaghae, Eghosa E. 2005. "State, Constitutionalism, and the Management of Ethnicity in Africa." *African and Asian Studies* 4(1–2): 83–105.

Paek, Hye-Jin, So-Hyang Yoon, and Dhavan Shah. 2005. "Local News, Social Integration, and Community Participation: Hierarchical Linear Modeling of Contextual and Cross-Level Effects." *Journalism and Mass Communication Quarterly* 82(3): 587–606.

Page, Janet. 2005. Knowledge Economy and Forecast on Africa's Development. From the African Economic and Financial Data. *African Development Indicators*, World Bank.

Pareto, Vilfredo. 1935 (reprinted 1965). *The Mind and Society: A Treatise on General Sociology.* New York: Dover Publications.

Peter, Jochen. 2003. "Country Characteristics as Contingent Conditions of Agenda Setting: The Moderating Influence of Polarized Elite Opinion." *Communication Research* 30(4): 683–712.

Philippart, Michel. 2000. "Media status report: Burundi." Retrieved April 11, 2009, from http://www.gret.org/parma/uk2/ressource/edm/pdf/burundi.pdf

Pitts, Gregory. 2000. "Democracy and Press Freedom in Zambia: Attitudes of Members of Parliament toward Media and Media Regulation." *Communication Law and Policy* 5(2): 269–294.

Podpiera, Richard, and Martin Cihaik. 2005. "Bank Behavior in Developing Countries: Evidence from East Africa." IMF Working Papers. The International Monetary Fund.

Posner, Daniel. 2005. *Institutions and Ethnic Politics in Africa.* Cambridge, MA: Cambridge University Press.

Przeworski, Adam. 1991. *Democracy and the Market.* New York: Cambridge University Press.

Przeworski, Adam. 2003. "Minimalist Conception of Democracy: A Defense," In *The Democracy Handbook,* ed. R. Dahl, I. Shapiro, and J. Cheibub. Cambridge, MA: MIT Press.

Pye, Lucien W. 1962. "Armies in the process of political modernization." In *The Role of the Military in Underdeveloped Countries,* ed. J.J. Johnson. Princeton: Princeton University Press.

Ramaprasad, Jyotika. 2003. "The Private and Government Sides of Tanzanian Journalists." *The Harvard International Journal of Press and Politics* 8(1): 8–26.

Raudenbush, Stephen and Anthony Bryk. 2002. *Hierarchical Linear Models: Applications and Data Analysis Methods.* Thousand Oaks, CA: Sage Publications, Inc.

Raudenbush, Stephen, and Anthony Bryk. 2002. *Hierarchical Linear Models: Applications and Data Analysis Methods.* 2nd Ed. Thousand Oaks, CA: Sage Publications.

Reyntjens, Filip. 2004. "Rwanda, Ten Years On: From Genocide to Dictatorship." *African Affairs* 103(441): 177–191.

Robertson, David. 2004. *The Routledge Dictionary of Politics*. London and New York: Routledge.

Robertson, Graeme. 2007. "Strikes and Labor Organization in Hybrid Regimes." *American Political Science Review* 101(4): 781–98.

Rose, Richard, William Mishler, and Christian Haerpfer. 1998. *Democracy and Its Alternatives: Understanding Post-communist Societies*. Baltimore: Johns Hopkins University Press.

Rotberg, Robert, and Thomas Weiss. 1996. *From Massacres to Genocide*. Cambridge. MA: The World Peace Foundation.

Rubongoya, Joshua. 2007. *Regime Hegemony in Museveni's Uganda: Pax Musevenica*. New York, NY: Palgrave MacMillan.

Ruteere, Mutuma. 2006. "Politicization as a Strategy for Recognition and Enforcement of Human Rights in Kenya." *Human Rights Review* 7(2): 6–16.

Sarikakis, Katharine. 2004. *British Media in a Global Era*. London: A Hodder Arnold Publication.

Schapiro, Leonard. 1972. *Totalitarianism*. London: Pal Mall.

Schatzberg, Michael. 2001. *Political Legitimacy in Middle Africa: Father, Family, Food*. Bloomington, IN: Indiana University Press.

Schedler, Andreas. 2010. "Authoritarianism's Last Line of Defense." *Journal of Democracy*, 21(1): 69–80.

Scheufele, Dietram. 2000. "Agenda-Setting, Priming, and Framing Revisited: Another Look at Cognitive Effects of Political Communication." *Mass Communication & Society* 3: 297–316.

Schiller, Herbert I. 1992. *Mass Communications and American Empire*. Boulder, CO: Westview.

Schiller, Herbert I. 1994. "Communication, Technology and Ecology." In *Mass Communication Research: On Problems and Policies: The Art of Asking the Right Questions: In Honor of James D. Halloran*, ed. Cees J. Hamelink and Olda Linne. Norwood, NJ: Ablex Publishing, 333–341.

Schmitz, Hans P. 2006. *Transnational Mobilization and Domestic Regime Change: Africa in Comparative Perspective*. Hampshire, UK: Palgrave Macmillan.

Schumpeter, Joseph. 2005. *Capitalism, Socialism and Democracy*. New York: Taylor and Francis.

Schwarzmantel, John.1994. *The State in Contemporary Society, an Introduction*. Harvester Wheatsheaf/Hemel Hampstead.

Sekalala, Aga. 1968. *The Press*. Kampala, Uganda: Milton Obote Foundation Press.

Semujanga, Josias. 2003. *Origins of Rwandan Genocide.* Amherst, NY: Humanity Books.

Sen, Amartya. 1999. "Democracy as a Universal Value." *Journal of Democracy* 10(3): 3–17.

Shaw, Donald, and Maxwell McCombs. 1977. *The Emergence of American Political Issues: The Agenda-Setting Function of the Press.* St. Paul, MN: West.

Shivji, Issa. 1995. "The Rule of Law and Ujamaa in the Ideological Formation of Tanzania." *Social and Legal Studies* 4(2): 147–174.

Sklar, Richard. 2006. "Nigeria: Completing Obasanjo's Legacy." *Journal of Democracy* 17(3): 100–115.

Smith, Daniel Jordan. 2005. "Oil, Blood and Money: Culture and Power in Nigeria." *Anthropological Quarterly* 78(3): 725–740.

Snyder, Jack. 2000. *From Voting to Violence: Democratization and Nationalist Conflict.* New York, NY: W. W. Norton & Co.

Snyder, Jack, and Karen Ballentine. 1996. "Nationalism and the Marketplace of Ideas." *International Security* 21(2): 5–40.

Sonwalkar, Prasun. 2004. "Out of Sight, Out of Mind: The Non-reporting of Small Wars and Insurgencies." In *Reporting War: Journalism in Wartime,* ed. Stuart Allan and Barbie Zelizer. New York, NY: Routledge, 206–223.

Spector, Regine A. 2007. "Authoritarianism." In *Encyclopedia of Governance,* ed. M. Bevir. California: Sage Publications.

Steeves, Jeffrey. 2006. "Presidential Succession in Kenya: The Transition from Moi to Kibaki." *Commonwealth and Comparative Politics* 44(2): 211–233.

Stepan, Alfred. 1990. "On the Tasks of a Democratic Opposition." *Journal of Democracy* 1(2): 41–49.

Stromseth, Jane, David Wippman, and Rosa Brooks. 2006. *Can Might Make Rights? Building the Rule of Law after Military Interventions.* New York: Cambridge UniversityPress.

Sturmer, Martin. 1998. *The Media History of Tanzania.* Dar es Salaam: Ndanda Mission Press.

Suberu, Rotimi T. 2007. "Nigeria's Muddled Elections." *Journal of Democracy* 18(4): 95–110.

Takirambudde, Peter, and Kate Fletcher. 2006. "Civil Society in Governance and Poverty Alleviation: A Human Rights Perspective." In *Democratic Reform in Africa: Its Impact on Governance and Poverty Alleviation,* ed. Muna Ndulo. Oxford, UK: James Currey.

Tanner, Andrea. 2004. "Agenda Building, Source Selection, and Health News at Local Television Stations." *Science Communication* 25(4): 350–363.

Teer-Tomaselli, Ruth, and Keyan Tomaselli. 2001. "Transformation, Nation-Building and the South African Media, 1993–1999." In *Media, Democracy and Renewal in Southern Africa,* ed. K. Tomaselli and H. Dunn. Colorado Springs, CO: International Academic.

Tesfaw, Desta. 2007. "Insights on Broadcasting Service in Ethiopia." In *Broadcasting Situation in Ethiopia: Opportunities and Challenges.* Dialogue Report by Panos Ethiopia and Ethiopian Broadcasting Authority, 51–79.

Tettey, Wisdom. 2006. "The Politics of Media Accountability in Africa: An Examination of Mechanisms and Institutions." *The International Communication Gazette* 68(3): 229–248.

Therkildsen, Ole. 2002. "Uganda's Referendum 2000: The Silent Boycott." *African Affairs* 101: 231-241.

Thorne, Barrie, and Nancy Henley. 1975. "Difference and Dominance." In *Sex and Language,* ed. Barrie Thorne and Nancy Henley. Rowley, MA: Newbury House.

Tripp, Aili. 2000. "Political Reform in Tanzania: The Struggle for Associational Autonomy." *Comparative Politics* 32(2): 191–214.

Tripp, Aili Mari. 2004. "The Changing Face of Authoritarianism in Africa: The Case of Uganda." *Africa Today* 50(3): 3–26.

Tronvoll, Kjetil. 2008. "Human Rights Violations in Federal Ethiopia: When Ethnic Identity Is a Political Stigma." *International Journal on Minority and Group Rights* 15(1): 49–79.

Uche, Luke Uka. 1989. *Mass Media, People and Politics in Nigeria.* New Delhi: Concept Publisher Company.

Uvin, Peter. 1997. "Prejudice, Crisis, and Genocide in Rwanda." *African Studies Review* 40(2): 91–115.

Uvin, Peter. 1998. *Aiding Violence: The Development Enterprise in Rwanda.* West Hartford, CT: Kumarian Press.

Uvin, Peter. 1999. "Ethnicity and Power in Burundi and Rwanda: Different Paths to Mass Violence." *Comparative Politics* 31(3): 253–271.

van de Walle, Nicolas. 1999. "Economic Reform in a Democratizing Africa." *Comparative Politics* 32(1): 21–41.

van de Walle, Nicholas. 2002. "Africa's Range of Regimes," *Journal of Democracy* 13(2): 66–80.

Vestal, Theodore M. 1999. *Ethiopia: A Post-Cold War African State.* London: Praeger.

Wanta, Wayne. 1997. *The Public and the National Agenda: How People Learn about Important Issues.* Mahwah, NJ: Lawrence Erlbaum Associates.

Wanta, Wayne, Guy Golan, and Cheolhan Lee. 2004. "Agenda Setting and International News: Media Influence on Public Perceptions of Foreign Nations." *Journalism and Mass Communications Quarterly* 81: 364–377.

Wanyande, Patrick. 1996. Mass media-state relations in post-colonial Kenya. *Africa Media Review* 9(3): 54–76.

Wanyeki, Muthoni. 2000. "The Development of Community Media in East and Southern Africa." *Promoting Community Media in Africa.* UNESCO, 25–41.

Weaver, David and Swanzy Elliot. 1985. "Who Sets the Agenda for the Media? A study of Local Agenda Building." *Journalism Quarterly* 62: 87–94.

Weber, Max. 1968. *Economy and Society.* Berkeley: University of California Press.

Weiler, Joseph. 1997. "Legitimacy and Democracy of Union Governance." In *The Politics of European Treaty Reform: The 1996 Intergovernmental Conference and Beyond,* ed. Geoffrey Edwards and Alfred Pijpers. London, UK: Pinter Publications.

Weintein, Jeremy N. 2009. Forum: "Is It Africa's Turn?" *Boston Review.* Boston, MA: MIT Press.

Welch Jr., Claude. 1970. "The Roots and Implications of Military Intervention." In *Soldier and State in Africa,* ed. Claude Welch. Evanston, IL: Northwestern University Press.

Wiking, Staffan. 1983. *Military Coups in Sub-Saharan Africa: How to justify illegal assumptions of power.* Sweden: Africana Publishing Company.

Wood, William C. 1985. "The Educational Potential of News Coverage of Economics." *Journal of Economic Education* 16(1): 27–35.

Young, Crawford. 1976. *The Politics of Cultural Pluralism.* Madison, WI: University of Wisconsin Press.

Young, Crawford. 1998. *Ethnic Diversity and Public Policy: A Comparative Enquiry.* United Kingdom: Palgrave Press.

Zafliro, James. 1988. "Regional Pressure and the Erosion of Media Freedom in an African Democracy: The Case of Botswana." *Journal of Communication* 38(3): 108–120.

Index